More Praise for *The Two-Minute Drill*

"You don't even have to be a fan of the game to wonder what it is about a two-minute drill that allows a team to move the ball and score quickly. Spend a minute thinking about how impressive your results could be if you could apply these same principles in your workplace. That's what this book will help you do when you learn to run your own two-minute drill!"
—Joe Napoli, general manager, The Toledo Mud Hens

"In an organization such as ours, where speed is critical, the two-minute drill represents a powerful and very effective approach to turning challenges, apparent problems, or defeat into victory. *The Two-Minute Drill* provides a perfect mental model for how to prepare, execute, and win!"
Donald L. Warner, vice president, director of quality and training, SSOE, Inc.

"I think *The Two-Minute Drill* is a fantastic analogy. It is easy to explain, easy to remember, and drives home the importance of TEAM. So many of the ideas about change in the organization today talk about team, but don't really incorporate it in action. To organize chaos, instill team spirit and measure results. How can you go wrong?"
—John Walton, president, Davidson Plyforms, Inc.

"*The Two-Minute Drill* is a clear and concise blueprint for achieving better results. The findings present a simple and effective approach for successfully managing the real time issues impacting companies today. *The Two-Minute Drill* provides an excellent technique for dealing with the rapid change in today's economy in a way that can be understood from the top to the bottom of the organization. Great read!"
 —**John S. Szuch, chairman, Fifth Third Bank (NWO)**

"I'm a huge football fan and believe there are many parallels between team sports and business, and *The Two-Minute Drill* is one of them that really works. Approach your next change using *The Two-Minute Drill* and you'll see what I mean."
 —**Janie Miller, CEO, Central Travel**

"What a great idea! *The Two-Minute Drill* combines two passions—business and football—into exceptionally useful reading that had an immediate impact on my ability to lead rapid change. The connection to the two-minute drill in football provides a unique and very helpful method to apply the successful organizational change principles. The self-assessment tools are a quick method to identify the areas that need to improve to achieve better results faster. I recommend *The Two-Minute Drill* to any manager leading a team in today's rapidly changing global business environment."
 —**Tom Handel, CFO, Sunrise Windows**

"Thinking about change as a two-minute drill can help leaders energize their people and make better use of both time and talent. It works!"
 —**Dr. Randy Oostra, president and COO, ProMedica Health Systems**

"The speed of today's business environment opens the door for chaos. *The Two-Minute Drill* provides a fast-paced, disciplined approach to creating a sense of urgency while eliminating delays that are costly. I see it as the playbook for success that I can pass down through the organization."

   —**Mike Riccio, senior vice president and CFO, La-Z-Boy Incorporated**

"The authors frame years of experience and research in getting results into a unique and memorable framework for creating a sense of purpose and urgency in leading successful change and improvement. Whether your organization is trying to implement lean or some other improvement initiative, *The Two-Minute Drill* can help you get better results."

   —**Dave LaHote, president, Lean Education, Lean Enterprise Institute Inc.**

JB JOSSEY-BASS

THE TWO-MINUTE DRILL

Lessons for Rapid Organizational Improvement from America's Greatest Game

Clinton O. Longenecker

Greg R. Papp

Timothy C. Stansfield

BICENTENNIAL
1807
WILEY
2007
BICENTENNIAL

John Wiley & Sons, Inc.

Published by Jossey-Bass
A Wiley Imprint
989 Market Street, San Francisco, CA 94103-1741   www.josseybass.com

Wiley Bicentennial logo: Richard J. Pacifico

Jossey-Bass books and products are available through most bookstores. To contact Jossey-Bass directly
call our Customer Care Department within the U.S. at 800-956-7739, outside the U.S. at 317-572-3986,
or fax 317-572-4002.

Jossey-Bass also publishes its books in a variety of electronic formats. Some content that appears in
print may not be available in electronic books.

Library of Congress Cataloging-in-Publication Data

Longenecker, Clinton O.
    The two-minute drill : lessons for rapid organizational improvement from America's greatest game/
Clinton O. Longenecker, Greg R. Papp, Timothy C. Stansfield ; foreword by Marvin Lewis. – 1st ed.
        p. cm.
    Includes bibliographical references and index.
    ISBN 978-0-7879-9490-7 (cloth)
1. Organizational change. 2. Organizational effectiveness. 3. Organizational behavior.   I. Papp,
Greg. II. Stansfield, Timothy C. III. Title.
    HD58.8.L6625 2007
    658.4'06—dc22

                                                                                            2007024497

FIRST EDITION
HB Printing 10 9 8 7 6 5 4 3 2 1

CONTENTS

We dedicate this project and subsequent book to our wonderful, supportive, and loving families. They are truly God's gift to us.

To Cindy, Clint, Shannon, and Steve; my parents, Clint and Rita Longenecker; and my in-laws, Chuck and Ginny Breese

To Carolyn, Laura, Emily, Patrick, and Emma; my parents, Frank and Julia Papp; and my in-laws, Richard and Ruth Bryant

To Carol, Mark, Luke, and Ellen; to my parents, Charles and Beverly Stansfield; and my in-laws, Leo and Donna Poeniche

FOREWORD

Every coach that I have known during my football career goes into each and every contest with a game plan designed to help him win. As coaches we place great emphasis on scouting our opponents, seeking out favorable match-ups, and developing various offensive and defensive schemes that play to our strengths and exploit our opponents' weaknesses wherever and whenever possible. Our goal is to prepare so that we can execute that game plan in the heat of battle and win. Yet with competition being what it is today, close games are becoming a bigger part of the landscape of the game of football in every league. In fact, a significant number of football games these days are decided by a touchdown or less.

In today's game, it is easy to find yourself behind on the scoreboard in a close game with your original game plan not working as you had hoped and time running out. As a player and coach, I have found myself in this situation many times. Learning to come from behind is a real challenge that creates a true test of the quality of preparation, strength, and character of your team. The bad news is that you and your team are losing. The good news is that you are still in the game with an opportunity to win if you can execute an effective two-minute drill offense and do the things necessary to close out the game.

Successful two-minute drills have made a real difference in my career, and I only have to think back to our 2004 win over the Baltimore Ravens to be reminded of the power of the two-minute drill. Going into the fourth quarter, we were down 20 to 3 and scored three touchdowns, but still trailed the Ravens 26–24 with 1:42 left in the contest. Our offense executed a winning eight-play drive that covered 60 yards and culminated in a 24-yard field goal in front of a capacity Baltimore Raven crowd, with 0:00 left on the clock. Our two-minute drill made the difference in the outcome!

Because of increased competition in the NFL, the two-minute drill has become one of the most essential aspects of the game of football in the twenty-first century. And the difference between winning and losing can be what you do when you find yourself behind late in the game.

On my team, we dedicate a key segment of our Thursday practices to the mechanics of the two-minute drills that we hope we will *not* have to use against our next opponent. We take great care in preparing our team for the contingency and necessity of having to run a two-minute drill if that is what it will take to win. Long hours of planning and practicing are devoted to this preparation, which is a real priority for my team. Although our coaches are always hopeful that our established game plan will get us through sixty minutes of play with a victory, the last two minutes of a football game often require rapid action and adjustment to get a win. It is in the final minutes of a close game when those hours of planning and preparation can really pay off in execution.

Although a team's commitment to preparation is critical for success, a number of other factors also are paramount in executing a successful two-minute drill. Winning two-minute drills requires defining exactly what it will take to win, great quarterbacking, exceptional teamwork, selecting the appropriate plays, getting the ball into the hands of the right players, executing individual assignments, managing the clock, and maintaining a sense of urgency. All these things must take place while communicating above the roar of the crowd and remaining poised and organized. The players on the field must align their roles to a single goal to ensure that they succeed. For these reasons, the two-minute drill is a very demanding enterprise, but one that holds great promise for a team willing to develop this talent. It is frequently the tool that separates a winning team from the rest of the pack.

In the book that you are about to read, Clint, Greg, and Tim have made a very strong case that the practices associated with a two-minute drill in football have direct application to real and rapid improvement in the workplace. I agree with their conclusion. The two-minute drill is a perfect analogy as it relates to organizational change and improvement. In your world of work, as in mine, it is easy to find yourself behind on the scoreboard and in need of a quick come-from-behind score. If your organization is serious about winning in the challenging arena of organizational improvement, you would be well served to think of yourself as a quarterback who must seize control of the improvement game and execute an effective two-minute drill when you find yourself behind on your scoreboard.

As business quarterbacks, you must learn to apply the key practices prescribed in *The Two-Minute Drill* so that you can leverage all the power and energy associated with people's desire to come from behind and *win*. With the guidance and proper execution of this useful playbook, you can use the same principles that we use on the football field to win at work. This book will help you draw the parallels between football and improvement in a way that I am confident you will find to be very useful, simple to apply, and easy to remember when you need to achieve real and rapid organizational change. Remember, when you are behind on the scoreboard in a close game, there is always hope if you know how to execute an effective two-minute drill. *In the end, it's how you finish that really counts, regardless of your playing field!* I wish you well in all your improvement endeavors.

Marvin Lewis
June 2007

THE TWO-MINUTE DRILL

SPEED AND EXECUTION ARE THE KEYS TO SUCCESS

Today, football is all about speed... and execution!
—BOB DAVIES, TV FOOTBALL COMMENTATOR AND FORMER
NOTRE DAME HEAD FOOTBALL COACH

*Executing one's business plan is critically important
to success, but the key factor is frequently the timing
and speed of the action. Without quick and effective
execution, the best-laid plans can become outdated
and ineffective, and we are struggling with this right
now ourselves.*
—SENIOR VICE PRESIDENT OF BUSINESS DEVELOPMENT,
FORTUNE 1000 HEALTH CARE ORGANIZATION

When the first recorded football game was played on November 6, 1869, between Rutgers and Princeton universities, few people, if any, could have possibly imagined what football would look like more than a century later. The one hundred fans watching the game observed a contest that more resembled an "ugly rugby match" than our modern version of American football. Two twenty-five-man squads faced off in a battle of physical prowess replete with running, kicking, head butting, and tackling in an environment of surprise and chaotic disorganization. The Rutgers student newspaper, *Targum*, offered the following account of the game: "To sum up, Princeton had the most muscle but didn't kick very well and wanted [lacked] organization.... Our men, on the

1

other hand, though comparatively weak, ran well and kicked well throughout. But their great point was the organization, for which great praise is due to the captain. The right men were always in the right place."

Rutgers won the contest 6–4, and American-style football was born in New Brunswick, New Jersey.[1] Although the game was primitive by today's standards, it is interesting to note that leadership, talent, and organization were keys to Rutgers' victory.

FAST-FORWARD TO THE TWENTY-FIRST CENTURY

When we fast-forward to today, we see a vastly different game played in four quarters with eleven offensive players pitted against eleven defensive players on a 100-yard-by-51-yard playing field. There is a clearly defined set of rules. Offensive schemes are designed to score either touchdowns or field goals; defensive schemes are designed to prevent this from happening. Today's playbooks are virtual encyclopedias of various sophisticated offensive and defensive schemes that are used to get the best of the opponent.

Today's players have become offensive and defensive specialists who train year-round to get bigger and stronger. Modern players wear highly developed equipment that is designed to prevent injury, although injuries of all sorts are still a significant part of the game. These innovations in the game, coupled with the development and evolution of leagues and rivalries at all levels of the sport, have created the phenomenon that makes football America's greatest game. Today people swarm to stadiums and camp out in front of their television sets because of the excitement and bigger-than-life persona of the game.

HOW FOOTBALL'S "TWO-MINUTE DRILL" CAN HELP YOUR ORGANIZATION CHANGE FASTER—AND SUCCEED

Winning in football today is all about teamwork, utilizing offensive and defensive talent, and developing and executing well-designed game plans. A potent combination of speed and effective execution

---

Exhibit P.1: Ten Critical Success Factors for Implementing Change

1. Clear focus
2. Effective leadership
3. Knowledge of your opponents
4. A sense of urgency
5. A solid game plan
6. Talented and motivated personnel
7. Proper execution
8. Performance measurement and management
9. Feedback on performance and reinforcement of effective actions
10. Organizational learning from mistakes and successes

---

is a delight to offensive-minded coaches and fans, and it's a thorn in the flesh to coaches and fans whose defenses are struggling. Speed and execution in the game of football contain great lessons for business leaders interested in winning at work. *The purpose of this book is to help you, the reader, better execute and accelerate change and improvement in your organization.*

Although sports analogies are frequently overused in today's workplace, we believe that the concept of the *two-minute drill* (TMD) from football holds great promise for you in your quest for better performance through fast and effective change. We do not make this claim lightly! Rather, we want to demonstrate that using the key principles of rapid scoring from American football can help you as a leader in your organization improve both the effectiveness and speed of nearly any change effort. Change efforts will fail when they lack the critical success factors we've listed in Exhibit P.1; therefore, if you are serious about transformation, you must deal with these factors effectively.

HOW THE TWO-MINUTE DRILL WORKS IN FOOTBALL

Whether it is a USC quarterback trying to score a last-second touchdown against Notre Dame in a game affecting national rankings, or the New England Patriots kicking a last-second field goal to win the Super Bowl, two-minute drills can be used to snatch victory from the jaws of defeat. A two-minute drill is an offensive strategy in which one team attempts to move the ball rapidly down the field to score when it is losing late in a game. The quarterback must demonstrate great poise and must seize control of the game. The other team members will use plays that they are confident will enable them to move the ball while controlling the clock. Successful two-minute drills are run with a sense of urgency but without a sense of crisis, panic, or despair. Teamwork becomes paramount as each individual must perform his assignment on each play for the team to be successful. Two-minute drills are exciting to be part of and are fun to watch when your team has the ball and is in control of its own destiny.

HOW THE TWO-MINUTE DRILL CAN WORK FOR YOU

Business organizations can use the same disciplined mind-set and practices of the TMD to accomplish any and all of the following goals:

- Accelerate sales growth
- Implement a lean manufacturing initiative
- Accelerate a cost reduction program
- Roll out an improved customer relationship management process
- Implement any type of change faster and with greater effect

So what is a Two-Minute Drill from a business perspective? The Two-Minute Drill is a critical leadership practice of creating rapid and real organizational change and improvement by using the fundamentals of rapid scoring from American football. The Two-Minute Drill is designed to give you a vehicle that you can use to drive real improvement when the stakes are high, time is short, and real results are needed.

Why this sports analogy? Here are just some of the benefits of adapting the concept of the two-minute drill to change efforts and performance improvements at work:

- The two-minute drill is a powerful metaphor *that captures the most critical components* of the change process.

- The two-minute drill is about *winning the game of change,* not just going through the motions.
- The two-minute drill *creates a vivid picture* in the mind of the team.
- The two-minute drill is *simple and straightforward* in its approach to change.
- The two-minute drill requires *the leader to be cast in the role of the quarterback.* And nearly everyone has an opinion and view of what makes a good quarterback: that's what "Monday-morning quarterbacking" is all about!

But before we describe in detail what football can teach you about business success, let's look at a case study of an all-too-common scenario in business today.

"WE HAVE TO MOVE FASTER AND EXECUTE BETTER . . . AND EVERYBODY KNOWS IT!"

This proclamation was recently made during a sobering and heartfelt discussion with the president of a diversified service enterprise that was experiencing very hard times. This executive's situation illustrates the importance of speed and change in today's marketplace. His declaration made it clear that things in his organization needed to change faster and more effectively, and also reflected the fact that people on his leadership team were in agreement with his position (although whether they were willing to speak publicly to that end might be another matter).

With increasing regularity and frequency during the past several years, we have heard various versions of this proclamation made by thousands of leaders in hundreds of organizations in nearly every industry in America. This president's comment, "We have to move faster and execute better!" is the driving force behind the book that you are about to read. Ask yourself the key question given on page 6.

This leader's organization had experienced more than a decade of uninterrupted growth and profitability, and it had carved out a nice niche for itself in its industry, which it could

> **Key Question**
> Is real change happening fast enough in your organization to help you get the results you need for success?

defend from its traditional competitors. Margins were strong, shareholder value was growing, and life was good. The company had invested heavily in technology and automation, and it had reengineered the organization and streamlined processes at all levels. In addition, the company was ISO certified and had implemented a formal continuous improvement process that had yielded sound and solid results during the early years. It made steady progress in investing and developing its workforce to improve productivity, reduce unwanted turnover, and make the organization an employer of choice, which allowed the company to compete in the "war for talent."

In short, this organization appeared to have done all the right things, yet it was now struggling to hit its performance goals and achieve the results it so desperately needed. What had happened? Was this just another case of ineffective top management? Was it bad strategy? Was it the competition? Could it be blamed on forces beyond the company's control?

An in-depth analysis of this organization's situation revealed that the root of this enterprise's dilemma was not that it did not know what to do to successfully compete. Rather, the problem was that *it was ineffective at executing real and rapid organizational change to achieve better performance.*

This organization was constantly running a long list of improvement initiatives. The words of one manager captured the essence of this organization's current state: "We are all scrambling to make things happen to get at better performance, but scrambling gets old fast." This scrambling typically led to a rather lengthy and cumbersome process for arriving at the decisions to make needed changes. It seemed as if every serious change this organization tried to make required

- Large formal committees
- Diverse improvement teams

- Lengthy analytical procedures
- Endless meetings
- Fancy PowerPoint presentations
- Tiresome report writing
- A myriad of other time-consuming and distracting activities

Collectively, all this activity tended to suck the momentum and vitality out of the company's change efforts before the organization was able to deliver better performance. Further, by the time the company implemented the decisions, the improvement opportunity or the marketplace had frequently moved on. Large quantities of time and resources had been expended, with little tangible return on investment in the last several years. Managers and workers alike had become cynical about "change misfires," "talk without action," and "treading water." In the words of one jaded middle manager in this organization, "We're good at everything but actually changing." It is our opinion that these views are widespread among organizations.

Although some might say this is nothing new, a deeper look across the competitive landscape suggests that the state of the game has changed significantly in recent years. An organization's ability to transform itself rapidly and to execute change flawlessly has become the name of the game (and this organization was currently losing that game). This organization's culture and leadership had developed an approach to change and improvement that had worked in the past, but the current business environment now demanded more speed and effectiveness than this organization was in the habit of delivering. This president and his lieutenants were worried about their organization's long-term viability, but they were equally concerned about keeping their jobs, and rightfully so.

BETTER RESULTS ARE REQUIRED FASTER

Recent trends in management terminations and downsizing suggest that this president's concerns are well justified. Business is adapting a football mind-set: when business leaders can't achieve desired results fast enough, their tenure is in question. Football coaches at all levels are on a very short leash when it comes to developing and maintaining *winning* programs. Institutions, alumni, and fans all want success *now!* Because of this, the tenure of both professional and college coaches is in a downward trend. The same is true of quarterbacks who might experience Super Bowl success one year, only to find themselves on the bench or even traded the next year. Personnel changes are a critically important part of developing and maintaining a winning team.

In the words of the CEO of a large service conglomerate, "The global economy is increasing competitive pressure in every industry, which almost always requires change…and change requires real leadership to get results.…If the leader can't get better results, they are sitting on a career powder keg." Business leaders today must lead the change process more effectively and at a faster tempo than their predecessors, or they run the risk of losing their jobs and, in the worst-case scenario, maybe even their organizations. Open up any business periodical or publication these days, and you'll see eye-catching headlines that reflect the growing need for better performance. For example:

- "Business as Usual; Formula for Disaster"
- "Change or Die"
- "Memo to Top Management: Improve Results or Go"
- "Managers Experience Growing Profit Pressure"

It is important to note that improving performance and getting better results almost always require change. To this end, the ability to lead and execute change becomes paramount to a leader's long-term success and survival. Research findings have made it clear that the current state of the game in organizations demands that managers get better results for their enterprises sooner rather than later.

Five Sobering Reasons Why You Need to Improve the Performance of Your Organization

1. CEOs are being replaced at a record rate at organizations across the United States as shareholders are placing increasing pressure on sustaining performance and improving shareholder value.[2]

2. A recent survey of corporate management downsizing decisions found that the number one factor used in deciding which leaders were let go was the individual's ability to achieve desired results on an ongoing basis.[3]
3. Organizations are much more likely to remove managers who do not hit performance goals than they were a decade ago, regardless of the cause of failure.[4]
4. A large sample of managers recently reported that the abilities to get results and sustain performance were the single most important factors for career success and survival in their organizations.[5]
5. Improving performance on an ongoing basis has been directly linked to a leader's propensity to keep his or her job, be promoted, and improve his or her compensation situation.[6]

Although achieving results has always been critical, the imperative for achieving better results *more quickly* is becoming increasingly powerful. Ask yourself the following question:

> **Key Question**
> Are you achieving the results that you need to advance your career?

WHAT ARE YOU DOING TO GET BETTER RESULTS?

Alfred DuPont Chandler, the noted Harvard business historian, concluded that businesses typically change primarily when they are forced to change, whether by internal or external factors.[7] His findings carry an important message for today's leaders, in that there is a tendency in all of us to *avoid* change when possible, thus creating a myriad of problems for both our careers and our organizations.

We have found that organizations pursue performance improvement in a wide variety of ways, including the following:

- Reengineering and process redesign
- Six Sigma

- Lean manufacturing
- Toyota Production Systems and Kaizen
- Restructuring and workforce reductions
- Customer and supplier partnerships
- Enhanced operating technologies
- Improved human resource management efforts

These initiatives are designed to improve operating performance, customer satisfaction, and the bottom line, and to demonstrate to owners, shareholders, managers, and employees that the enterprise is serious about getting better performance. In the words of one CEO, "Knowing that we have formalized improvement processes in place helps me sleep at night."

We have found, paradoxically, that embedded in most organizational attempts at change and improvement are the very seeds of ineffective and sluggish change. Through our research and experience with rapid organizational improvement, we have learned that the keys to real change are leadership, speed, and execution. Remember, *real change* requires *real leadership*, regardless of what performance metric you are trying to improve or what kind of change you are trying to implement. Although teams, committees, and task forces can be useful tools, they are not an effective and meaningful substitute for leadership in any improvement effort. Thus a leader's performance in the twenty-first century is more critical than at any other point in business history. To this end, we would like to briefly review some research findings that might be of interest; they also form the basis for this book.

WHAT WE LEARNED FROM OUR RESEARCH ON CHANGE

For the past decade, we have conducted an ongoing applied research study on successful and unsuccessful organizational efforts at change. We have chronicled both the factors that are the driving forces for successful organizational transformations and those that have led to change failures and meltdowns. In essence, this has really been an effort to understand the change process in organizations that *had* to do things differently to get better performance and remain in the competitive game.

We used a wide variety of data collection methodologies, including interviews, focus groups, and surveys. Our sample of more than one thousand managers across all our studies included 31 percent senior, 36 percent middle, and 33 percent frontline managers. Without going into a great deal of detail on our findings, we would like to share a quick summary of what we have learned, which has given us cause for concern and a burning passion to help business leaders and their organizations become more proficient at winning the game of change. The following "challenges of change" emerged from our research findings.

Typical Problems That Get in the Way of an Organization's Efforts to Change and Improve

- *Most improvement in organizations is not continuous;* rather, it is discontinuous: changes take place, things settle down, habits and routines develop, and the need for change emerges again at a later point.
- *Time is the enemy of most change efforts,* because the longer the change takes to plan and implement, the more difficult it is for leaders and teams to maintain focus, enthusiasm, and momentum.
- Frequently, managers and employees are asked to make *changes that have little or nothing to do with improving real performance.* A similar problem is that often no one has clearly defined the desired outcome of the change—which causes a lack of commitment, motivation, and confidence.
- A *sense of importance and urgency* on the part of those involved with making the change is a critical ingredient of any successful change effort.
- *Change typically represents hardship* for those involved in the process (regardless of how positive the change may be), because the additional activities associated with making change happen take place on top of an already busy schedule.
- *Planning change is frequently a game of extremes:* leaders and participants tend either to underplan or to overplan for the rollout of change initiatives, with negative outcomes at either end of the continuum.

- *A leader must ultimately be responsible for every change initiative* if it is to be successful, and the credibility of the leader carries great weight in the success or failure of any change effort.
- If not properly maintained, *formal improvement processes can cause a myriad of dysfunctional problems,* including
  - Improvement bureaucracies
  - Organizational caste systems of participants
  - Paperwork jungles
  - Leaders' abdicating their roles and responsibilities in the change process
- *Many change efforts are too complicated* to be properly executed in the real world of the workplace.
- *Communication breakdowns are a primary cause of failure* in change efforts, and leaders frequently overestimate their own effectiveness in sharing critical information with those who must make the change work.
- At some point, *all change must become personal and individualized,* because people must be equipped and motivated to act differently if things are going to actually change collectively.
- In many organizations, *so many change initiatives are in action at any one time that they are not taken seriously* by those involved.
- When positive change and improvement do take place, *organizations are frequently prone to backsliding* and allowing old behaviors and practices to reemerge, which nullifies improvement.
- *Politics are inevitably something that either accelerates or decelerates the change process,* regardless of the size of the organization; politics must therefore be taken into consideration in any attempt at making change.

We share these general findings with you to reinforce what you already know: that change is by no means an easy process. Clearly the nature of the change game requires a special mind-set and mode of operation if an organization is to be successful at overcoming these challenges. Can you relate to any of these findings? If you can, you are like most of us. With this background, ask yourself the following very important question. As you read this book, we are confident that your thinking on the subject will be greatly stimulated in a very practical way.

> **Key Question**
> As a leader, what must you do to lead and execute
> change initiatives more effectively to achieve better
> results faster?

HOW THIS BOOK IS ORGANIZED

Chapter One is an overview of the entire book; it includes a
detailed description of the two-minute drill in football and a pre-
view of the eight TMD principles you can apply to improve the
performance of your business. Chapters Two through Nine then
discuss each of the eight TMD principles in detail. In each chapter,
we recount a two-minute drill from a great moment in football
history to provide the context for the principle described. We
also include a detailed business case study that vividly illustrates
how different problems often play out in the workplace. Please
note that the organizational and managerial examples provided
throughout this book are all real. The names have been changed
to protect confidentiality and competitive advantage; however,
we use direct quotations from study participants throughout the
book to illuminate the points we illustrate.

In addition, we've included Key Questions throughout the
book, as well as end-of-chapter checklists and "momentum builders" to help you think through how you can apply the eight principles of the Two-Minute Drill to improve the performance of your
own organization.

LET'S GET STARTED!

As we conclude our introduction on the state of the game, we ask
you to complete the exercise that follows. We are confident that
it will help you draw the parallels between effective change and
a successful two-minute drill in football. As you approach learning how to run an effective workplace two-minute drill, remember
the words of Tony Dorsett, the legendary Dallas Cowboys running
back and Heisman trophy winner: "To succeed...you need something to hold onto, something to motivate you and something to

inspire you!" It is our hope that this book can do just that. Let the game begin.

A STARTING TMD WORKOUT: THINK ABOUT YOUR OWN ORGANIZATION'S CHANGE EFFORTS

Stop right now and think of an *unsuccessful* change initiative that your organization recently implemented—one that did not produce real change or improvement. What were the causes of this failure? Make a list and be specific. Now do the same for a successful change initiative that you have recently experienced. Set these lists aside for the time being. Later in the book we will ask you to compare what you wrote with our findings about successful organizational change efforts. We're going out on a limb in asking you to do this, but we are very confident about what you will find. *Go for it!*

THE TWO-MINUTE DRILL MIND-SET

Eight Winning Principles Business Leaders Can Learn from the Great Game of Football

Accelerating change requires skill, determination, and considerable imagination. It requires challenging an accepted paradigm of how change is introduced and managed and the searching for ways of doing things differently and better.
—TODD DICK, AUTHOR OF *MANAGING CHANGE*

People who work together will win, whether it is against complex football defenses, or the problems of modern society.
—VINCE LOMBARDI, LEGENDARY COACH OF THE GREEN BAY PACKERS

The Power of the Two-Minute Drill: David vs. Goliath—the Toledo Rockets vs. the Pittsburgh Panthers, September 20, 2003

When fans filed into the Glass Bowl Stadium to see the unheralded University of Toledo Rockets of the Mid-American Conference take on the ninth-ranked University of Pittsburgh Panthers in fall 2003, they were coming to see a classic case of David versus Goliath.

Toledo, a mid-major program with an untested starting sophomore quarterback named Bruce Gradkowski, was pitted against Big East powerhouse Pitt, with a high-powered offense and the nation's number one receiver, Larry Fitzgerald. Pitt clearly controlled the first half of the contest: at halftime, Pitt led 24–14.

The Rockets took the opening second-half kickoff and engineered a strong fourteen-play, 82-yard drive to bring the score to 24–21. The teams then traded punts, but Pitt's next possession culminated in a seven-play, 60-yard scoring drive that put them up 31–21 with 2:43 remaining in the third quarter. Pitt's offense was beginning to control the line of scrimmage, and the Toledo defense was having a difficult time putting pressure on the mobile Pitt quarterback, Rod Rutherford.

Toledo received the kickoff but fumbled on the next possession, turning the ball over to Pitt on its own 37-yard line. Pitt was deep in Toledo territory with an opportunity to put the game away, until an interception gave the Rockets the ball back on their own 2-yard line. The Toledo quarterback then led a twelve-play, 98-yard scoring drive that included a gutsy fourth-down-and-6 conversion on the Rockets' own 45-yard line. The score was now Pitt 31, Toledo 28. The Panthers took possession on their own 20-yard line, but failed to keep their drive alive and were forced to punt the ball to Toledo, which took possession at its own 17-yard line.

As time was running out late in the fourth quarter, both teams knew exactly what they had to do to win this game. There was tremendous excitement in the air, and both head coaches knew that what happened in the next several minutes would have a profound effect on their teams, their seasons, and their programs. Both teams had practiced for this very moment. A defensive stop would mean a win for Pitt. But a successful 83-yard drive would mean a win for the underdog.

The players and fans on both sides were all staring at a scoreboard that showed a 4-point deficit for the Rockets. This score ruled out a field goal and forced the Rockets to go for a touchdown to win. The Toledo offense would put its best players on the field for this final drive. The offense would execute a two-minute drill, with a package of plays and players that they were very confident would allow them to move the ball down the field while controlling the clock. They would have to communicate intensely above the roar of the capacity crowd that had now risen to its feet. The Rocket quarterback would need to exercise great leadership, demonstrate poise, and make wise decisions on every play if his team was to be successful.

Final score: Rockets 35, Panthers 31. Toledo's Gradkowski drove his team to score, covering 83 yards in fifteen plays and completing nine out of ten passes, including a 13-yard completion on a "do-or-die" fourth down and 2. The offensive line gave the QB solid pass protection, although Gradkowski had to use his scrambling abilities on several occasions to "make things happen." The winning scoring play occurred when he hit wide receiver Lance Moore in the right corner of the end zone, and Moore made a "circus catch" for the touchdown. The Rocket defense rose to the occasion to close out the game by breaking up several deep passes to Larry Fitzgerald, as Pitt attempted to get into field-goal position and put the game into overtime.

In Gradkowski's first big start as a college quarterback, the Pittsburgh native completed forty-nine of sixty-two passes for 461 yards and three touchdowns. He had demonstrated his ability to take a hit and had shown great poise, despite the fact that his team was behind for all but the final forty-three seconds of this contest. After the game, head coach Tom Amstutz said, "We prepared for this challenge, everyone did their job, we had great leadership, and we executed our game plan. . . . Coming from behind makes this an awesome win and makes a real statement about our program and the quality of our players and coaches! We played to win!"

ORGANIZATIONAL CHANGE GONE WRONG: A CULTURE OF NOT SCORING AND NOT PLAYING TO WIN

Five years ago, a Fortune 500 manufacturing organization made a strategic decision to implement Six Sigma as a continuous improvement process to respond to increasing domestic and international competition. Over several years, Six Sigma had been rolled out on a corporation-wide basis and had demonstrated some success in reducing costs, improving processes, and providing the organization with a common set of tools to use in planning and executing change.

In recent years, however, the Six Sigma process had "lost steam" and had become what some described as a "sluggish, bureaucratic money-pit." The organization had spent millions of dollars in creating the Six Sigma culture, and senior managers had taken great comfort in the fact that Six Sigma was in place. Now, serious questions were being raised about the overall value and contribution of this process.

In response to these concerns, CEO Jim Armstrong commissioned a study to assess the current state of Six Sigma; it revealed the following key findings:

- People who were part of the Six Sigma team were individually committed to the effort, and they strongly believed they were making a difference in the organization's performance, but they viewed lack of teamwork as a barrier to organizational change.
- Managers within the organization believed that the Six Sigma process had become somewhat of a bureaucracy, that the company was frequently involved with far too many initiatives that might not be contributing to its bottom-line performance, and that results were not always evident.
- Managers believed that the measures used to assess Six Sigma performance were not as meaningful as they should be and that there was an overemphasis on giving credit to training programs and the development of more "black and green belts," rather than on actual performance improvement.
- Managers in many parts of the organization admitted to relinquishing their responsibilities for driving improvement efforts, handing them over to Six Sigma team members.
- Employees believed that the organization was undertaking too many initiatives at any one time, which created a loss of focus, and there was a strong opinion that the overall program was cumbersome and that actual improvements were very slow in coming.
- There was a certain level of animosity and tension between those responsible for executing change and the black and green belts who facilitated the development of the change initiative; this suggested that a "caste system" existed that elevated "the belts" in relation to the rest of the organization.
- There was a belief that black belts were receiving far too much credit for successful efforts and not taking enough responsibility when initiatives faltered or failed to produce real change and improvement.

This organization was at a crossroads: the very process it was counting on to drive change and continuous improvement had become, in the minds of far too many people, an *impediment* to change. The CEO wondered if they were playing to win. At this point, top managers were analyzing what they needed to do to revitalize this initiative; needless to say, they were experiencing anguish and frustration over the whole situation.

Jim Armstrong came to the conclusion that Six Sigma could not help move this organization forward unless managers at all levels of the enterprise increased their direct involvement in the change process. Although the Six Sigma process was sound and proven, it could achieve nothing without leadership and momentum. If his organization was going to get a return on investment for Six Sigma, Armstrong needed to get his managers to come off the sidelines, step onto the playing field, and become *leaders* in the change process, rather than simply spectators. It was becoming increasingly apparent to all that the process wasn't working, yet few (if any) leaders were willing to openly discuss the situation.

APPLYING THE TMD'S RAPID SCORING TO BUSINESS SITUATIONS

Every football fan has a favorite game that ended in a "big finish" that he or she can remember, and we are no different. We opened our discussion of the TMD model with the Pittsburgh-Toledo game for several reasons:

- All three of us were at this same game, and we know many of the people involved; we could compare notes, feelings, and memories of this terrific comeback win. We all witnessed firsthand the power of an effective two-minute drill.
- This game involved an underdog performing at an exceptional level when it had to do so to be successful. From a business perspective, we find this taking place more and more often as domestic organizations frequently find themselves to be the underdogs competing on a global playing field.
- This game exemplifies the ingredients that are critical to producing rapid scoring in a very competitive environment where time is of the utmost importance.

Now let's shift the focus from football to the workplace. Armstrong's organization had created a playbook for change and continuous improvement; it had started out with great promise and fanfare, but was currently struggling with the execution of that game plan and was disappointed with its results. (Recent research on this subject tells us that this company is not alone.[1]) With the passage of time, the factors that drive real and successful change had eroded away. The big Toledo win illustrates what these factors are:

- Recognizing the importance of leadership
- Knowing the score
- Having a sense of urgency
- Using an appropriate package of plays
- Having the right players on the field
- Moving the chains
- Creating momentum
- Using the talents of individual players for the good of the team

These attributes of a successful two-minute drill in football are the very factors that our research indicates are the ingredients of successful and faster organizational change.

Although fans whose teams have just executed a successful two-minute drill experience the elation and "adrenaline rush" that comes with a last-second win, they frequently fail to realize a deeper issue: the use of a two-minute drill or of a "hurry-up offense" means that the team is not winning the game: it is behind on the scoreboard, and the players must do something very different soon or they will lose! The team running the two-minute drill is not in this position by choice but rather because it has fallen behind on the scoreboard and because an opponent has imposed its will on the losing team. But there is good news hidden here. Although no one intends to be behind in a football game or in a business setting, the circumstances and tension created by being behind (or losing) can be used to cause very good things to happen quickly—if you know how to tap into this reservoir of energy. You might be behind, but you're still in the game with an opportunity to turn things around if you systematically execute a plan of attack that is aimed to score quickly.

A starting point for unlocking the power of the TMD mind-set is to analyze a TMD that you have witnessed and draw out your own lessons from that experience. Think now of a successful and memorable two-minute drill that you have personally experienced as a coach, a player, or a football fan. Then think about each of the following questions and write out your answers:

- How did your team get into the position where it would have to run a successful TMD to win?
- As a team, how did the team members perform differently in the final minutes of the contest, as compared to the rest of the game?
- What specific things did the quarterback do during the TMD to help the team win?

Your responses to each of these questions can shed light on the important issue of how to lead successful change. If you are like most of us, you are currently facing a situation at work in which you are behind on the scoreboard on some important performance dimension. You're probably under increasing pressure to do something differently, sooner rather than later, to bring about the changes—and this is where the Two-Minute Drill can help you make real change happen fast.

TMD BUSINESS SUCCESS STORIES

We have chronicled and been part of numerous workplace two-minute drills in which organizations used TMD principles to implement successful improvements quickly. Here are just a few examples:

- A financial services organization analyzed and implemented changes in its supply chain, creating a 16 percent cost savings in forty-five days.
- A health care organization implemented a new system for managing patient and customer satisfaction information in two months, giving leaders real-time data for decision making.
- A domestic manufacturer began importing 40 percent of its component parts and created and implemented an effective delivery and distribution system to its domestic plant operations in one quarter.

- A Fortune 1000 service organization redesigned and executed a new sales strategy and selling model to better meet changing customer demographics, with an improvement in top-line sales within six months.
- A manufacturing plant shaved 11 percent off of its cost of sales in three months to respond to demands from its customers for price reductions.

All these initiatives achieved rapid and effective change because leaders and followers were willing to approach improvement with a TMD mind-set.

Of course, if you are currently winning "across the board" on all the results that are critical to your success, then count your blessings and stick with your current game plan. You are to be commended that your game plan is working and that you are winning! But when you find yourself needing to change quickly to improve performance, to execute a new business plan, or to change a current process, then you might consider applying the TMD mind-set to make things happen. In doing so, it is important to remember the words of author Todd Dick in this chapter's opening quotation: "Accelerating change requires skill, determination, and considerable imagination."

OVERVIEW OF THE TWO-MINUTE DRILL FOR ORGANIZATIONAL CHANGE

Now we'd like to walk you through our TMD model, which has emerged and evolved from our research and practice on rapid organizational change and improvement. We're confident that when we have finished, you will look at your approach to change somewhat differently. Let's start with the what, who, how, when, why, and where of the Two-Minute Drill.

- **What is a TMD?** A TMD is the critical leadership practice of applying the principles of rapid scoring from American football to the process of organizational change. The TMD is designed to give you as a leader a vehicle that you can use to drive real change and improvement when the stakes are high, time is short, and real results are needed.

- **Who is involved in a TMD?** The most important person in running a TMD is the quarterback of your team. Your team is made up of the members of your organization who are ultimately responsible for making change happen.
- **How is a TMD run?** The key to running a successful TMD is applying each of the critical scoring practices to your change and improvement initiatives in a concentrated and flawless fashion.
- **When is a TMD appropriate?** When a change effort is required for your organization to be successful and it needs to happen sooner rather than later.
- **Why is a TMD appropriate?** A TMD is about serious change. If a change is worth making, it must be taken seriously by you and all the people engaged in this effort. The TMD gives you a time-sensitive tool for executing change.
- **Where do you use a TMD?** A TMD can be conducted in any type of initiative or at any level of an organization. The key is to identify the unit of operation to be engaged in this process.

If you don't take the change effort seriously, or you just go through the motions, you damage your credibility as a leader, which can have far-reaching implications. At the end of the Prologue, we asked you to identify an unsuccessful and a successful change initiative in which you participated and to describe the causes of failure and success. Pull out that TMD workout homework and review your response. As we walk you through the TMD process, compare what you wrote down with the research findings that are the basis of the TMD and see what you learn. We believe that all leaders need to engage their imaginations and develop their own interpretations of the key components of a TMD, keeping in mind that the TMD principles should be viewed as "absolutes" that are necessary for successful change and improvement.

The cornerstone of an effective TMD is to never waste time, so let's get started with our review of the TMD model, illustrated in Exhibit 1.1. The rest of this chapter gives an overview of the eight TMD principles in the model. We want to repeat that each principle of the TMD is derived from our research findings on successful organizational change, which we highlight in Winning with TMD boxes throughout the chapter.

Exhibit 1.1: The Two-Minute Drill Model for Organizational Change and Improvement

Know the Score and Define Winning
- Know the score
- Use the scoreboard to define winning
- Communicate what it means to win

Develop Scouting Report and Match-Ups
- Know what you are up against
- Determine match-ups

Create an Extreme Focus and a Sense of Urgency
- Declare the importance of the win
- Create extreme focus
- Ratchet up the sense of urgency
- Rally the team—fast

You Are the Quarterback
- *Be energized to play at a new level*
- *Seize control of the game*
- *Communicate above the roar of the crowd*
- *Create ownership of the drive*
- *Keep the play clock in your head*
- *Make adjustments on the field quickly*
- *Have the courage to take a hit but avoid being sacked*
- *Find a way to win*
- *Be a cheerleader*
- *Demonstrate poise*

Develop a Winning TMD Package
- Identify the right people to have on the field, ready to play with requisite skills
- Use the right plays
- Take ownership of the drive
- Clarify individual assignments

Execute the Right Plays and Score
- Establish a TMD scoreboard
- Snap the ball and move the chains
- Make necessary adjustments fast
- Manage the clock and keep the team hustling
- Execute in the red zone and score

Close Out the Game, Then Celebrate
- Make sure you are really scoring
- Wait to celebrate
- Make sure the score holds up
- Celebrate the drive and the win
- Hand out the right trophies

Conduct a Postgame Analysis and Press Conference
- Analyze the game for lessons
- Share the lessons
- Avoid politics

TMD Principle 1: You Are the Quarterback

Very few, if any, successful TMDs are executed without effective leadership on the part of the quarterback, who must possess a special skill set. And although most business supervisors, managers, and executives have been encouraged to think and act like coaches in recent years, leading rapid change and improvement requires hands-on, trustworthy, on-the-playing-field leadership that is *much more* demanding than simply being a coach.[2] Here's why:

- Coaches stand on the sidelines or sit in the press box, where they have a clearer and more perfect view of the field of play and the opponent.
- Coaches do not face career-ending injuries on every play, and they do not have to make decisions in nanoseconds with large people trying to hurt them on every down.
- Coaches can insulate themselves from the noise and clamor of the stadium with headsets, and they can dress to minimize the cruelties of the weather and playing conditions.
- Coaches might call the plays, but the quarterback is the one whose execution of the plays will determine the outcome of the game and the fate of the team.

None of this is to say that being a coach is easy, but rather to emphasize that coaches are not the ones who have to overcome the harsh realities on the field of play in order to succeed. (For this very reason, QBs are frequently called "field generals.")

As the manager in charge of a business unit that must implement real and rapid change—whether that unit is a work group, a department, a division, or an entire enterprise—you must be on the field of play, quarterbacking your team during the change process. You must enact your role as leader, instilling confidence in your players and convincing them that they must take this effort seriously—that the purpose of everyone's efforts is to win and not simply to go through the motions. As the quarterback, you must demonstrate your commitment to the cause and must make everyone on the team realize that success is possible if everyone executes his or her assignments on every play. In the words of Hall of Fame quarterback Terry Bradshaw, "The quarterback's job is to make everyone believe that the team can win, and that takes commitment and courage."

In a nutshell, as a leader playing the quarterback role you must

- Make effective decisions
- Communicate intensely
- Encourage hustle
- Be able to take a hit
- Create the momentum necessary to win

So if you are serious about leading a successful organizational change, you must start to think of yourself as a quarterback. And if someone else is going to lead a change for you, that person must be empowered to be the team's quarterback, with all the requisite skills and authority. We will discuss the quarterback's critical role in Chapter Two.

WINNING WITH TMD

Real and rapid change does not happen without effective, trustworthy, hands-on leadership from the person in charge of that unit.

TMD PRINCIPLE 2: YOU MUST KNOW THE SCORE AND DEFINE WINNING

Going into a two-minute drill, everyone involved knows

- Exactly what score the team needs to win
- Where the team is on the field
- How much time the team has to work with
- How many time-outs remain

Using scoreboard information effectively correlates strongly with a successful outcome of any TMD and any organizational change. As a leader, ask yourself the following questions:

- Do I have a clear sense of whether or not I am currently winning or losing the performance game in which my superiors or shareholders (or both) have asked me to compete?

- Do I work hard to always know how my work group is performing against the performance variables that are most critical to success?
- Do I use my scoreboard to make rapid adjustments?

Although these questions may seem elementary, they are critical to your ability to implement rapid change and needed improvement. An appropriate scoreboard can be an invaluable source of information, inspiration, and motivation.

Back in the earliest days of football, teams kept score on large slates with a piece of chalk. Players had to look around individually to locate where they were on the field and find the down and distance chains to know what was needed for a first down. In addition, they had to ask the officials repeatedly how much time remained in the game. It was difficult for every player to have complete information on the team's status on every play. This undoubtedly led to confusion and lost opportunities. Then scoreboards evolved that allowed the score to be hung up on placards, which were easier to see, and large game clocks began popping up in stadiums across the country. As football entered the "modern era," scoreboard technology advanced rapidly, and scoreboards became a complete and accurate running source of information on the status of each game, including metrics for down and distance, location on the field, time-outs remaining, and giant instant replay screens (which have been a source of pain for football officials since day one).

In TMD situations, the team members must know exactly what it takes to win the game. They must know the outcome they seek and must be led to develop a game plan to achieve it. The successful execution of two-minute drills—both in football and the workplace—requires clearly defined improvement goals and accurate performance data on key metrics that players can view on a scoreboard that is seen and understood by all. We discuss these topics in detail in Chapter Three.

WINNING WITH TMD

Successful change efforts are triggered by the realization that performance on a specific metric is not where it needs to be, that things must change, and that the unit must set clearly defined goals.

TMD PRINCIPLE 3: YOU MUST KNOW YOUR OPPONENT(S)

Going into any football game, teams expend great resources scouting their opponents so they will know what they are up against and how their team's talents match up. Teams do this so that they can formulate a clear game plan based on actual knowledge of their opponent's strengths, weaknesses, and tendencies. Football teams are very careful to make sure that they have accurately assessed their opponents so that they can create match-ups that give them a competitive advantage. Both in business situations and on the football field, we need to take a different twist on a familiar adage: what you don't know *can* hurt you. Going into a change effort without analyzing your real opponent(s) is naive and shortsighted, and it can lead to career-ending injury for a quarterback (who might get blindsided or sacked).

In today's workplace, however, leaders frequently engage in improvement processes without doing any sort of assessment of the true nature of what they are up against. Although leaders are quick to realize that their competitors are their opponents, they might be less quick to realize that *people within their own organization* might also attempt to stop their improvement drive, for any number of reasons. They might even find that their team or even their own leadership style might hurt their efforts. These issues are discussed in detail in Chapter Four, where we'll give you an opportunity to assess who your real opponents are as you're going into your next organizational improvement initiative.

WINNING WITH TMD

Leaders of successful change efforts know who their opponents are, as well as their team's strengths and weaknesses in developing improvement plans.

TMD PRINCIPLE 4: YOU MUST CREATE CLEAR FOCUS AND A SENSE OF URGENCY

When a football team finds itself on its own 20-yard line with 1:53 left in the game and it needs 3 points to win, every player focuses his energies on helping the team get into position to kick a field goal. In such a situation, there is an exceedingly clear focus on the fact that a field goal can win the game, and the time factor creates a sense of urgency for players, coaches, and fans alike.

Similarly, once a business organization knows the score and realizes what performance outcome is necessary for success, it must create a clear focus and a sense of urgency around that performance outcome and the process it will use to get there. That score and the information on the scoreboard help team members maintain their focus on how well they are performing in relation to their goal.

After a TMD victory, people frequently ask football coaches, "Coach, your team just drove down the field and won the game, so why didn't they just move the ball like that the entire game?" This may be a logical question, but it fails to recognize two of the most important factors that galvanize players to achieve a higher level of performance: focus and urgency. The lack of time energizes the team, increasing the pace, tempo, and intensity of the final minutes of the game exponentially. When business organizations approach the change process, these key ingredients are frequently found lacking. Thus, if you're a leader interested in executing rapid change, you must find healthy and creative ways to develop and communicate a clear sense of focus and urgency for those involved in the change initiative. We discuss this in further detail in Chapter Five.

WINNING WITH TMD

Real and rapid change takes place when people have a clear focus on achieving a specific, desired outcome and when they believe that the changes are important and must happen sooner rather than later in order for them to avoid negative consequences.

TMD PRINCIPLE 5: YOU MUST DEVELOP A WINNING TWO-MINUTE DRILL PACKAGE

Successful football teams know their opponents and their own strengths and weaknesses, and they go into every game with a collection of plays that are designed to help them achieve success when they are behind, with time running out. This collection of plays and the players who execute them is called a TMD package and is special in a number of important ways:

- Every play in the TMD package is designed to use time sparingly and to get the ball into the hands of the team members who are "difference makers," "go-to guys," and "money players."
- Each and every play has a starting and stopping point, and it's practiced and rehearsed so that team members know their assignments well and are capable of making adjustments at the line of scrimmage.
- Each play in the TMD package is designed for a specific outcome to advance the ball and put the team in a position to score.

It is not surprising to find that teams at the high school, intercollegiate, and professional levels devote significant practice time on a daily basis to TMD preparation. This is because coaches and quarterbacks don't want to blow an opportunity to win a close game because of something that they could have controlled with planning and practice. As Penn State's legendary coach Joe Paterno said, "The will to win is important, but the will to prepare is vital."

Because of their preparation, most teams enter TMD situations with confidence; they know they have a chance to win, using plays and a plan of attack that they believe in and own. Teams use plays specifically designed to get them the results they need to win the game.

In business, however, organizations frequently take an extreme approach to the change and improvement process. Sometimes they approach change in a lackadaisical and cavalier fashion, despite the fact that the stakes are extremely high. These efforts at change can be poorly planned or halfhearted, or they are simply exercises in compliance without commitment or passion. At the other extreme, organizations frequently develop momentous change plans that are too complicated, complex, and rigorous to have any real effect down in the trenches among the people who have to execute the plan and live with the changes.

For you to develop change plans that have a high probability of success, you must balance complexity with common sense, analysis with action, and processes with people. To go into a TMD without taking great care to make sure that the right people are in the right positions with the right talents is to invite failure. The difference between winning and losing is almost always the quality of play of your players on the field. Business organizations, like football teams, must know and understand the skill sets necessary for each position on the field when serious change is required. Imagine asking a quarterback to play center and a center to play quarterback for just one play! Although the outcome of such a decision might be humorous to watch, the impact on the team's ability to score would most likely be catastrophic. Yet all of us have seen similar personnel decisions made during our careers, with the same sad outcome.

As a leader, you must have a TMD package of plays that represents your game plan for change. Sometimes your play package comes from your boss or from a corporate initiative. Sometimes you develop your own change package or use a problem-solving team to do so. At other times you employ a continuous improvement team from a Six Sigma, Kaizen, or Lean manufacturing process. Regardless of the source of your TMD package of improvement plays, you must link those plays to the outcome you are trying to improve on and follow the guidelines that we discuss in more detail in Chapter Six.

Winning with TMD

Effective change is based on plans of action that are realistic, understandable, designed to get a specific result using the talents of the right people, and highly likely to succeed when properly executed.

TMD Principle 6: Snap the Ball, Execute the Right Plays, and Score

In a successful TMD, time is the single most important resource, and each play is of critical value. Wasted plays kill scoring opportunities. In football, knowing the snap count for each play is a basic yet vital component in a team's efforts to score. When a team is executing a TMD, stadium noise can be a significant barrier to effective communication. It can cause a multitude of problems—for example, players might not hear the play that is called or miss the snap count. When a player jumps offside and starts a play prematurely, his team will be penalized. When a player comes off the ball late, the team's ability to properly execute their assignment diminishes quickly. Receivers are suddenly behind in their pass routes, running backs are late taking the handoff, and offensive linemen are frequently beaten by defensive linemen because they started late.

Successful TMDs are characterized by a clear starting point in which coordinated action commences at the direction of the quarterback. Successful efforts at change are characterized by individuals' and groups' knowing that it is time to execute the individual assignments necessary to support each play in your TMD change package. One of the key components to any successful TMD is the principle of "moving the chains": executing your plays so that your team achieves first downs and so that the scoring drive can "stay alive."

Getting off to a proper start in any change effort increases the likelihood of success by avoiding false starts that have a debilitating effect on the morale and confidence of team members. Once the ball has been snapped, every person on the team must execute the assignment that he or she has been given to support the team's effort at change and improvement. A team may have a great play on paper, but if individuals and groups do not execute their assignments, the likelihood of failure increases significantly. Successfully executing all the plays in a TMD package will help the team score the desired outcome. Chapter Seven discusses the importance of snapping the ball and executing the right plays.

WINNING WITH TMD

Successful change initiatives have a clear and specific starting point; individuals and groups clearly understand that their performance will determine the success of the effort and that it will be measured and critiqued accordingly.

TMD PRINCIPLE 7: CLOSE OUT THE GAME, THEN CELEBRATE

Closing out the change game is critically important, because it means that before celebrating victory, leaders and their teams take the steps necessary to ensure that an improvement effort holds up. We have all seen teams come from behind and get ahead on the scoreboard, only to see their opponents defeat them in the final seconds because they did not do the things necessary to protect their advantage. This highlights the crucial role leaders play in motivating their team members through every phase of an improvement initiative. The desire to win and be successful in the workplace can be a powerful motivator when people feel part of a team doing important and real work that is making a difference for coworkers, customers, owners, and other stakeholders.

One of the most exciting things about experiencing a TMD is the anticipation prior to the snap of the ball or when the pass is in the air or when the kick is on its way. People are anticipating that something big is going to happen, and when it does, they go crazy. When a team scores the go-ahead touchdown or field goal at the culmination of the TMD, everyone watching the game knows that the team has scored. Scoring has a powerful motivating effect on the players and the fans because everybody likes to win.

In the workplace, people frequently do a good job at improving performance, making a significant change, fixing an urgent customer problem, or streamlining a process. Sadly, these high performers often are not reminded or told that they have done a great job—that they have scored. Why is there no celebration?

In truly successful change efforts, people know what score they need and what they need to do to get that score. They also know that they will be congratulated for scoring and helping their organization win.

But scoring celebrations should be held in check until the game is closed out and the effects of the change efforts have been maintained and have become part of the team's operating fabric and daily modus operandi. At that point, the organization should celebrate the team's successes in a meaningful way, at both the group and individual levels. These important issues will be discussed in more detail in Chapter Eight.

> **WINNING WITH TMD**
> Leaders must let performers know when they score, make the changes stick, and celebrate the success.

TMD PRINCIPLE 8: CONDUCT YOUR POSTGAME ANALYSIS AND PRESS CONFERENCE

One of the marks of a winning team is that it is constantly looking for new and better ways of doing things, and learning not only from its mistakes but also from its successes. A successful team will always review game films and statistics, not simply to relive the glory of the moment (although this is one reason for reviewing game films), but also to better understand what went right, what could have gone wrong, and what could have been done better.

Change is a never-ending process in business organizations, too: the more a team can learn about why a change effort was successful, the better off it will be when it's time to make the next major change. In addition to simply knowing and understanding the causes of success, it is important to *share* that information with others in your organization. Just as coaches hold press conferences to share their insight on their winning ways, business leaders can do something similar to create benchmarks and encourage others in the organization to make change happen. This process can also provide your team with an additional opportunity for reflection and celebration. These practices will be discussed in detail in Chapter Nine.

> **WINNING WITH TMD**
> Organizations should review and analyze their change efforts so that they can document lessons and share them with others.

CONCLUSION AND A CALL TO ACTION

Our purpose in sharing this chapter's overview of our TMD model was to give you an opportunity to engage your imagination in creating a TMD mind-set as it pertains to the process of change. As the quarterback of any change effort, you need to remember that each of these key principles represents a set of imperatives that, if properly executed, are *momentum builders* that increase your likelihood of success in the change game. Conversely, if these principles are not part of your change mind-set and actions, they represent *momentum busters* that can cause your efforts to be bogged down, stifled, and fraught with frustration and ultimately failure.

As you prepare to use this book in your daily business life, please take several minutes to complete the TMD self-assessment in Exhibit 1.2 and score yourself on the extent to which you effectively practice each of the key components of the TMD model in your current approach to leading change. We will repeat this self-assessment at the conclusion of the book so that you can see what you have learned about your approach as a leader to organizational change and improvement.

Finally, we end this chapter on a humorous note, with the words of the immortal W. C. Fields: "All this change drives me crazy. I want to try something new and soon." Although we hope that the TMD mind-set is not something completely new to you, it just might keep you from going crazy when leading change.

Exhibit 1.2: The Two-Minute Drill Self-Assessment

Answer each of the following questions as they pertain to your approach to making change happen in your organization:

When approaching change do I...	Never	Rarely	Sometimes	Usually	Always
1. Take control of the change process and lead by example?	❏	❏	❏	❏	❏
2. Do all the things necessary to lead change so as to drive better results and performance?	❏	❏	❏	❏	❏
3. Know when change is required by using an accurate scoreboard?	❏	❏	❏	❏	❏

4. Clearly define what success means when entering a change initiative?   ❏ ❏ ❏ ❏ ❏

5. Know and understand the opponents we face when entering a change initiative?   ❏ ❏ ❏ ❏ ❏

6. Know the strengths and weaknesses of my team so as to create favorable match-ups in a change effort?   ❏ ❏ ❏ ❏ ❏

7. Create and communicate a clear sense of focus on what we are trying to change and how we are going to do it?   ❏ ❏ ❏ ❏ ❏

8. Create a sense of importance and urgency around the change initiative?   ❏ ❏ ❏ ❏ ❏

9. Have a clearly developed set of "plays" that advance the improvement effort and lead to improved performance and success when properly executed?   ❏ ❏ ❏ ❏ ❏

10. Have the right players on the field equipped and ready to play at an optimal level on each and every play?   ❏ ❏ ❏ ❏ ❏

11. Make sure we move the ball down the field, and take corrective action to make adjustments when performance is not where it needs to be?   ❏ ❏ ❏ ❏ ❏

12. Ensure that our players are doing the right things the right way at the right time so as to execute change?   ❏ ❏ ❏ ❏ ❏

13. Do the things necessary to   ❏   ❏   ❏   ❏   ❏
    ensure that the change
    or improvement sticks?
14. Let my team members know   ❏   ❏   ❏   ❏   ❏
    when we have won the game,
    and celebrate success?
15. Review and analyze change   ❏   ❏   ❏   ❏   ❏
    efforts when they are
    completed?
16. Share the lessons learned   ❏   ❏   ❏   ❏   ❏
    from an improvement
    initiative with others?

CHAPTER TWO

YOU ARE THE QUARTERBACK
Leading Your Organization to Improve

> *The toughest part of playing quarterback is the amount of information that must be processed in mere seconds while all Hell is breaking loose around him.*
> —TROY AIKMAN, DALLAS COWBOY HALL OF FAME QUARTERBACK

> *Leadership is the capacity and will to rally men and women to a common purpose and the character which inspires confidence.*
> —FIELD MARSHAL MONTGOMERY, BRITISH ARMY

WINNING IMPERATIVE: *Lead to Win*
You must demonstrate intense, time-focused, hands-on leadership to achieve success in your TMD drive for change.

"The Drive": Denver Broncos vs. Cleveland Browns, AFC Championship Game, January 11, 1987

In football circles, it has become known simply as "The Drive." In the NFL record book, it shows up as the 1987 AFC Championship game between the Cleveland Browns and the Denver Broncos. On a cold, overcast, dreary day in Cleveland, Ohio, Denver quarterback John Elway engineered a 98-yard fourth-quarter drive that helped put his Denver Broncos in Super Bowl XXI. "The Drive" was the prototype of an effective hurry-up offense and two-minute drill when the team is down and its back is against the wall. The Drive also helped propel John Elway's name into the stratosphere with the legends of the NFL.

With his offense struggling for most of the game and his team down 20–13, Elway led his team back in what many describe as one of the best winning drives in the history of the NFL. The Browns scored late in the game to go up by a touchdown, and all the momentum now favored Cleveland. The Broncos fumbled the ensuing kickoff, recovering the ball on their own 2-yard line, giving their team a terrible field position against a tough Cleveland Browns defense. This turn of events suddenly allowed Cleveland fans to imagine their team playing in their very first Super Bowl.

As the Denver offense took to the field, the playing conditions were as challenging as any team could face: the notorious wind off of Lake Erie was whipping through Cleveland Municipal Stadium, and the hostile Cleveland "Dawg Pound" fans were roaring boisterously (and throwing debris onto the field). Fifteen plays later, with 0:39 on the clock, Elway completed his sixth pass of the drive, with a 5-yard touchdown strike to wide receiver Mark Jackson. Rick Karlis's extra point tied the game at 23–23, and the silence in Cleveland stadium was suddenly deafening. The game was now in sudden-death overtime.

The game-tying 98-yard scoring drive showcased several critical plays, including two unscripted (yet confident) runs by Elway. The first was when Elway was forced to scramble when he was tackled for an 8-yard loss on the ninth play of the drive—yet remained composed enough to immediately call a time-out. The second impressive play occurred on third down, when Elway maintained his concentration when the ball bounced off the hip of wide receiver Steve Watson, who was running in motion, and Elway completed a daring 18-yard pass. His leadership in these tough situations kept his team in the game. Clock management also became a critical issue, as Denver covered the last 60 yards of the drive in seven plays, with 1:52 remaining in the game. Elway used all his talents to lead his team down the field with great confidence in the face of great adversity.

Cleveland won the toss in the sudden-death overtime, but gained only 8 yards on its first possession and was forced to punt. On Denver's first possession of the overtime, which started at its own 25-yard line, Elway picked up right where he left off, marching his Broncos 60 yards in nine plays to set up Rich Karlis's game-winning 33-yard field goal, clinching a spot in Super Bowl XXI.

Truly, it was a remarkable team effort, but every great team effort demands a great team leader. On that day, and in forty-seven other games during his sixteen years in the NFL, John Elway quarterbacked his team to game-winning or game-saving drives in the fourth quarter. His competency at coming from behind earned him recognition as the best TMD quarterback in NFL history. Elway was quoted after the Cleveland game as saying, "Great quarterbacks make great plays in great games. That's what it's all about, isn't it?"[1]

Constar, Inc.—Change in a Leadership Vacuum: A Sad Tale of a Poor Leader and a Lost Opportunity

The same characteristics of winning quarterback leadership have direct application in the workplace, when your team must get better results and time is of the utmost importance. What happens when an organization tries to execute change without real leadership? In case after case of studying both successful and unsuccessful efforts at organizational change, we have seen that leadership tends to be an extremely strong predictor of success. You have no doubt seen this during your career. When an organization attempts to improve, leadership is paramount. Without effective leadership, your organization is entering a game that will be very difficult to win and where your opponents just might get the best of you. Let's look at an example to illustrate this point.

Background: Retail Chain Needs Stronger Distribution Centers to Compete

Constar was a regional retail chain with a very strong market share across the Midwest and central states. It fought off competition from some of the national chains with exceptional customer service, an excellent selection of hard-to-find products, and value pricing. Although their retail operations were very solid, the lifeblood of the enterprise was its five distribution centers, which were responsible for providing each retail operation with the lion's share of the products on each store's shelves. These distribution centers had experienced a lot of pressure in recent years to control costs and to improve the quality of service to help this retailer fight off the competition. The organization had used the distribution center closest to the corporate headquarters as a test site for a wide variety of improvement initiatives—ranging from redesigning inventory flow, introducing better information technology, and developing better ways of engaging its large unionized workforce, among others.

As these improvement efforts were implemented and refined at the "corporate" distribution center, they were exported to the four other distribution centers for implementation. One of the distribution centers had a wide variety of ongoing problems that seemed immune to the organization's "packaged" solutions. This particular distribution center was constantly plagued by incomplete orders, shipping damage, inventory losses, service delays, improper documentation on orders leaving the center, and a history of ongoing labor-management conflicts that were viewed as a primary barrier to this distribution center's progress.

A NEW MANAGER IS HIRED—BUT HAS A HANDS-OFF MANAGEMENT STYLE

Several years ago, the company hired Tom White, a new but seasoned distribution center manager who had come in with a great deal of hoopla. Tom was well educated, well dressed, and well connected to the senior leaders at the corporate headquarters. He was viewed as a smooth-talking, hands-off manager who was big on delegation and liked e-mails. Tom had an extensive collection of best-selling business books strategically placed throughout his office, and he frequently used outside consultants. He was often described as a very political manager who did not like to get his hands dirty, who deflected responsibility and avoided taking risks.

Other managers in this operation believed Tom had ego problems, had a tendency to "look down on the little people," and insulated himself from problems and the changes that needed to be made in the operation. It was also widely believed that Tom hid behind labor-management conflicts as the cause of his organization's flatlining performance. It was said that he was simply biding his time in the field before moving up to a corporate position.

A NEW APPROACH: IMPLEMENTING A TOTAL PERFORMANCE MANAGEMENT SYSTEM

Eighteen months into his tenure, Tom's operation had shown marginal improvement at best. Corporate management then mandated the implementation of a new initiative called the Total Performance Management System (TPMS), which had been developed and tested at the corporate distribution center with solid performance outcomes. In addition, the corporate office insisted that Tom's operation produce significant measurable results within six months with the new system. The TPMS was an integrated approach to performance improvement that used a combination of information technology, effective industrial engineering work design, and self-directed work teams. It also boasted of more effective supervision techniques and an ongoing system of performance measurements and feedback.

Tom's response to this initiative followed suit with his modus operandi: he set up a steering committee and delegated responsibility for the implementation to his "number two" person (and his team of frontline supervisors). He followed this with a steady stream of e-mails about the importance of this change, and he had HR conduct the needed training while using the assistance of a consultant to drive the process. This change initiative was viewed as another "flavor of the month" effort by both management and labor alike, and people were often heard saying, "If we hold our breath long enough, this TPMS thing, and maybe Tom, will go away."

The implementation of this effort required a coordinated plan for implementing technical software and training, redesigning the workspace, and conducting frontline supervisory training and team development. Although people at the corporate distribution center believed that the TPMS initiative had been well designed and thought out and was a "foolproof, plug-and-play" program, the effort failed in terms of producing real results during the six-month implementation period. In a nutshell, the TPMS initiative fell flat on its face because it was never taken seriously by the people in this operation.

WHY THE NEW SYSTEM—AND THE NEW MANAGER—FAILED

Corporate headquarters was not pleased with the status of this change effort, and it sent a lead engineer into the operation to interview key personnel and review performance data to determine why the organization had faltered. Here is what she learned:

1. The distribution center manager (Tom) was viewed by his staff as *not providing the leadership necessary* for this effort to be taken seriously; it was business as usual, and he failed to clearly establish the purpose and vision for this initiative.
2. There was *minimal planning* concerning how this effort would be rolled out, who would be responsible for what, and the timelines for implementation.
3. There was virtually *no teamwork or cooperation* among the people in this facility because of the long-standing performance barriers between labor and management, which created all sorts of operational, communication, and performance problems.
4. *Resistance to this change effort* was found primarily in the ranks of the frontline supervisors, but was also present among union leadership and informal leaders throughout the distribution center.
5. *Performance metrics, measurement, and feedback processes were never fully utilized,* causing the organization to operate in the dark, struggling to know where it stood on any given day.
6. There was virtually *no individual accountability* for making the necessary changes to support this initiative, and when people began to realize that this effort was struggling, there was no attempt to make adjustments.
7. The outside consultant was making decisions and driving the TPMS program initially with some success, but he *failed in his efforts to get management personnel to change and lead the charge.*

In contrast to Tom's distribution center, the other four facilities that implemented the TPMS did so successfully, with real performance improvement in the areas of service, quality, and efficiency.

In summary, Tom's facility was now in worse shape than it was before this improvement initiative was undertaken. The reasons for this included a real loss of confidence in the organization on the part of all parties involved, and growing cynicism and frustration in the ranks, due to the simple fact that the organization had damaged the credibility of an improvement initiative that actually could have made a difference. There was widespread belief that this operation was not serious about getting better and that change was something that could be avoided. Further, bad labor-management relations got worse as workers became even more doubtful of the trustworthiness of their leaders.

The engineer's report was submitted to corporate headquarters, and after a series of high-level meetings, Tom White was unceremoniously terminated despite his political connections and lofty career expectations. Constar suffered because it attempted to implement change in a leadership vacuum with sad, yet predictable, consequences.

THE QUARTERBACK POSITION: THE PLACE FOR LEADERSHIP

Are you up to the task of quarterbacking your team to a successful scoring drive? We sure hope so, but let's find out. In Chapter One, we asked you to engage your imagination as you consider developing a TMD mind-set as it applies to the subject of organizational change and improvement. It is important to note that just as the quarterback is central to the success of a TMD in football, the business leader is the force that influences all the other critical factors in the TMD approach to organizational change. The parallels between being an effective quarterback and being an effective business leader in driving change in the twenty-first century are both readily apparent and powerful.

John Elway led his team to victory over the Cleveland Browns by his personal actions, his decision making, and his attitude that failure was not an option despite the adversity facing his team. In contrast, Tom White, the Constar distribution manager, was the complete opposite of an effective quarterback and winner in the game of change. He failed to demonstrate even minimal leadership in attempting to implement TPMS, costing him and his operation dearly. The Broncos experienced victory and Constar, defeat. The difference was leadership. We predict that if you think back to the exercise that you did in the Prologue of this book concerning your analysis of a successful and unsuccessful improvement effort, you will see the importance of leadership leap off the page.

Many sports experts would say that the quarterback is the single most difficult position to play of *any* in team sports. Success for a quarterback is not a matter of luck. In the words of Don Shula, the legendary coach who led the Miami Dolphins to two Super Bowl victories: "Sure, luck means a lot in football. Not having a good quarterback is bad luck."

It is also heralded that QBs have the greatest influence as an individual on the outcome of any sporting contest. The quarterback touches the ball on every offensive play and choreographs the team's efforts through a highly unpredictable series of events. The quarterback must use his physical, intellectual, and emotional talents to make things happen. He is generally the first one to be blamed for defeat and the first one to receive praise in victory. Being a quarterback is a very demanding and extremely stressful (and dangerous) position, to say the very least, as all eyes are on him during the entire game.

On the organizational playing field, however, *the task of leadership is even more daunting.* A high school quarterback will play only ten or eleven games a year during the regular season. A college quarterback will play eleven to thirteen games, and a professional quarterback will play sixteen games. But think about it: business leaders quarterback their teams in a minimum of 250 games (work days) a year and are required to keep their teams performing at a high level on a daily basis. Being a business leader is more demanding and stressful than being a quarterback because the stakes in business are infinitely higher. Cutting costs, improving market share, enhancing productivity, implementing new processes, and reducing cycle time are serious actions that organizations need to take if they are to survive and succeed. Let's be honest: success in these contests is extremely difficult to achieve without effective leadership and persistence.

Quarterbacks are judged on a wide variety of measures that include their passing yards, completion percentage, touchdowns, interceptions, and passer rating (which is an efficiency measure). But the most important statistic from a team's perspective is its win-loss percentage: Does the quarterback and his team win more games than they lose?

We would like to ask you some questions along the same lines:

- What is your win-loss percentage when it comes to implementing change and making improvements in your operation? Are you undefeated? 8–3? 6–5? 0–11? What number would you attach to this important metric?
- If sportscasters were making the call, how would they describe your performance as the quarterback and leader of your team during a recent change initiative?

Base Skills of a Good Quarterback-Leader

So what does a quarterback really do? To fans in the stands, it seems rather straightforward. The quarterback works the huddle, gets his team to the line of scrimmage, calls the cadence, takes the snap, and either hands the ball off, passes it, or runs with it. In reality, it's a bit more complicated. A good quarterback must possess what coaches refer to as the *base skills* necessary to lead his team. These talents include the following:[2]

- Strong presence and confidence
- A strong arm and good throwing mechanics
- Mobility and good feet
- Excellent peripheral vision
- Mental and physical toughness
- Great hand-eye coordination
- Superb memory and ability to process information quickly
- Ability to analyze opponents
- Effective communication skills
- Poise and composure

Along similar lines, our research with successful leaders has led us to conclude that there are base skills that are universally applicable to any leadership position and are necessary for a leader to be effective and achieve desired results.[3] Leaders must be able to

- Clarify the unit's mission and goals
- Analyze, plan, and make decisions skillfully
- Select and develop people
- Empower others and delegate
- Communicate effectively
- Motivate others to achieve results
- Develop teamwork and cooperation
- Measure performance and provide feedback
- Remove performance barriers and improve processes
- Develop personally and maintain balance

Possessing these skills will get you in the game as a leader; employing, developing, and perfecting these skills will help you be successful during the normal course of business. These basic skill sets allow quarterbacks and business leaders to compete successfully in normal times and under normal game conditions.

But are there different skills that are critical for success when your team is behind in a football game or in periods of rapid organizational change and improvement? Our research allows us to proclaim resoundingly, YES!

ENHANCED TALENTS OF A TMD QUARTERBACK

During a football season, a quarterback will be faced with leading an average of two or three TMDs. These usually require him to shift away from the normal game plan and demonstrate a specific set of talents that are needed in this demanding situation. Not every quarterback is a great TMD quarterback. Similarly, managers who are effective in more stable or normal times frequently struggle in dynamic and hyperactive business environments. Driving change is truly problematic for some managers. Business leaders responsible for driving change must have the base leadership skills we just identified, but they also need a special set of talents that are critical to running a TMD in the workplace. Let's look now at these talents.

MOMENTUM-BUILDING LEADERSHIP IMPERATIVES

As a leader, you must perform the correct actions in driving the change process, but, equally important, you must energize and infuse a passion for winning into such an effort. Change initiatives in far too many organizations become very bureaucratic, rigid, routine-driven, and antiseptic affairs. When these qualities are taken to an extreme, organizations can fail to recognize and address the importance of the *human* side of change.

A superb TMD quarterback must be extremely capable of tapping into the human component of the change process. This human component is necessary to generate both the *momentum* and *speed* necessary to score in the time that remains on the clock. In fact, there is a rather interesting list of critical leadership imperatives that have emerged from our study of successful change initiatives; these imperatives draw heavily on the power of people and must be applied to each component of the TMD model (see Exhibit 2.1).

MOMENTUM BUILDER 1: BE ENERGIZED TO PLAY AT A NEW LEVEL

Have you ever noticed that when a football game is on the line, some quarterbacks suddenly "shift gears" into a higher level of play and intensity? They seem to have greater strength, focus, and energy, which

---

Exhibit 2.1: Key TMD Leadership Momentum Builders

1. Be energized to play at a new level.
2. Seize control of the game.
3. Communicate above the roar of the crowd.
4. Create ownership of the drive.
5. Keep the play clock in your head.
6. Make adjustments on the field quickly.
7. Have the courage to take a hit, but avoid being sacked.
8. Find a way to win.
9. Be a cheerleader.
10. Demonstrate poise.

allows them to lead their team at a higher level. We have seen this exact same practice demonstrated among highly successful change leaders in a wide variety of organizations. When improvement and change are necessary, they come to work with a new level of intensity and energy that will help them drive the change process forward.

These leaders know that change requires them to pump up the volume on what they are doing and how they are doing it. There is a significant body of research that suggests that change requires extra energy and intellectual capacity on the part of both leaders and followers.[4] Effective leaders recognize this need and begin change initiatives by marshaling their own energy. They might do this by taking better control of their work schedule, getting extra sleep, minimizing meetings, getting more exercise, and communicating more intensely with their people.

The intangibles of the two-minute drill in football include the leader's ability to use adrenaline, excitement, passion, and a desire to win to help shake off the fatigue that sets in late in the fourth quarter. For leaders driving change, the same must be true. *Successful TMD business leaders develop the ability to infuse their teams with energy, excitement, and passion with their actions.* When real change is needed, people want to know if their leader knows what he or she is doing and is motivated and energized to do it. If you, as the leader, approach change with a business-as-usual attitude, you will get off to a bad start.

Momentum Buster

Leaders who are not excited, energized, and willing to take their game up a notch in leading change will have a debilitating effect on their team's performance.

Key Question
When change is required, do you demonstrate your willingness to *elevate your own level of play* in leading change?

Momentum Builder 2: Seize Control of the Game

Football coaches frequently state that in TMD situations, it is imperative that they "turn over control of the game" to their quarterback: because of time constraints, their role as coach becomes less important because the QB is on the field of play and can directly affect the outcome of the contest more than they can. For example, Tom Brady, the famous New England Patriot's quarterback, is notorious for taking control of the game through his commitment to winning and effective decision making.

The workplace should be no different where change is concerned. Yet in many organizations, leaders frequently delegate or abdicate their responsibility for driving change to teams, black belts, consultants, experts, and subordinates. The equivalent on the football field would be sending the trainer, equipment manager, or even water boy out onto the field to quarterback the team in a TMD situation. In a football game, this would be ludicrous, but in business, this practice is far too common. When a business leader turns over control of the game to others, it increases the likelihood that the change effort will not be properly led or taken seriously.

In our Constar example, this is exactly what happened. Tom White turned over a serious change initiative to other people, with dire consequences. He wanted to stand on the sidelines, where he thought he was safe from the dangers of the game, and watch others implement the change. As he found out, failing to step up to one's responsibility as a leader and seize control not only influences the outcome of the game but may also determine if your name shows up on next year's roster.

One of the powers of the TMD is manifested when the leader recognizes *all* the elements that can affect the progress and eventual outcome of the game and takes appropriate action to influence each of them. It's that observable leadership talent that allows team members to know both emotionally and intellectually that the leader is in control and is confident of pulling together all the key components of the TMD.

In football, this is where the TV announcers start using such phrases as

"He's in the zone."
"He's definitely in control of this drive."
"Losing doesn't seem to be an option for this quarterback."
"At this point, this quarterback is in control of his own destiny."

Similarly, when change is necessary, you as a leader need to step up and take control of the change process. Your passion and will to win must infuse your actions to influence and monitor every phase of the change process. These actions must include

- Publicly endorsing the effort
- Tying the effort to specific outcomes
- Measuring performance
- Asking tough questions
- Providing resources
- Holding others accountable for progress
- Ensuring execution
- Generating excitement

Without demonstrating your personal commitment, you as the leader are only creating problems for yourself and your people.

Momentum Buster

Failing to take control of a change effort sends the message to people that the leader is not really serious about change.

Key Question
When approaching any effort at change, how do your people know that you are truly *committed* to this effort and that you have *taken charge* of this initiative?

MOMENTUM BUILDER 3: COMMUNICATE ABOVE THE ROAR OF THE CROWD

Organizations are very noisy places to begin with, but the noise level rapidly rises when change is brought to the organizational playing field. What with hallway gossip, e-mails, meetings, formal organizational proclamations, data overload, political haggling, training programs, performance reviews, feedback sessions, newsletters, casual conversations, and web boards, organizational information can turn into a communications roar. Yet ironically one of the primary reasons managers fail to achieve desired results during periods of rapid organizational change is *their inability to communicate effectively* with the people they depend on to execute change.[5] As a leader, you must communicate about goals, required actions, individual roles, timelines, and a myriad of other issues that are necessary to keep your team focused and informed. All too often, the other noise in the organizational stadium drowns out attempts at communication and drags down improvement efforts.

This is not unlike a quarterback starting a TMD in a hostile stadium, where the roar of the partisan crowd attempts to drown out the quarterback's ability to communicate in both the huddle and at the line of scrimmage. Great quarterbacks always find a way to keep their team members in the communications game so that they can perform their assignments. For example, the legendary All-Pro quarterback Joe Montana used every communication tool available to him to make sure his team members always knew the play, the snap count, their assignments, and any change of plans at the line of scrimmage. Joe was famous for supplementing hampered oral communication with hand gestures, arm waving, foot wagging, and eye movements to let a receiver or a running back know what to do.

Similarly, when you as a manager view a change effort as a TMD, you must make communicating above the noise of the organization both a priority and an art form so that members of your team are able to execute the TMD game plan. You must take great care to communicate such that you *understand* what is going on with your team and *are understood* by your team at every phase of the change process. Simplicity is key!

Momentum Buster

Communication breakdowns will cause any change effort to falter when team members are not sure what is going on or when, where, and how the game plan is to unfold.

> **Key Question**
> When implementing change, do you *make sure that all the players on the field know what is going on* and know their role and the overall game plan?

MOMENTUM BUILDER 4: CREATE OWNERSHIP OF THE DRIVE

In our research, we have found that one of the most critical leadership skills necessary for successful change is the leader's ability to create *ownership* of and *accountability* for the change process among the members of his or her team. Although leaders need to be in control of the overall change process, they must also create a sense of commitment and ownership among the members of their team who are responsible for the execution of the change. In the words of Missouri's head football coach, Gary Pinkel: "The quarterback and the ten other players on the field need to *own* the drive." This comment makes it clear that winning a football game is a team effort, as is the proper execution of any desired change. It's not the coaches on the sidelines or the scouts in the press box who will make the real difference in a successful scoring drive. You as the leader and your fellow players on the field are the "difference makers."

In organizations, it is not uncommon to hear managers say things like these:

"I'm the only one around here who cares."
"Nobody else seems to give a hoot about what we're trying to do."
"Does anybody else realize that this change is in everybody's best interest?"

These statements are indicative of an environment where a leader has failed to create ownership of the change process among the members of his or her work unit. In contrast, successful TMD leaders create an environment where

- Individuals have clearly defined roles and responsibilities in the change process.

- Their input is encouraged and valued.
- They have a say in both creating and executing the plan for improvement.

The TMD quarterback's goal is to make sure each and every member of the team owns his or her piece of the TMD drive for improvement. Without this ownership, the quarterback just might find himself without blocking, without receivers, or without anyone to hand the ball off to. As a leader, you have to master a delicate balancing act of taking control of the change process while simultaneously engaging your people so that they take ownership of their part of it.

Momentum Buster

Any change effort that does not have buy-in and shared ownership will struggle to reach its full potential.

Key Question
What specific things do you need to do to ensure that your team *takes ownership* of your change initiative?

Momentum Builder 5: Keep the Play Clock in Your Head

One of the most notable characteristics of a TMD in a football game is the large number of plays that can be run and the significant distances the ball can be moved in a relatively short period of time. Successful quarterbacks and business leaders share a common attribute: they tend to be extremely sensitive to the issue of *time*—both theirs and others'. In organizational settings, however, time is frequently treated as a commodity rather than as the precious resource that it really is.

In business, people are overwhelmed with meetings, e-mails, paperwork, and more meetings, which tend to consume much of the time and energy needed for results-oriented activity, including change. In some of our research, we found that the average professional has *only two to two-and-a-half hours a day of actual productive time to do his or her job* and achieve results. This makes it clear why implementing change is frequently a hardship, as it takes additional time on top of schedules that are already full to the breaking point. Therefore, to be an effective leader of change, you need to demonstrate extreme sensitivity around the issues of meetings, e-mails, paperwork, training, and other activities that are necessary in planning and executing change. You need to keep a running clock in your mind of how time is being spent in a change initiative and of whether or not progress is being made toward established timelines. You need to realize that time is your most important resource and must be used with the utmost care in executing change.

Momentum Buster

If time is used ineffectively, change efforts can overwhelm participants, lose momentum, and end up in stalemate.

Key Question
When you are leading change, are you *time sensitive* in each and every activity surrounding your initiative?

MOMENTUM BUILDER 6: MAKE ADJUSTMENTS ON THE FIELD QUICKLY

As Dallas QB Troy Aikman pointed out, "The toughest part of playing quarterback is the amount of information that must be processed in mere seconds when all Hell is breaking loose around him." On the football field, executing under pressure means

- Making decisions in nanoseconds
- Calling audibles when the defense changes
- Managing huddles (or playing without a huddle)
- Ensuring that the right players are in position and ready for the snap
- Identifying the tendencies identified in the scouting report
- Managing the clock

And all these decisions must be made *quickly*.

Every football fan has witnessed the impact of a delay-of-game, illegal formation, or illegal procedure penalty on the momentum of a drive. Often it throws the entire team out of rhythm, leading to a multitude of problems. In business, unfortunately, there is no referee to throw a flag when the wrong people are on the project, when people spend more time than necessary on planning, or when excessive meetings cause the effort to stagnate. These types of situations often go unnoticed until the cumulative negative effect takes momentum out of the drive.

On the upside, however, a skilled TMD quarterback or business leader manages the team so as to effectively anticipate and reduce or eliminate these momentum busters. One of the most important findings about successful leaders of TMDs in the workplace is that they tend to be *very quick* at doing all of the following:

- Making decisions
- Solving problems
- Removing roadblocks
- Fighting the tyranny of the *urgent* at the expense of *what's really important*

TMD leaders make decisions and adjustments quickly and effectively so as to maintain and build momentum. As mathematician James Yorke noted, "Most successful people are those who are good at Plan B." TMD business leaders are always ready with a Plan B.

Turning to the Constar case study once again, we could legitimately question if the outcome would have been the same had Tom White taken quick action to make adjustments when his improvement drive stalled. Too bad for him that his first real taste of a quick decision came when senior management brought him before the corporate firing squad and summarily dismissed him.

Momentum Buster

Failing to take quick and effective action to make adjustments when a change effort is struggling can spell disaster.

> **Key Question**
> When leading a change initiative, are you *decisive in making adjustments* to keep the change process moving?

MOMENTUM BUILDER 7: HAVE THE COURAGE TO TAKE A HIT, BUT AVOID BEING SACKED

During his entire career, Green Bay quarterback Brett Favre was a role model for his team in being willing to take a hit if that's what it took to help his team advance the ball. Brett had a reputation for being courageous, getting up quickly, and getting back in the game after taking a "monster hit." One of the worst things that can happen in a football TMD is a quarterback sack. It not only costs time and generates a loss of yards and a wasted down but also wreaks havoc on that critical element of *momentum*. It can shift players' mental energy from the offense to the defense, making it even tougher to move the chains.

Accordingly, a skilled TMD quarterback is a master at avoiding the sack and dealing effectively with potential opposition. A QB's bag of tricks includes all of the following:

- Stepping up into the pocket
- Scrambling
- Exhibiting bursts of speed
- Having great peripheral vision
- Being able to create alternative plays instantly
- Having a sense of when to throw the ball out of bounds
- In some cases, having the raw strength to avoid going down

Again, you can apply these same talents to the organizational world. In many situations, a leader is operating in an environment where (to put it politely) some people do not want to see a change succeed and are willing to undermine these efforts. Successful leaders of change have the courage to do the right thing when change is truly needed, but this can lead to being hit. Sacks or "hits" in the workplace can come in a wide variety of forms, but they can be driven by such factors as

- Workforce resistance
- Lack of frontline supervisory support
- A nonsupportive superior
- Political rivalry
- Internal or external competition
- Lack of resources

These are just a few of the factors that can threaten to throw your improvement efforts for a loss. In these settings, change can become a test of wills and perseverance. In the words of legendary college coach Lou Holtz: "I've never known anybody to achieve anything without overcoming adversity."

A key skill of a TMD quarterback in this type of environment is that of avoiding the sack. It is critical to develop an awareness of the factors that can damage the scoring efforts. Although a pregame scouting report can help develop awareness of some of these factors, it's the unanticipated factors that can really hurt.

We have all watched quarterbacks as they are about to be blindsided by a defensive end, and many of us have even shouted a warning at a deaf TV. In the complex world of business, though, it can be tougher to see the blindside sack coming. Nevertheless, the effective quarterback-leader has a knack for doing so, and typically this knack improves with experience. Keeping your eyes open for "things that just don't seem right" is imperative when attempting to make any organizational change.

Unfortunately, sacks do happen in both football and business. Despite your efforts, opponents do at times get the upper hand and throw you for a loss. Facing the reality of a sack or a big hit, you need to ask yourself, *How will I handle the next play?* Recovering from a hit of any kind requires courage on the part of the quarterback. Similarly, overcoming organizational inertia and resistance requires courage on the part of an effective leader. Will you recover and regain momentum? Or will the sack cause you to flounder as a leader, never quite getting the ball moving downfield again?

Momentum Buster

All change efforts experience resistance and problems that, if left unchecked, can overwhelm any efforts at improvement.

Key Question

Do you *demonstrate courage* when your efforts at change meet resistance, and do you avoid taking unnecessary hits by *anticipating potential problems and threats* to the success of your change efforts?

MOMENTUM BUILDER 8: FIND A WAY TO WIN

Johnny Unitas, legendary quarterback of the Baltimore Colts, was famous for his unvarnished commitment and passion for winning and letting opponents know that when the game was on the line, he was willing to find a way and do whatever it took to win within the rules of the game. Winning quarterbacks find creative ways to win, whether it is by scrambling, using a pump fake, calling an audible at the line of scrimmage, or blocking downfield for a running back.

Similarly, when change in a business organization is needed, real leaders need to demonstrate their willingness to look for creative solutions and new and better ways of doing things at each step of the change process. Leading change requires you and your team not only to think outside the box but also, more important, to *operate* outside the box. Performance is always a function of a team's *ability* × *motivation* × *support.* To be a successful leader of change, you need to look for ways to address each of these factors creatively and find ways to make your change efforts successful. Creativity can play a great role in enhancing a team's ability, motivation, and support, but you must both sanction and then stimulate such creativity.

If you are going to make full use of the talents of your team in finding winning solutions in the change process, you as the leader must be willing to observe and listen to everything going on around you. When a teammate comes back to the huddle with a suggestion on what might work in a given situation on the football field, good quarterbacks listen. When a change is required, the input of your team at every phase of the TMD is critical, whether you are attempting to implement a "packaged" change or creating your own.

As an important side note, we need to point out that all organized sports have rules, and they have officials to ensure that these rules are followed by all the participants. In contrast, it's sad to say, we live in an era when a few business leaders who desire to win at all costs have become "creative" to the point of employing unethical business practices to increase sales and profits. A quick review of the cover stories of major business publications in the recent past reveals a rogue's gallery of business leaders who are caught doing just that, with horrific organizational and personal outcomes. Obviously, their actions were completely wrong. Creativity should not be defined as a way to escape moral, ethical, and legal parameters. Successful leaders find ways to win playing by the rules, lest they be tossed out of the game and banned for life.

Momentum Buster

When leaders are unwilling to think creatively or innovatively or are driven primarily by tradition, they throw away opportunities to increase the likelihood of success in change efforts.

Key Question
In driving the change process, do you *encourage people to be innovative and creative* in finding new and better ways of winning?

MOMENTUM BUILDER 9: BE A CHEERLEADER

An important but frequently overlooked role of successful quarterbacks is that of cheerleader for their team, especially in situations when the team is behind. Most of us have seen quarterbacks like Terry Bradshaw, Donovan McNabb, and Kurt Warner cheer for team members when they made a big play, or encourage teammates after a dropped pass or a lost opportunity on the playing field. Successful quarterbacks look for ways to motivate team members and to keep them in the game, particularly during TMDs.

In the business world, a leader's emphasis tends to be different. Most managers see it as part of their job description to look for things that could be done better and problems or situations that need to be fixed. Thus it is not surprising to find that during periods of change and uncertainty, managers can easily and unknowingly provide their people with an unhealthy dose of criticism, disapproval, and negative feedback.[6]

Successful leaders of change counterbalance this tendency by providing their people with a steady dose of praise, encouragement, and positive feedback to help keep change initiatives in the forefront of people's minds and to motivate the team to keep doing the right things. On the football field, high-fives, back slapping, belly butting, and helmet smacking are ways that quarterbacks encourage their teammates to continue doing a great job. Similarly, to be a successful TMD leader, you should look for meaningful ways to "cheer for" and encourage your team to continue doing the right things to keep the change process moving forward. Although the word "cheerleader" can have a negative connotation in some situations, successful TMD business leaders make sure they infuse large doses of encouragement into their improvement drives.

Momentum Buster

When people receive only negative feedback (or no feedback at all) during a change initiative, their motivation and willingness to go the extra mile can be destroyed.

> **Key Question**
> When implementing change, do you *encourage and praise your people* on a regular basis when they deserve it?

Momentum Builder 10: Demonstrate Poise

It is said that when John Elway stepped onto the field in a situation requiring a quick score, you could see fear in the eyes of the defense. What element of leadership led to such a strong reaction? Despite being down on the scoreboard, Elway was *confident, composed, poised,* and *ready to play to win.* The defense knew that the odds were not in its favor, and the fans knew they were about to witness something special. Neither the opponents nor the fans knew how Elway was going to do it, but they all knew there was a good chance that he would get it done.

The ability to execute under pressure and demonstrate poise at all times has always been an admirable trait of effective leaders, but nowhere is this more true than when change is required. We have all heard people describe leaders who lost their poise and composure in the heat of battle:

"He just lost it."
"She just sort of snapped."
"He just couldn't hold it all together."
"She went postal."
"He went off the deep end."

The problem with not being poised and composed during the change process is twofold: First, "losing it" has a detrimental effect on your ability to process information and make effective decisions. Second, a loss of composure has a detrimental effect on the morale and confidence of the people who are depending on you to lead them forward.

Composure is important because your people will follow your lead, and panic always begets panic. Consider the words of veteran NFL coach Herm Edwards: "When you're a leader, you can never panic, no matter what happens. The building could be falling down. Fire could be going all places. Somebody has to make a decision on how to get out."

And if you're the quarterback, that person is *you*. When things are going well, it's easy to demonstrate your poise. It's when the situation gets tough and people are struggling that poise and composure become critical.

Momentum Buster

When a manager leading change breaks down and does not demonstrate poise, his or her behavior has a detrimental effect on all facets of the change process, with unpredictable outcomes.

Key Question
As leader, do you *maintain your composure and poise* during periods of change, or are you prone to "losing it"?

CONCLUSION AND A CALL TO ACTION

Leadership is without question one of the most important and widely discussed topics of the day, to a great extent because of its stature in the change process. Your basic leadership skills lay the foundation for successful change. Beyond them, the ten TMD momentum builders discussed in this chapter are talents that you can develop if you are serious about improving your ability to drive change. And they are imperatives: maintaining and building momentum are key during all phases of the TMD process. When you as a leader do not demonstrate these momentum builders, you unknowingly create momentum busters by your very action or inaction.

Take the time now to assess the extent to which you effectively build momentum into your change efforts through your approach to leading others. Exhibit 2.2 can help you see if your leadership style is serving to build momentum or bust it when you lead change. Any response that falls into the No category is an opportunity to accelerate your change efforts by targeting one of the ingredients for leading change that our research has found to be important.

Exhibit 2.2: TMD Leadership Momentum Builder Checklist

Answer each of the following questions as they pertain to your approach to leading change in your organization:

When approaching change, do I...

Momentum Builders	Yes	No
1. Come energized and ready to play at a new level?	❏	❏
2. Seize control of the factors that will affect the outcome of the change or improvement process?	❏	❏
3. Communicate effectively above the roar of the crowd during the change process?	❏	❏
4. Create ownership of the improvement drive?	❏	❏
5. Keep the play clock in my head and demonstrate extreme sensitivity to the issue of time?	❏	❏
6. Make adjustments quickly to the factors that threaten to derail or slow down our efforts at change?	❏	❏
7. Have the courage to take a hit when resistance to change occurs, and avoid unnecessary sacks?	❏	❏
8. Look for creative and innovative ways to win in our efforts at change?	❏	❏
9. Serve as a cheerleader and encourager to the members of my team, providing praise and positive feedback when deserved?	❏	❏
10. Maintain my composure and poise during the change process?	❏	❏

CHAPTER THREE

KNOW THE SCORE AND DEFINE WINNING

How Is Your Organization Really Performing, and What Do You Really Want to Achieve?

If winning isn't everything, why do they keep score?
—VINCE LOMBARDI

*How can we really change when we haven't even
clearly defined what it means to win?*
—VICE PRESIDENT OF OPERATIONS, FORTUNE
500 AUTOMOTIVE SUPPLIER

WINNING IMPERATIVE: *Know What It Means to Win*
Every change initiative comes down to being either successful
or pointless.

---

*"The Sneak": USC Trojans vs. the Notre Dame
Fighting Irish, October 15, 2005*

Notre Dame Fighting Irish football teams have a strong and storied
history of knocking off nationally ranked, undefeated football
opponents. The 1946 Army team saw its twenty-five-game winning
streak end in South Bend in a 0–0 tie. Notre Dame also stopped
the longest winning streak in the history of college football at

forty-seven games when they defeated the Oklahoma Sooners 7–0 in their home stadium in 1957. In 1971, the Texas Longhorns watched their thirty-game winning streak evaporate at the hands of the Irish. And in 1973, the USC Trojans were defeated at Notre Dame, their twenty-three-game winning streak halted in South Bend with a final score of 7–0.

In 2005, the top-ranked USC Trojans brought their twenty-eight-game winning streak to South Bend for a contest against the ninth-ranked Fighting Irish under first-year head coach Charlie Weis. There was a great deal of hoopla and hype surrounding this big game, and the contest was predestined to live up to it. At halftime, the scoreboard read Notre Dame 21, USC 14, after a first half that saw both teams take the lead at various points. With 5:09 left in the game, the scoreboard showed Notre Dame trailing 28–24 with the ball on its own 13-yard line. Irish quarterback Brady Quinn led his team on an eight-play, 87-yard scoring drive that culminated with Quinn running the ball in from 5 yards out. Notre Dame now had the number one team in the country on the ropes, 31–28, with 2:04 showing on the game clock.

USC's hopes for a "three-peat" of the national championship depended on the team's ability to execute a two-minute drill in a stadium filled with boisterous Notre Dame fans aching to see history repeat itself. USC defined winning not just as beating Notre Dame but as keeping its national championship goals on track. USC began its drive with an ineffective start, as 2004 Heisman trophy winner Matt Leinart had an incomplete pass and was sacked for a 9-yard loss on the first two plays of the drive. USC called time-out with 1:44 remaining and a third down and 19. On the next play, Leinart passed to 2005 Heisman trophy winner Reggie Bush for 10 yards, creating a do-or-die fourth down and 9 on USC's own 26-yard line. The Trojans' hopes rested on this play to keep the drive alive. Leinart launched a "picture-perfect" 61-yard pass to wide-out Dwayne Jarrett, who scampered to the Notre Dame 13-yard line. After an incomplete pass, Leinart handed the ball off to Reggie Bush twice, for gains of 6 and 5 yards, respectively, creating a first and goal.

All eyes in the stadium looked at the scoreboard, which showed the ball resting on the Notre Dame 2-yard line with no time-outs left, 15 seconds remaining in the contest, and USC trailing by only 3 points (making a field goal an option to tie and put the game into overtime). Leinart snapped the ball and attempted to scramble into the end zone, but he was stopped at the 1-yard line and fumbled the ball out of bounds. The game clock showed 0:00. Notre Dame had won 31–28; its fans erupted and poured out onto the field, and head coach Charlie Weis began celebrating with his team. The TV shots of the stadium showed the scoreboard and the celebrations on the field.

But USC head coach Pete Carroll charged out onto the field and argued that the fumble stopped the clock. After a rather lengthy huddle, the officials agreed, and they reset the game clock to show 0:07 remaining with the ball on the Notre Dame 1-yard line. On the final play of the USC drive, Matt Leinart took the snap and attempted a quarterback sneak behind the left side of his offensive line. His initial momentum was stopped cold, but a push from running back Reggie Bush propelled Leinart into the end zone for the winning touchdown with 3 seconds left on the clock.

Leinart could have spiked the ball to set up a game-tying field goal and put the game into overtime, but in the postgame news conference, Coach Carroll confessed that his team had never considered settling for a field goal. USC had clearly defined the purpose of its final drive as a game-winning touchdown. The team was not playing to get to overtime: it was playing to win. Time ran out on the ensuing kickoff when the Notre Dame player was tackled on the 10-yard line. Final score: USC 34, Notre Dame 31.

SoCal AirPack, Inc., Defines Winning

Knowing the score, defining winning, and using the scoreboard information had significant implications for the USC Trojans in the team's big win. This game also offers strong lessons for business leaders responsible for implementing and executing change. Such is the case with SoCal AirPack, Inc. (SAI), a fifteen-year-old company that enjoyed a niche business supplying nonperishable food products to regional air carriers in the western United States.

Background: Food Distributor Seeks to Expand Business as a Subcontractor

Carrie Herrington and Josh Bryant, cofounders of SAI, had done a good job of leading their company to significant growth during tumultuous times within the airline industry. They had succeeded in matching the delivery and quality performance of larger caterers, who primarily serviced the national and international carriers. SAI packaged bulk shipments of crackers, cookies, peanuts, and other snack munchies, and delivered them directly to the regional aircraft at nearly sixty-five airports. Its workforce comprised unskilled labor that packaged the products and delivered them using company vehicles on a predictable delivery schedule.

Approximately fourteen months ago, Quad States Airlines, a regional carrier, sought to attract additional business, so it initiated a plan to add an in-flight meal to any flight over five hundred miles. Quad States then contracted with SAI to package and deliver attractive nonperishable box lunches that contained five food items and a small brochure and survey. The program was to be rolled out over four months in a series of steps, adding additional cities to the in-flight meal program until all fifty Quad States Airlines locations were participating.

SAI agreed to package the products and deliver the flight-specific number of box lunches directly to the individual aircraft, meeting the ramp-up schedule outlined by Quad States. Doing so would be a challenge, and margins were expected to be relatively thin, but SAI wanted to be on the front end of what some thought could be a reverse trend in the airline industry.

PROBLEMS ARISE WHEN MOVING FROM CENTRALIZED TO REGIONAL DISTRIBUTION

SAI management determined that it would be efficient to package the new products at seven locations throughout ten western states. This approach would differ from the company's current approach, in which SAI's entire packaging and order fulfillment process occurred at a single location. Moving to a regional structure required the hiring and training of staff and managers at each of the seven locations. As most of the work was light-duty and manual, the physical facilities were easily leased at industrial parks near several airports.

Once regional managers were hired, they were given full authority to hire local staff for the packaging and delivery processes, but trucks were supplied from the central location.

To conserve needed capital, owners Carrie and Josh decided to work with the computer and software system currently in place, even though it was designed for bulk shipments from a single location.

As the program rolled out, normal launch problems popped up, such as incorrectly packaged meals, damaged boxes, and shipments with incorrect quantities. Regional managers assured the owners that these issues were quite fixable and were to be expected.

Quad States Airlines saw the problem differently. The airline had advertised a program to attract customers, but the program was beginning to have the opposite effect as customer complaints began to increase. The comment of one of Quad States' passengers said it best: "Telling a passenger that everybody else on the plane gets a boxed lunch except them causes some people to go crazy, and they did!"

SAI's information system indicated that a problem existed, but it was ineffective at portraying the magnitude and source of the problem. SAI's owners were lulled into thinking that time and "the learning curve" alone would solve their quality problems. By week five, every region (except region 4, which was doing quite well) was in an outright panic: employee turnover was running high, as low-paid workers moved on to better-paying jobs; the information system was inconsistent with results on schedule performance; and Quad States management was continually on the phone, demanding a solution from whichever regional location was creating the greatest number of problems that day.

Josh and Carrie knew that they personally had to change the game plan and that they had very little time to do it. Quad States had given them two weeks to achieve 98 percent on-time delivery, with a 95 percent quality rating. (Both categories were currently averaging only approximately 60 percent.) Otherwise Quad States would, with great embarrassment and a potential loss of passengers, cancel the meal program, leaving SAI holding the bag.

It had become obvious to both Carrie and Josh that the reputation of the company they had built was on the line. They could not trust the numbers being generated by the information system. As they pored over records, it became apparent that the situation was much worse than they had originally thought. Poor quality and delivery swings were disappointingly frequent, and time for corrective action was short. They had to move quickly.

SOLVING THE PROBLEM BY KNOWING THEIR PERFORMANCE "SCORE" AND CLEARLY DEFINING WHAT "WINNING" WOULD MEAN

Carrie and Josh requested that five of the seven regional managers clear their schedules for the next couple days and join them at the main office for a midnight meeting. In preparation, Carrie painted a dramatic eight-by-twenty-foot graph on the lunchroom wall. The huge grid included blank squares for each of the next ten days (which was SAI's version of a two-minute drill; after all, ten days in a business is a very short time period), with room to enter two daily numbers, Quality % and On-Time Delivery % (which represented SAI's performance "score"). At the left end of the graph, Carrie painted twelve-inch-high bright red numbers for both of their current statistics: Quality 60%; On-Time Delivery 63%. At the right end of the grid, she painted similar numbers for the goal to be achieved by day 10: Quality 95%; On-Time Delivery 98%. The owners also hung five whiteboards adjacent to the graph.

Seeing the large visual display, the arriving managers sensed that something big was going to happen, and they knew they were in for a long night. Josh laid out the situation and emphatically assured everyone in the room that SAI, as a team, was going to succeed: "Our game to turn this situation around starts right now (12:55 A.M.). Our goal is to achieve the delivery and quality requirements outlined by Quad States Airlines within the next ten days. We, as a team, will do it. I will assume direct control of operations, and Carrie will lead the effort to get the information system fixed."

Having clearly defined what winning meant for SAI, Josh and Carrie outlined a program to immediately centralize the process into the main facility:

- The five regional managers present were requested to remain with the organization, acting as liaisons with Quad States at the airports to ensure that a personal SAI presence was felt by the airline staff.

- Packing personnel already in place at the central location were requested to work overtime to handle the added workload, and a hiring program (headed up by the region 4 manager) was initiated immediately.
- Each of the managers was assigned specific roles with immediately measurable outcomes.

Before the meeting ended at 4:00 A.M., the team had developed specific goals for each of the five managers and listed them on the new whiteboards. By the close of the meeting, everyone in the room clearly knew the team's goals, his or her individual role, and the specific assignments designed to meet those goals. The definition of winning was complete. Communication with the customer and implementation would follow shortly according to the tight time schedule that had been established.

Josh and Carrie personally presented their plan to Quad States management the following morning, assuring them that they had defined specific goals throughout SAI and had put the resources in place to be successful. As Carrie summed it up: "SAI plans to win. And we will, and everyone knows exactly what has to happen to do so!"

Starting Your TMD Initiative

The great sports strategist Yogi Berra once remarked, "If you don't know where you are going, you are sure to get there." Walt Disney expressed the same idea in a more positive tone, proposing that "If you can dream it, you can do it." As the TMD model in Chapter One illustrated, a TMD initiative actually begins with the definition of winning. Why? It's quite simple. As Yogi and Walt framed it, you need to create a definite picture of where you want to go or what you hope to accomplish. This is essential before you can take action toward achieving it. Otherwise, you may not succeed, and you might not even realize that you failed.

USC coach Pete Carroll made it clear that USC was driving for a winning touchdown and not a field goal to put the game against Notre Dame in overtime. Carrie and Josh at SAI made it clear that 95 percent quality and 98 percent on-time delivery represented winning for their company. Similarly, as the quarterback or leader of change in *your* organization, you are responsible for getting things moving, and that starts with knowing the score. You may or may not be the one who initially decides to make a change, but you definitely are the one who must make change happen. You are the person your team looks to for guidance and to generate momentum when change is needed. In this chapter, we discuss three factors that are critical to setting the stage for an effective organizational change. These factors entail a number of actions that you must perform as a leader to get your improvement effort moving:

1. **You must know the real score.** Is there a valid scoreboard that indicates the need for change? Do you really know the score?
2. **You must define winning across multiple levels of the organization.** How is winning defined for the enterprise as a whole, for the team, and for each individual?
3. **You must communicate the definition of winning to all appropriate parties.** Does everyone understand what winning means and how he or she fits into the overall picture?

The concept of defining goals at the beginning of an initiative is far from novel.[1] Wrapping the element of speed around the three activities outlined here, however, adds a new dimension to the practice. In a TMD situation, where the team is behind and time is critical, being able to perform these actions rapidly is paramount. The three elements of scoreboarding, defining, and communicating should be seen as one seamless step in laying the foundation for real change. Each element alone is important, but the effective combination of all three of them is priceless.

If you address each of these three elements effectively, your TMD effort will be off and running. Failure to address them appropriately up front will lead to confusion and almost certainly will result in an ineffective effort or, in a worst-case scenario, failure of the initiative altogether. In the end, *every change initiative comes down to being either successful or pointless.* Building a foundation at the outset of the effort will contribute immensely to ensuring that it is a success. In our discussion with senior executives, four of the top six factors critical to successful change were significantly related to the initial steps of defining what it means to win. Those six factors are

1. Ownership
2. Direction
3. Focus
4. Speed
5. Metrics
6. A clearly defined process

All were deemed to be vital in any successful effort. Yet do you find yourself at times jumping into a change initiative without clearly knowing why or knowing what desired outcome you are seeking? If so, you are not alone!

Before we address the momentum builders that will help you kick off the initial phase of a TMD, take a moment to review two scenarios:

1. Recall a vivid memory of a season-making football game in which the clock was winding down and your team needed a quick score to win.
2. Think of a recent significant change initiative in your work environment or personal life in which you needed to move quickly to succeed.

Mentally place yourself at the beginning of each of these two scenarios. What stands out in your mind as the defining moment when the drive to win the game or the change initiative actually began?

- Was it the time-out on the sidelines when the coach was barking instructions in the face of the quarterback above the roar of the crowd?
- Was it your boss pulling the team into his office on a Saturday morning for a not-so-pleasant kickoff of a cost reduction project?
- Was it you gazing into the mirror and deciding, for example, that you needed to knock off thirty pounds to get back into shape?

If you think about it, each of these scenarios had a definitive point where the effort actually began. This "realization" or commitment was critical to what would follow.

Thinking of these past events again: What stimulated the coach, your boss, or you personally to decide that a change was necessary? Once a decision was made that a change should occur, what parameters did you use to decide if it was eventually success-ful? Essentially, we are asking you to determine *how you defined winning*. When serious change is on the table, answering these questions is not optional. Your answer to each of them is pivot-ally important at the beginning of any change process, and it's even more critical when a lack of time is a factor and the need for speed is a priority.

TMD KICKOFF MOMENTUM BUILDERS

As a TMD unfolds, each step of the process—including defining a game-winning set of plays, selecting and motivating the team, and executing the package—hinges on initially defining what you mean by a win. Clear, crisp, well-communicated definitions of outcomes, timing, and personal expectations will lead to efficient execution and an increased likelihood of a successful outcome. In stark contrast, vague or incomplete treatment of these initial parameters will result in wasteful, reiterative activities that will cre-ate delays and potentially lead to failure.

MOMENTUM BUILDER 1: START BY KNOWING THE REAL SCORE

Many organizations are in a state of continual flux, and change is the norm. Unfortunately, *successful* change is not the norm. In our ongoing research, many executives have expressed con-cern over the meager success rate of major change efforts in their organizations. Immense amounts of resources—time, people, goodwill, and money—are thrown at projects with-out significant return. One key deficiency has stood out as an important cause of these failures: the lack of really knowing and understanding the score across key metrics and then using that score to trigger action.

Filtering out the noise of information overload and drawing attention to the areas of importance are always challenging, as most organizations employ a wide range of methods for measuring how well they are doing, including financial and nonfinancial scorecards, customer satisfaction surveys, and employee focus groups.

One should consider, however, whether the information is useful as a trigger to initiate change or whether it's simply a way of recording history. Is the information really reflective of the goals of the organization? If it is, management can be armed with the knowledge to act or not. If it isn't, management can flounder, take no action, or blunder forward, perhaps taking the wrong course. In the case of SAI, it became apparent (but only after the company was deep into the launch) that the owners and managers were using invalid data, which provided a false sense of security and an inaccurate portrayal of the success of the launch. As it turned out, they were further behind than they had believed, and needed to take drastic action to recover.

For a scoreboard to be valid, useful, and effective as a trigger for leaders to consider change, it must include the essentials shown in Exhibit 3.1.

Exhibit 3.1: Factors Essential to an Effective Business Scoreboard

1. **Clear performance metrics (in other words, the score).** The scoreboard must *incorporate metrics that measure the success factors of the organization* (for example, profitability, customer satisfaction, on-time delivery, time to market) and should compare those results to those of the competition.
2. **Schedules and deadlines.** The scoreboard must *project outward to a time horizon that allows the organization to react.*
3. **Widespread visibility.** The scoreboard must *be visible to all people* in the organization who need the information to take action. For example, note what SAI did in transforming the lunchroom wall into a huge performance graph.

4. **Accurate information.** The scoreboard metrics must *be quantifiable, simple, accurate, consistent, and current,* because making today's decisions with yesterday's data leads to disaster.
5. **Business synchronicity.** The scoreboard must *be in sync with the cycle of the activity or business that it monitors.* For example, using a monthly scoreboard to trigger action on an activity that changes *daily* is useless.

As a word of caution, beware of "scoreboard creep." How many of us have seen or participated on teams or in organizations where every month, management added supplementary metrics to the scoreboard, eliminating none? Typically, the list grew so long that it was necessary to include yet another index, perhaps a ratio of the number of metrics that were positive this month to those that were negative, to capture overall performance. For example, in the early days of process improvement, we witnessed a Fortune 500 company develop (in secret) a list of sixty-seven measures that each operating division would track monthly for bonus purposes. This type of scoreboard activity makes leading and managing change more difficult than it needs to be. Knowing what needs to change and when an improvement effort is really needed is critically important to every business leader. So give the following key questions some serious thought.

Key Questions
1. Does a scoreboard exist in your organization or work unit that will act as a trigger for rapid change?
2. Does it encompass the proper metrics?

So what happens if the scoreboard indicates a problem? Obviously, two broad choices come into play: either someone can interpret the scoreboard and make a decision, or the organization can choose to ignore the scoreboard and allow things to proceed.

Too often, organizations that are faced with definite bad news become mired in the complexity of the situation, and take no action. Yet imagine your disbelief if the TV cameras trained on the sidelines of an NFL team in trouble showed the coaching staff and players blankly staring at the scoreboard as time ticked away. Unfortunately, some organizations get into that type of paralysis mode because the complexity of the scoreboard freezes their decision-making process.

Would SAI have avoided the entire crisis had management interpreted the scoreboard correctly and taken action earlier? Think about the last time an indication of a problem surfaced in your organization. Who made the decision to do something? Your boss? The corporate office? You? Your team? Was that person or team capable of correctly reading and interpreting the scoreboard before acting? Was a nervous executive moving too soon or maybe too late?

Clearly, defining who is responsible for making a change is important. One of the prime drivers of successful change as outlined by executives whom we interviewed is the issue of *owner-ship:* if you own an idea or an action, you are more committed to seeing it work. We all know that. At times, however, you are not the originator of the idea. You may simply be the quarterback with the assignment to get out on the field and get the job done. In these situations, it is very important to you as a leader to develop the skills and attitude to be an implementer. It's time to address certain critical questions.

Key Questions
1. Does the organization respond rapidly when the scoreboard indicates that a problem exists?
2. Who decides that action should be taken?
3. Has that person or team interpreted the scoreboard correctly?
4. Does that person or team act in a timely fashion?

MOMENTUM BUILDER 2: DEFINE WINNING FOR YOUR ENTERPRISE, YOUR TEAM, AND EACH INDIVIDUAL

In their book describing General Douglas MacArthur, one of the greatest military leaders of the twentieth century, Donna and Theodore Kinni point out, "Leaders are responsible for defining what victory means, focusing the intention of the organization on it, and shepherding their followers in the quest to attain it."[2] The sequence of these responsibilities is not random: it reflects the logical progression necessary to put points on the board in a football drive or to succeed in an organizational change effort. Here's why defining winning is so important:

- By defining victory, you can build a road map to success; without a definition, a team can be left to wander.
- With a victory road map comes order; without it comes confusion and chaos.
- With a road map, you can act quickly; without it, you lose precious time.

But *how* do you define victory in your organization? In its most basic sense, winning is the achievement of a goal. To be effective in driving rapid change, however, the definition of winning must be more specific and encompass all the characteristics listed in Exhibit 3.2.

Thinking about the characteristics listed in Exhibit 3.2, consider the nebulous goals so frequently heard in meeting rooms across the country:

"Sell more."
"Improve your processes."
"Be the best."
"Think bigger."
"Deliver faster."
"Cut costs."
"Improve our product."

These goals only leave people wondering what the "goals" really mean and what they can really do to achieve them! Such

---

Exhibit 3.2: Characteristics of an Effective Definition of Winning

1. **Clear.** All parties must understand the definition. Avoid ambiguity, confusion, and complexity. For example, think of the simple visual scoreboard that SAI's owners created on the lunchroom wall as they kicked off their recovery initiative.
2. **Actionable.** The team must be able to execute activities to achieve the goal. For example, USC head coach Pete Carroll gave his team a play he knew they had practiced before, not one based on some wild, spur-of-the-moment idea.
3. **Measurable.** The goal must be specified such that results can be measured. Again, think of how SAI approached the plan to fix its business: specific actions with specific goals were publicly listed on the whiteboards in the lunchroom.
4. **Time-oriented.** The definition must include the element of time, especially in a TMD situation. Remember, *speed* is the prime differentiator of a TMD from normal activity. Consider how SAI was able to successfully turn things around in its ten-day time window.

---

statements may make good slogans, but they fall very short in accurately and quantifiably defining what winning really means. Exhibit 3.3 illustrates ineffective definitions of winning from the realm of football and business, along with improved versions. When it comes time for you to define winning for an initiative, use the four characteristics listed in Exhibit 3.2 as a checklist to determine if the goal you set forth makes sense.

In a world where organizations are multilayered, it is important to address the issue of defining winning across various levels of the enterprise. Should the definition of winning for your initiative be identical for the enterprise as a whole, for the team as a subset of the organization, and for each individual on the team? Our

Exhibit 3.3: Examples of Definitions of Winning

Ineffective Definitions of Winning	Better Definitions of Winning
IN FOOTBALL	
Put some points on the board fast.	Score a TD within the next minute, then hold the opponent to no score until the game is over.
Get in position for a field goal.	Move within the 30-yard line in the center of the field in the next two plays.
IN ORGANIZATIONS	
Improve productivity.	Improve output of product A by 20 percent with the same resources within forty-five days.
Deliver faster.	Improve on the delivery rate from 65 percent to 98 percent by July 1.
Beat the competition.	Create a 3 percent favorable price spread with similar delivery capability for the fourth quarter.
Achieve better results.	Improve ROI from 11 percent to 15 percent across all divisions for the coming year.

feedback from management interviews would emphatically say no. Managers indicated that in many cases, a senior executive specifies the goal or definition of winning; consequently, it's usually a broad-brush statement. Too often, that statement is never fleshed out in terms of specific support targets further down the organization. As a result, even dedicated and committed employees are unable to use their skills and talents effectively and efficiently to support the overall goal. They simply don't know what is expected of them.

For organizations that do cascade targets and goals through various levels, a TMD situation brings one additional challenge: the element of *speed*. The competency of an organization to rapidly develop and interpret the definition of winning across multiple levels is itself a measure of success. Getting it right *quickly* is important simply because time constraints may not allow you another shot.

In the mind of USC coach Pete Carroll, winning the game was clearly the overall goal. He stated afterward that they had never considered going for the tie to put the contest in overtime. To quarterback Matt Leinart, the objective was a bit more specific. In the back of his mind, Leinart understood that the overall objective was to win the game and eventually shoot for a national title, but his focus at that moment was the goal line. At that moment, he needed to run one play that would gain 1 yard (a very measurable outcome). His attention was directed at the match-ups of linemen and the need to take a clean snap, find a hole, and punch it in.

You can bet that Pete Carroll (as upper management) didn't just tell Leinart on that final play to "do whatever you want to win the game." Things became a bit more focused and specific. In fact, the tailing running back, Reggie Bush, had the same goal—that is, to make sure Matt Leinart crossed the goal line (even if a little push was necessary). In a business situation, although "improving the corporation's ROI from 8 percent to 13 percent" may be an appropriate marker for an executive vice president, that goal may not be actionable or clear for the preventive maintenance team that is responsible for achieving better equipment uptime. Even though their actions may contribute to the improvement in ROI, they need *specific targets* related to factors within their control, such as equipment uptime and maintenance spending, as goals that they as individuals can own. They must know what *they* can do now to win.

Similarly, when SAI initiated its recovery plan, an appropriate definition of winning for the people working on the software may have been "create a tracking system with 100 percent data integrity and implement it within forty-eight hours." To them, winning was defined as an actionable and measurable objective that fit within the overall plan of SAI to meet customer demands. Taking the definition to that level freed the team to fix the information system creatively while knowing the boundaries that defined winning from both a time and content perspective.

Throughout the book, we refer to the reality that in some cases, someone other than you may initiate a TMD and charge you with making it happen. The same situation holds true for defining victory. Ideally, the individual or group that decides to kick off the TMD effort should also define winning for the program. Our discussions with business leaders indicate that too often, *the person responsible for initiating the activity fails to specify what it means to win.* Such commands as "Fix it now!" or "Do whatever it takes" or "The ball's in your court" offer an emotional direction, but they provide little meat. Why does this happen? Three reasons stand out:

1. The person demanding change *may not know how to define victory.* In large, diverse organizations, senior management may be quite conversant in specifying overall goals, but they are often quite inadequate at defining the specifics that apply further down the ladder. If you are the quarterback functioning at the "action level," you need to acknowledge the reality of this situation and take it upon yourself to define winning targets. If you don't do it, it probably won't happen.

2. The individual demanding change *may totally skip the step of defining winning* or may define it without addressing the key characteristics, such as clarity and time orientation. Again, if you are the quarterback with the responsibility for making it happen, you may need to call a time-out and convene with the appropriate people to flesh out the definition. *Do not start the initiative without identifying the target!*

3. The individual who kicks off the demand for change *may intentionally decide to be vague.* Often, organizationally savvy people who want to maintain their track record of winning (or not failing) tend to be very ambiguous about clarifying what they hope

to achieve. It's much easier for them to define victory after the game is over, thus providing themselves with the luxury of being proud of an achievement that actually falls short of a true victory or, worse yet, passing the blame for the shortfall to others. In the SAI case, notice that owners Carrie and Josh took on the responsibility of defining winning at the *front end* of the recovery effort, specifying *clear, measurable targets* to be achieved *in a specified time frame*. They did it right.

As you kick off initiatives in your organization, even if they are not of your choosing, ask yourself the following questions:

Key Questions
1 Is your definition of winning clear, actionable, measurable, and time-oriented?
2. Does your definition effectively cross appropriate boundaries, with the necessary specificity at each level?
3. If you did not create the definition, are you, the quarterback, satisfied with its workability?

One last point in defining winning: take the time at the start of your change effort to *define losing*. This can be a very useful group exercise to help solidify understanding of what you are trying to achieve and, equally important, what outcomes will be unacceptable. We have seen this practice used with great effect; conversely, we have seen many a change effort that could have benefited from this exercise.

MOMENTUM BUILDER 3: COMMUNICATE WHAT IT REALLY MEANS TO WIN

In the words of Paul Danos, dean of the Tuck School of Business at Dartmouth, "Leadership is an unbelievably hard communications job. You must have a firm grasp of your competitive environment, encapsulate the spirit of an organization, package it in strategic statements, and then emphasize those statements repeatedly, so that the message becomes part of the conversation." Danos's statement comprises several actions mandatory for success in TMD situations. Defining winning is only meaningful if the right people—that is, those who must act to produce the win—know what they need to know, when they need to know it. Once again, in a TMD situation, speed of communication is critical.

Check out any winning quarterback and you will undoubtedly find a successful communicator. A QB is incessantly shouting above the roar of the crowd (or speaking softly below it), moving around behind the line, and using hand, eye, and body gestures to direct the team. The most important communication task that a quarterback performs is calling a specific play and clarifying the snap count. Although the goal of the play might be to pick up 11 yards and a first down, the quarterback must translate that goal into individual assignments that are known and understood by all.

Several characteristics of communication are vital to ensuring that the message gets to the right people at the right time. For your next initiative, try using the checklist in Exhibit 3.4 to help you determine whether your communication is effective.

We must emphasize that within every phase of a TMD, communication is the glue that holds the activity together. As the speed

---

Exhibit 3.4: Effective Communication Checklist

To be effective in a TMD situation, ensure that your communication is . . .

❏ Fast   ❏ Clear

❏ Simple   ❏ Visible

❏ Efficient   ❏ Flexible

❏ Specific   ❏ Actionable

❏ Two-way   ❏ Multifaceted

of physical activities ratchets up, enhancing the efficiency and effectiveness of discussion becomes paramount. For example, SAI began a rapid recovery once the owners began to communicate quickly, clearly, and simply with the management team and the customer. As you kick off your own initiative, ask yourself the following questions.

Key Questions
1. Does everyone who needs to know the definition of winning know it?
2. Does your communication meet the criteria for simplicity, clarity, and speed, as outlined in this chapter?

SoCal AirPack, Inc.: The Outcome

Revamping the organization and the flow of work from a decentralized structure with seven locations to a single source facility was not an easy task. However, SAI laid out the initiative quickly, defining what needed to be done, by whom, and by when. Carrie and Josh reprioritized cost below the goal of satisfying their customer, realizing that although they wanted to make money on this product line, they needed even more to preserve the reputation of the company and its viability for future contracts.

Within eight days, using the resources already available at their central facility, they hired and trained the additional packers and were delivering food boxes to each location on time. Essentially, they were able to strip unnecessary waste and friction from the change process by focusing on each defined target. Commitment of the owners and the work teams was critical, as was a continual line of communication with the airline's food services representative. By the end of day 10, the original defined target date for recovery, the team was able to take a brief time-out in the food kit assembly room to celebrate their achievement.

Enjoying a steak dinner, team members exchanged war stories, proud of how they were able to do what even they thought impossible just ten days earlier. The most rewarding moment was an unexpected visit from the vice president of flight operations from Quad State Airlines, who congratulated each employee with a handshake and a coupon for one round-trip ticket to any destination in the western United States.

CONCLUSION AND A CALL TO ACTION

In our research, we have seen time and time again organizations embarking on change efforts without clearly defining what they truly want to improve and without succinctly defining what it means for the change effort to be viewed as a success. The likelihood of a successful change effort increases when a business leader stakes out the desired outcome and regularly monitors the metrics that are most important for success. Effective leaders take appropriate action—without costly delay or political debates—when those metrics are not where they need to be. Real change requires defining what winning looks like for the enterprise, your team, and, very important, individual performers. This requires intensive communication on the part of the change leader at many levels, but everyone must be in agreement on what it will ultimately mean for this specific change effort to be viewed as a success when the clock runs out. If you as the quarterback do not properly define what winning looks like—what it really means to the organization and to members of your team—you are unnecessarily and unwittingly throwing yourself for a loss at the start of an improvement effort. To avoid this potential momentum buster, you will take great care to build momentum into the start of your TMD by using the momentum builders in Exhibit 3.5.

Exhibit 3.5: TMD Momentum Builder Checklist

Listed below are momentum builders for defining winning at the start of any TMD. Ask yourself the check-off questions to determine how well you stack up to the challenge!   ✔

TMD field winner: QB and coaches monitor the scoreboard to decide when a TMD is needed.

Your check-off: Do you have a physical or mental scoreboard   ❑
that serves to trigger the need for a TMD?

TMD field winner: QB effectively communicates the definition of winning with the team and his coaches.

Your check-off: Do you use appropriate communication tools   ❑
to ensure that the right people are informed of what outcomes
are desired and how improvement will be measured?

TMD field winner: QB ensures that everyone knows what score is needed and what that score means to the team and each individual player.

Your check-off: Do you clarify what winning and victory   ❑
mean for each level of the organization and for the players
and fans who have a vested interest in the outcome?

CHAPTER FOUR

CREATE YOUR SCOUTING REPORT AND GAME-DAY MATCH-UPS

Identify Potential Opponents to Change

It seems like when we are trying to make serious changes in this company, we often become our own worst enemy. . . . We have to better understand our competitors but also our own internal barriers to improvement that can hurt us daily, drive us crazy, and stop progress cold
—FRONTLINE SUPERVISOR, TRANSPORTATION COMPANY

We can't run. We can't pass. We can't stop the run. We can't stop the pass. We can't kick. Other than that, we're just not a very good football team right now.
—BRUCE COSLET, FORMER CINCINNATI BENGALS' HEAD COACH

WINNING IMPERATIVE: *Scout to Win*
Going into any change game, it is critically important to know your talents and what you are up against.

Know Your Match-Ups: Miami Dolphins vs. New York Jets, November 27, 1994

Hall of Fame quarterback Dan Marino did not become the most productive passer in NFL history (more than 60,000 career passing yards) without being a successful student of the game. Marino had a reputation for always knowing his opponent's defenses and looking for match-ups for his players to best exploit scoring opportunities. Nowhere were these leadership talents more evident than when Marino's Dolphins took on the New York Jets in a game late in the 1994 season played at the Meadowlands, with the divisional lead on the line.

The Dolphins were trailing the New York Jets by 18 points in the second half when they abandoned their running game and allowed Marino to utilize his throwing talents. Marino unleashed a 28-point second-half scoring barrage by exploiting the match-ups of his entire receiving corps with the Jets secondary. Marino was particularly successful in delivering the ball to journeyman receiver Mark Ingram, using routes designed to isolate the Jets defensive backs in one-on-one situations. The aggressive Jets defense pulled out all the stops. They employed strong man-to-man coverage, switching formations just before the snap of the ball and disguising their blitzes in an attempt to force Marino into making a mistake that never came. Marino's knowledge of his match-ups, coupled with his quick release, allowed him to lead his team from behind and to put them in a position to win in the waning moments of the fourth quarter.

Marino led his team in a two-minute drill, trailing 24–21, and drove the length of the field, getting his team to first and goal on the Jets 8-yard line with just seconds remaining in the game. Marino approached the line of scrimmage, motioning that he was going to spike the ball to stop the clock. But instead, he snapped the ball and faked the spike, which caused the Jets defense to freeze in its tracks momentarily. Marino took a short drop and passed the ball to streaking wide receiver Mark Ingram for his fourth touchdown catch of the game. Everyone in the stadium was stunned, with the exception of Marino and the Dolphins' offense that won the game 28–24.

The largest home crowd in the history of the Jets franchise had just witnessed not only a loss at the hands of "the best arm in professional football" but also the competitive advantage that comes with knowing your opponent's strengths and weaknesses and your own talents.

Dynamic Materials: Matching Up the Right People to Fix the Company's Price-Quoting Process

Knowing what you are up against makes a real difference not only in winning football games but also in an organization's success and survival. Let's take a look at a business case study that illustrates this.

Background: A Manufacturing Company's Price-Quoting Process Is Too Slow

Sonny Siravo was the vice president of new business development for Dynamic Materials, an East Coast metal-stamping organization. He was quickly coming to the realization that their current quoting process was too cumbersome and did not meet customers' needs in terms of speed and ease of use. The current assets of the corporation were operating at levels under 50 percent, and the continuous improvement efforts were not keeping up with Dynamic Materials' acceptable bottom-line profits. In addition, the quoting process was often inaccurate and contained incomplete data that created errors and delays in the final submission process. To make things worse, Dynamic's competitors had become more sophisticated and streamlined in their quoting processes and had made it easier for potential customers to solicit their product quotes in an expeditious fashion. Dynamic was in serious trouble, and Sonny knew it.

Further, the current cost structure and how it was manifested in the quoting system, combined with the company's targeted aggressive profit margins goals, were no longer bringing new business to their operations. Dynamic's performance had been critically damaged in the past two years by the deficient quoting process, and action needed to be taken *now*. Without serious improvement in the quoting process, the new business department would be seeking a new leader, and Sonny knew his job was on the line. He realized that something needed to change, and the change needed to occur yesterday.

SOLVING THE PROBLEM REQUIRES COOPERATION OF MANY TERRITORIAL DEPARTMENTS

Sonny made an executive decision to streamline and simplify the quoting system, but as he thought through how to do this, he began to realize that there were a myriad of internal conflicts and tensions among the sales, engineering, materials control, information technology, and accounting departments that might stop his efforts cold. He recognized that the traditional quoting system would affect a number of functional departments that had traditionally operated as silos and had been very territorial in almost every aspect. He realized that the success of any efforts at improving the Dynamic Materials quoting process would require the cooperation of a number of very strong personalities, all of whom had a vested interest in this critical organizational process but who, he believed, were waiting for someone to take the lead. Essentially, most of the key players were all acting like spectators. As he was pondering what to do, Sonny concluded that his own discomfort with conflict and confrontation had caused him to fail to bring these groups together to fix the problem.

For example, Sonny knew that Jeff Smith, the VP of sales, begged for speed and simplicity in the quoting process. Susan Walton, the engineering guru of the company, insisted on a thorough and comprehensive analysis of all new projects and quoting activity before taking action. She and Sonny had talked on numerous occasions about the need for changes in the quoting process, and she was ready to help when the time was right. John Weston, who led the materials department, was constantly demanding more lead time to secure accurate material costing data and delivery information. Bob Stone, a veteran "numbers guy," ran the accounting department and was a stickler for extreme accuracy in all phases of the quoting process. The information technology group had recently taken control of all computer applications in the company, and Saum Vijay would see that any new quoting technology met the guidelines established by the IT department. But Saum also had the ability to think through the true needs of new applications, and he liked a good challenge.

Sonny established a task force to map out the current quoting process in an effort to identify opportunities to improve its quality and speed, as well as to ensure that management could confidently understand the overhead rates applied to each new quote. The task force included each of the appropriate managers, including Saum from the IT group. Sonny knew there was a history of tension between some of the aforementioned personalities, yet he knew that real progress would require everyone's effort and approval. Dynamic Materials was an organization that craved stability and had a culture that tended to "treasure the status quo." The fact that they were losing market share on a monthly basis caused people throughout the organization to realize that serious change needed to be made—or they would lose the game.

The new quoting process had to drive deep into the mechanics of quoting, but it also had to address the reward systems, accountability, and growth issues. Knowing that he had a good sense of what he was really up against, Sonny felt better going forward with the change initiative. He realized that he wasn't just taking on the quoting system but also facing the challenge of dealing with the personalities, agendas, and needs of all the key players, which he found somewhat discomforting. At the same time, he was glad to know what he was really up against and would adjust his game plan accordingly.

SCOUTING REPORTS: KNOW YOUR MATCH-UPS

Dan Marino's win and Dynamic Materials' difficulty illustrate the importance of knowing what you are up against and understanding what it will take to win. Many business gurus—Michael Porter, Henry Mintzberg, John Kotter, Tom Peters, and others—have made a strong case for knowing your marketplace competitors, but our experience with successful organizational change tells us that your competition is only part of the challenge of change. The real issue is not simply understanding your external competitors, but understanding *all* the factors that can damage your efforts at change and improvement.

Most change efforts can be accelerated by anticipating and developing plans to deal with potential opponents of change. And although we are excited to continue our discussion of the

TMD as an organizational change tool, we need to conduct a brief "game-day discussion" about the importance of scouting and of understanding what you are really up against in your efforts at change. So let's start with a question.

> **Key Question**
> Going into a change effort, how do you and the members of your team match up against the challenges that you are about to face in the change process?

Football teams are all about winning. When teams win, life for coaches and players alike can be very good. Fans swarm to stadiums to watch their heroes compete, revenues increase, billboards and team posters are plastered everywhere, television appearances become commonplace, endorsements abound, team jersey sales spike, and the Internet blogs talk about the team. When teams lose, critics and other Monday-morning quarterbacks line up to second-guess coaches, players, and their franchises or schools. Watch or listen to the commentators on ESPN, *College Football Today*, or *NFL Round-up*, or any of the myriad of talk shows, when a team is losing or not performing up to expectations. Their commentary is brutal and merciless! Stop right now and think about the great football dynasties like Notre Dame, the Green Bay Packers, Ohio State, the Pittsburgh Steelers, USC, the Dallas Cowboys, and the New England Patriots. When we ask fans to explain the phenomenon of these teams' success, they are quick to point out the obvious. The teams have great coaches, excellent player personnel, tremendous facilities, or terrific offensive or defensive schemes.

Yet beneath the surface and behind the scenes, every successful football program typically approaches each and every contest with exhaustive and up-to-date research and reports. Football teams are constantly scouting their opponents, seeking out any information that will allow them to create a competitive advantage when the two teams go head-to-head. An offensive lineman's stance might be a consistent indicator that the team is going to throw the ball, or a defensive back's position prior to the snap can indicate when a blitz is coming. This kind of knowledge can be a powerful tool in helping you know what you are up against and what you need to do about it prior to battle.

SCOUTING YOUR POTENTIAL OPPONENTS

Scouting is the act of systematically analyzing your opponents to ascertain their strengths, weaknesses, and tendencies, whether in football or in a business setting. Scouts are the people responsible for collecting and analyzing this competitive information. Football scouts need to be able to endure sitting in the stands and watching an opponent play in the rain, critiquing hours of game film, and gathering and analyzing statistical data from previous contests. Although the task may be mundane, tedious, and at times outright boring, it is nonetheless critical if a team is serious about winning. Without this critical information, football teams would go into games ill prepared, with unpredictable consequences. The same is true in business, yet organizations and leaders frequently enter the change arena without accurate knowledge of who their real opponents are and what they are really up against in their efforts to drive change and improvement. To borrow from the frontline supervisor in this chapter's opening quotation, they become their own worst enemy.

In football, scouting information is packaged into a document called a *scouting report*. Football scouting reports typically contain the following:

- Coaches' background, experience, and win-loss records, and a rating of their approach to the game in terms of risk taking and predictability
- Players by position: height, weight, age, and speed
- Team performance metrics—for example, points per game, yards per game, pass-to-run ratios, and turnover ratios
- Individual performance leaders—for example, leading rusher, leading tackler, and sack leader
- Various offensive, defensive, and special team capabilities
- Tendencies for action in various game situations
- Match-ups between the opponent's players and the members of one's own team

Scouting reports contain a significant amount of information that has been systematically compiled; they are then studied in detail and used to create a game plan that helps the team anticipate what will be coming at them on game day. Businesses can benefit from the same type of information. So ask yourself this important question:

> **Key Question**
> If you were compiling a scouting report to prepare for an organizational change, what information would you want in your report that would help you "win"?

In the case of Dynamic Materials, Sonny (the VP of new business development) instinctively began to develop a scouting report for his change initiative. He did this because he understood his own shortcomings and realized that the opposition he faced wasn't just his marketplace competitors. Because his scouting report forced him to think through how he and his colleagues (the players) at Dynamic Materials matched up against the challenges of developing a better quoting system, it increased the company's chance of successfully implementing that system.

SCOUTING REPORTS IN AN ORGANIZATIONAL GAME SETTING

Our research and experience with successful and rapid organizational change indicate that success is frequently predicated on understanding what you are up against in trying to implement needed change. A senior health care executive expressed this idea when she stated, "When we are trying to change anything in our operations, it's critical to not only understand what our competitors are doing but also our own tendencies towards changes in the past. . . . We need to determine if we are capable of making the changes successfully and being able to overcome the forces for the status quo."

Yet if you ask managers about their experiences with organizational change, they will tell you that scouting is generally *not* part of the equation. Organizations frequently engage in change activities without stopping to analyze what they are up against. In our interviews with business leaders concerning unsuccessful change efforts, we frequently heard leaders make these kinds of comments:

"We ran into unexpected resistance in this effort."
"Problems with this implementation seemed to come out of nowhere."
"We just couldn't get people to buy into what we were trying to do, and we walked right into the problem."
"Our top management went into this change with rose-colored glasses on, and we were all bitten by reality."
"Dealing with our competitors is sometimes easier than dealing with our own organization, which is something we seem to consistently fail to look for."

These business leaders share a commonality with losing football teams that failed to properly scout their opponents. They were confessing that they were not prepared for the opposition that they faced. Conversely, successful change efforts are almost always accompanied by a thorough analysis and understanding of all the following factors:

- Competitors
- Internal culture
- Team members' strengths and weaknesses
- Organizational and interpersonal dynamics facing the leaders of change

In our research, we have found that developing "pregame" scouting reports will help you understand who your real opponents are in the change process and help you think through how you match up.

Successful change leaders make a practice out of collecting and analyzing the information that will help them go into any change effort with their eyes wide open. In our research, five themes emerged that are typically part of a pregame scouting report. These factors represent areas that can stop you cold in your drive for change and improvement if you don't properly match up. As a quarterback-leader, you must know

- Your competitors
- Yourself
- Your team
- Your organization
- Your situation

Just as in the game of football, this information must be monitored and kept up-to-date every time you are about to attempt a new organizational change. *Making today's decisions with yesterday's data can be fatal.* Each change initiative can be a new game with new players, new opponents, and a new field. Without a thorough pregame assessment of who your real opponents are, you run the risk of being caught off guard, sacked, or blindsided in your efforts.

We all understand the inclusion of strengths and weaknesses as factors in a scouting report. Most of us have encountered this information when given personal performance reviews. But the term *match-ups* may be a bit foreign to some from an organizational appraisal perspective. It's not foreign to the world of football. Walk the practice field or visit the locker room during the week before any game, and you will hear that term kicked around more than a freshman walk-on. Football is a game of statistics, and much of the data and statistics compiled by the scouting team are boiled down to a series of match-ups. These match-ups—of individuals, the coaches, the team, and how the opponents act or react in certain circumstances—become the guidelines for the team to create a winning game plan. For example, the scouting team wants to know:

- When will an opponent pass?
- When will an opponent run the ball?
- When does the quarterback get rattled?
- What formation gives away a trick play?
- How do the personnel on the field hint at what is coming?

A significant purpose of a scouting report, both in football and in organizations, is to identify *tendencies*. Think about the tendencies of your organization, your team, and yourself to react in certain ways when faced with the need to do something different:

- Do you overanalyze?
- Do you avoid assuming authority?
- Do you develop realistic and detailed action plans?
- Do you make clear decisions and execute?
- Do you hold too many meetings?

Your attention to tendencies, coupled with a review of match-ups on strengths and weaknesses, will increase your ability to move quickly and win.

Knowing What You Are Up Against Is Critical

A CEO who participated in several of our research studies made a telling comment: "We have to get better at looking at ourselves in the mirror." As you think about preparing for an organizational change or serious improvement effort, you should look in the mirror and include in your scouting activities the key *potential opponents* described in the rest of this chapter.

Momentum Builder 1: Know Your Competitors

In business, it is important that you know your customer, but it is *imperative* that you know your competition. Most organizations are competing on some combination of cost, quality, customer service, speed, or innovation. In the concise words of management legend Peter Drucker, "Organizations exist to meet customer needs." An organization's ability to survive and thrive is predicated on its ability to meet and exceed its customer's needs when compared to its competitors.[1] We have found that customer needs and expectations are increasing at a rapid rate because of the increase in competition.

> **Key Question**
> Do you know how well you match up against the talents of your competitors?

For example, Sonny at Dynamic Materials recognized that his company's quoting process was obsolete, and its competitors were beating Dynamic on three fronts: cost, speed, and quality. The current system needed not merely evolutionary but rather *revolutionary* change to put the company in a winning position against its competition. This knowledge gave Sonny a tool to help create focus and a sense of urgency around his change effort.

Organizations frequently collect large quantities of customer-based information that tell them how they match up against their competitors. But what do they *do* with this information? Often it just ends up entered into a spreadsheet, listed in a document, or placed in a filing cabinet, without even crossing a leader's desk or mind!

It is one thing to say that change is needed. It is another thing to make a case that change is necessary because your competitors are doing a better job of meeting your customers' needs. Understanding how you match up against your competitors is a powerful starting point if you want to create momentum around a needed change. Successful change quarterbacks focus their scouting activities to keep up-to-date information on their competitor's strengths, weaknesses, and tendencies so that they will be in a position to exploit favorable match-ups or realize more quickly when real change is needed. Such knowledge of your opponent's game plan can help signal when and where you must execute change.

MOMENTUM BUILDER 2: KNOW YOURSELF

It has been said, "Knowing others is intelligence; knowing yourself is wisdom." When managers find themselves in situations where change is required, they frequently concentrate all their energies on the actual changes that have to take place. What they often omit in these intellectual analyses is an effort to assess themselves and how they match up with the change(s) that must be made. For example, when a leader with minimal technical expertise is asked to drive a technology change, or an executive is asked to implement a new business strategy that is beyond his or her current expertise, the individual simply may not be up to the task. In the rush to change, managers frequently do not stop and assess how their own skill set and leadership style match up against the requirements of the change initiative.[2]

Similarly, when a football coach is preparing for a new opponent, he may realize that his team needs to throw the ball more than he is comfortable with or is used to doing. The coach comes to the realization that they must do something outside their comfort zone if they are to win. Sonny at Dynamic Materials came to this understanding when he realized that his own aversion to conflict among the key parties in the quoting process was causing him to avoid addressing the problem. Further, though Sonny himself believed that the quoting system was broken, did the rest of the organization *share* that view? What did Sonny know about the technology that would be required to meet the needs of the customer? These were the match-ups that Sonny faced, and *his assessment of himself* was the first critical statistic of his scouting report for the new quoting process initiative. Your personal scouting report must determine how you match up with the demands of the change effort that you want to lead.

Key Question
Do you know your personal strengths, weaknesses, and tendencies when leading organizational change initiatives?

Momentum Builder 3: Know Your Team

As we know, a football team must have eleven players on the field at all times. A change initiative team, however, may be composed of a few people or dozens of people, all bringing different skills and playing a myriad of roles, depending on the task at hand. Although the word "team" is frequently used in business, it is our experience that very few work groups and improvement teams actually *function* as teams. Quite often, this is simply because key players are not matched properly to the activities that the changes require. Football players are always curious to see how they match up with the person playing opposite them, and the same should be true of business leaders. Although it is impossible to constantly put the "all-star" team on the field for every change initiative, understanding the individual player's strengths, weaknesses, tendencies, and potential match-ups will ensure that the team selected can still win.

For example, when Sonny at Dynamic Materials recognized the need for a new quoting process, he immediately established the match-ups for the key players that would be on the field for this initiative. The sales VP wanted speed and simplicity, yet the engineering and accounting department heads demanded thoroughness. Saum in IT would face the rigorous guidelines of corporate policy regarding information systems control, yet he had the ability to work well with the varied disciplines that were essential to success. Sonny's challenge was to ensure that this variety of skills and personalities worked synergistically to convert the quoting process to a competitive advantage.

In your own organization, in addition to determining match-ups, do you know your team's *tendencies* as they pertain to the change process? Ask yourself the following questions to make sure you know what those tendencies are, lest you be surprised to find at a later date that the members of your team are wearing the wrong color jersey and have become opponents in your quest for change.

Key Questions
1. Are members of your team willing to try new things, or do they have a tendency to cling to the status quo?
2. Do members of your team have a tendency to resist change regardless of the source?
3. Do you have people working for you who are going to try intentionally to cause failure?

MOMENTUM BUILDER 4: KNOW YOUR FRANCHISE

In football terms, a *franchise* comprises every facet of the team's organization, from the owners to the groundskeeper who is responsible for maintaining the stripes on the football field. In business, your franchise is the larger organization in which you and your team operate. Although most organizations talk about the need for improvement and the importance of change, some organizations have a stronger capacity for change than others. As W. Edwards Deming put it, "It is not necessary to change. Survival is not mandatory." But if you want your organization to survive, you must take into account its culture for change, which encompasses such critical factors as

- Senior leadership
- Risk-taking tendencies
- Leadership cooperation
- Rewards systems
- Resource deployment
- Accountability
- Political environment

Be sure you understand these factors as they play out in your organization, and ask yourself the following question:

> **Key Question**
> How will your organization react to the changes you want to make?

In our business case study, Sonny recognized that to continue to grow as an organization, Dynamic Materials had to rethink its quoting process and model. The organization had traditionally been comfortable with incremental improvements to its production processes and relied on them to stay competitive. Reengineering its quoting process would require both technical input and cooperation among the members of the upper management team.

Some organizations are very supportive and passionate about change and improvement; these organizations typically have creative top management, flexible organizational structures, open communication, and effective problem-solving mechanisms. In these environments, creating momentum and support for change can be less intimidating than in other organizations.

In contrast, many organizations simply give lip service to the need to change. When it is time to actually implement change, they are more comfortable talking about it, analyzing the need for it, and having committee meetings to discuss it. We would even go so far as to say that many thorough scouting reports will actually uncover fellow managers or departments (or both) that will mount direct opposition to *stop* an improvement drive. It is critical for you to know and anticipate the actions of potential opponents who will not only resist your efforts at change but even work against you. Without a doubt, these situations are unhealthy, but they are a reality nevertheless. Going into any serious change effort, you need to answer this question:

> **Key Question**
> How would you describe your organization in terms of its strengths, weaknesses, and tendencies in approaching change efforts?

MOMENTUM BUILDER 5: KNOW YOUR PLAYING CONDITIONS

In football, a wide variety of playing conditions can affect performance and the outcome of the game—for example, the distance traveled to the game, playing in the home stadium versus being on the road, the weather, playing in a stadium for the first time, and artificial turf versus natural grass. Leaders in the workplace are confronted with their own set of playing conditions, such as

- Current industry trends
- The pressure for change
- Management's desire for change or resistance to it
- Current financial performance
- Existing technological opportunities and constraints
- The current health of the overall economy

As the leader, you must take all these factors into consideration as part of preparing your scouting report. Although we all hope that playing conditions are conducive to change, keep in mind what inventor Charles Kettering observed: "People are very open-minded about new things—as long as they are exactly like the old ones." In other words, you must know and work within the reality of the playing conditions that you face in your organization.

Sonny recognized that the playing conditions for Dynamic Materials included a culture of resistance to change and an attitude of letting departments do their own thing. These were not conditions that made the change impossible, but *ignoring* them could lead to extended deadlines, budget overruns, and only marginal success.

Successful football teams react to mud, snow, and wind by changing their style of play and often their equipment. Similarly, successful organizations respond to difficulties and changes in their surroundings by using different methods and tools to build momentum for scoring. As pastor and noted speaker Robert Schuler has taught us, "Problems are not stop signs, they are guidelines."

Key Question
Going in to any change initiative, have you thoroughly analyzed the organizational environment and culture that you face?

Creating a Simple Scouting Report: Know Your Match-Ups

Although scouting reports can be voluminous collections of data, if they are to be useful to you and your team they must be condensed such that you can easily interpret the information and convert it into action. One way to do this is to work with the matrix in Exhibit 4.1. Take a few minutes to complete it when you begin a change initiative. Doing so will help you think through the various challenges that lie ahead. If you are really serious about getting a more accurate picture of what you are up against, ask members of your team and other fellow leaders in your organization to complete the same process. A facilitated discussion of the input from all the "scouts" who have a vested interest in the change can help you develop a thorough, highly useful understanding of what you are up against. This practice can also be a terrific team-building experience for participants.

Exhibit 4.1: Scouting Report—Match-Up Matrix			
Potential Opponents	Strengths and Weaknesses	Demands of the Change	Match-Up (Favorable or Unfavorable?)
Competitors			
Yourself			
Team			
Franchise			
Playing Conditions			

DYNAMIC MATERIALS: THE OUTCOME

So, did Dynamic Materials win or lose? Fortunately, the organization was able to assess its situation using the concept of a scouting report as a springboard to fixing the problem. As team leader, Sonny crafted a simple scouting report and solicited the input of all the "players," summarized in Exhibit 4.2, to highlight the match-ups and tendencies of the various parties associated with this change.

As its scouting report indicates, Dynamic Materials faced several hurdles in its effort to rapidly simplify the quoting process. Its competitors were way out in front with a more effective quoting process, which made Dynamic's task of creating something new to differentiate itself from the competition quite difficult. Sonny realized that his personal style of leadership was not well suited for this type of challenge. In addition, the people who were needed to fix the problem were not accustomed to working together and had their own agendas. Conversely, the engineering organization and the playing conditions from the top of the organization down made it clear that this problem must be fixed because of its effect on the organization's competitive position; this created a strong favorable match-up for Sonny and his team.

Incorporating this knowledge, Sonny, as the quarterback-leader, put another key player into the game to facilitate the process. A charismatic individual in the sales group who had developed strong relationships across the organization was drafted to spearhead the redesign team. Meanwhile, Sonny concentrated his efforts on working with

Exhibit 4.2: Dynamic Materials Scouting Report—Match-Up Matrix

Potential Opponents	Strengths and Weaknesses	Demands of the Change	Match-Up (Favorable or Unfavorable?)
Competitors	Competitors' quoting process is faster and more user-friendly	Beat our competitors on customer usability	Unfavorable
Yourself	Avoids confrontation and conflict but likes consensus building	Decisive action and strong leadership	Unfavorable
Team	Each member has own strengths but traditionally works in own silo, with no track record of cooperation	Teamwork, creativity, and speed	Unfavorable
Franchise	Tends to like slow change and status quo and frequently defers decisions to the engineering department	There is a strong realization of the need for real change in the engineering department	Favorable
Playing Conditions	Group tends to function best in slow, methodical environment	Group realizes the need for rapid change because of loss of market share	Favorable

Susan's group to standardize the engineering process to eliminate redundant paperwork and time. The IT experts found off-the-shelf web technology that could streamline the entire process.

The organizational change was made rapidly and effectively. In Sonny's words, "I realized, and we realized, that our competitors were not our only opponents. . . . This realization gave a common platform to attack this problem as a team and it really helped going in." The process was simplified, costs were reduced, Dynamic Materials' customers now had better and easier access to the company's products, and the competition was neutralized— all because the team used a scouting report. The likelihood of success goes up fast when you know your opponents!

CONCLUSION AND A CALL FOR PREGAME ACTION

As we conclude our discussion of developing your scouting report as a cornerstone of the TMD process, we must emphasize that generating an effective scouting report *going into each and every change initiative is critical.* Your scouting report is an important tool to help you understand and prepare for what you will face in your change game. The data you collect, the information you use, and the assessments you conduct must be both accurate and up-to-date if they are to be truly useful. Exhibit 4.3 provides you with an opportunity to think through the momentum builders that are critically important for creating your pregame scouting report, and to anticipate some of the potential problems and opportunities that you face when you step onto the playing field that represents your next change. There is no substitute for knowing how you and your team will match up against the challenges you face; in this case, what you don't know *can* really hurt you!

Exhibit 4.3: TMD Momentum Builder Checklist

Listed below are momentum builders for creating a scouting report. Ask yourself the check-off questions to determine how well you stack up to the challenge!   ✔

TMD field winner: QB determines match-ups and tendencies of the competition in this game.

Your check-off: Are you assessing the response the competition will make to your initiative?   ❏

TMD field winner: QB assesses his own tendencies and how his skills will match up to the needs of the drive.

Your check-off: Are you determining if you have the skills and commitment required for this initiative?   ❏

TMD field winner: QB checks team skills in relation to the chosen play package and the demands of the game plan.

Your check-off: Are you assessing your team's skills in terms of how they match up with the demands of the action plan?   ❏

TMD field winner: QB determines how all appropriate people (for example, the fans) can be useful in driving for the win.

Your check-off: Are you assessing the tendencies of the overall organization and adjusting accordingly?   ❏

TMD field winner: QB checks out the field conditions, weather, and so on and adjusts the play package accordingly.

Your check-off: Are you monitoring the overall business environment and modifying the action plan to stay on target?   ❏

CHAPTER FIVE

CREATE AN EXTREME FOCUS AND A SENSE OF URGENCY
A Plan for Implementing Rapid Change

Gentlemen, this is a football.
—VINCE LOMBARDI

Nothing focuses the mind better than the constant sight of a competitor who wants to wipe you off the map.
—WAYNE CALLOWAY

WINNING IMPERATIVE: *Get "Extreme"*
To achieve extraordinary results, you must ratchet up focus and a sense of urgency, from normal levels of operation to *extreme* levels.

"The Kick": New England Patriots vs. Carolina Panthers, Super Bowl XXXVIII, February 1, 2004

Playing in their franchise's very first Super Bowl, the Carolina Panthers arrived at Houston's Reliant Stadium intent on destroying the New England Patriots' hopes of winning two championships in three years. On that February Sunday in 2004, it initially appeared that both teams had left their offensive squads on the bus, as their powerful defenses dominated the first half, setting a record of 26:55 without a score. Miscues and strong defensive play led to both offenses' struggling to put points on the scoreboard.

The Patriots scored the first points of the contest with only 3:05 left in the first half, when QB Tom Brady hit wide-out Deion Branch for a 5-yard touchdown. Carolina responded with a seven-play scoring drive that took just 1:51 and culminated in a 39-yard touchdown pass from Jake Delhomme to wide-out Steve Smith. Things were heating up, and the offenses still were not done as New England drove the field and scored again, covering 78 yards in six plays using only 36 seconds. The Panthers got the ball back with 12 seconds left in the half, got into field-goal position with one play, and kicked a 50-yard field goal as time expired. Halftime score: Panthers 10, Patriots 14.

It appears that a sense of urgency began to develop for both offenses as the first half drew to a close. In around 3 minutes, fans had witnessed the spectacle of both offenses playing with a true sense of urgency, racking up 24 points. But more spectacles were in store, both at halftime and in the second half, for the fans in the stands as well as the 144.4 million people who were watching on national TV—which was the largest television audience in U.S. television history.

The halftime show featured the now infamous Janet Jackson–Justin Timberlake "wardrobe malfunction" that left fans and TV commentators in a funk, struggling to make sense out of what had just taken place on national television. Some argue that this funk carried over onto the offensive playing field, resulting in a scoreless and unfocused third quarter.

In the fourth quarter, however, the Patriots scored to go up 21–10, and the Panthers responded in kind with a touchdown and a failed 2-point conversion, making the score Carolina 16, New England 21. On the following possession, Patriots QB Tom Brady threw an interception, which the Panthers converted into a quick 85-yard touchdown pass. Again, the 2-point conversion failed, but Carolina now led New England 22–21. With 6:47 left, Tom Brady stayed focused on seizing control of the game and not on the fact that his interception had hurt his team; he engineered an eleven-play scoring drive with a 2-point conversion that put the Patriots up 29–22.

With less than 3 minutes left in the game, it appeared that the Patriots were in the driver's seat, but Carolina drove 80 yards in 1:43 to tie the game at 29–29 with 1:08 remaining. New England QB Tom Brady, known for his never-say-die attitude, led his team onto the field with one last shot to win the game and keep it from going into overtime. A six-play drive put virtuoso kicker Adam Vinateri into position for a 41-yard field goal with 0:04 remaining. Vinateri stayed focused on making the winning kick and not on the fact that he had missed his first-quarter field-goal attempt and had been blocked in a second attempt in the second quarter. The ball was snapped, and the kick was up. Good! The Patriots had won the Super Bowl 32–29, and QB Tom Brady was selected as the game's MVP. The ability of the Patriots to stay focused and execute their offense with a sense of urgency and yet without panic allowed them to secure their second Super Bowl victory in three years.

AMERISTEEL: WINNING THROUGH FOCUSED URGENCY

As he hung up his phone after an extended conversation with his controller, Charlie Hudak thought to himself that this was definitely shaping up to be a day when antacids would be part of his diet. Surging volumes, customer demands for price reductions, and a shortage of qualified workers all gnawed at his stomach as his stress level soared. But now this! Record-breaking low temperatures were beginning to take a toll on the availability of natural gas in the Midwest. Charlie's controller had just been informed by their utility supplier that unless the subzero temperatures suddenly abated, rationing to industrial users would begin within ten days. And the forecast was not favorable. Rationing would mean a 20 percent reduction from last year's average usage levels. Suddenly, as he sat alone in his soon-to-be-cool office, Charlie realized he had a real problem that would make the others pale in comparison.

BACKGROUND: A STEEL MANUFACTURER FACES A CRITICAL PRODUCTION PROBLEM

Ameristeel, a second-tier supplier of specialty steel to the automotive industry, was enjoying a banner year to date. Despite somewhat disappointing overall automotive sales, the company was positioned as the sole supplier of unique metals ultimately used on vehicles that were selling well. In their roles as leaders of Ameristeel's largest plant, located in upper Wisconsin, Charlie and his management team were quite adept at handling the typical issues and demands of the volatile automotive industry. Ameristeel had survived and even learned to prosper, becoming a valued member of the supply chain.

But the team had never before faced this type of situation: natural gas was critical to their production process, and a significant rationing would portend disaster to the entire supply chain. It was time for Charlie to relay the bad news upward to Greenwich Metal Industries (GMI), the parent company of Ameristeel.

Before dropping the issue in the lap of his boss, Charlie took a few minutes to assess his position. On the one hand, his management team and the entire two-thousand-person workforce at the facility had been working their way through an enormous degree of change in recent history. Ongoing new product launches, equipment conversions, system upgrades, and employee shortages were tasking the availability of management resources to the point that people were beginning to show signs of exhaustion. Charlie realized that adding one more major issue to their plates might cause some members of his team to snap. On the other hand, not facing and resolving the gas supply issue would relegate all their other initiatives to the trash heap. In his gut, Charlie was sure he would have to step up his own leadership to help focus the team and create the sense of urgency that would give them a shot at resolving this potential crisis. And they had only ten days to do it.

DAY 1: EXPLORING POSSIBLE SOLUTIONS AND MAKING A PLAN

As an initial step, Charlie decided to seek the advice of his trusted plant engineer, the man responsible for overseeing the massive gas system within the facility. Rather than initially getting the management team together in what could be an exercise in chaos, Charlie asked his confidant, Dwayne Carter, to drop what he was doing and head to Charlie's office. Dwayne had "grown up" at Ameristeel, rising from a junior civil engineer to plant engineering director, responsible for ensuring that nearly a billion dollars of capital assets worked 24/7. He had successfully handled equipment failures, skilled trade negotiations, and other normal requirements of the job. But he too had no experience in dealing with this sort of problem.

After several hours of bouncing ideas around, Charlie and Dwayne concluded that natural gas conservation efforts would help but would not be enough to solve the problem. Reaching back on his experience, Dwayne suggested the use of a liquid propane (LP) system to offset the shortfall. He proposed isolating one of the downstream processes from the natural gas supply, then converting it to an LP-based system. Off the top of his head, he thought the conversion was a monumental task, but he saw no other solution other than outsourcing production to another facility. A bit apprehensive, Charlie agreed.

With this alternative in mind, Charlie immediately called a meeting with his team, briefing them on the situation and Dwayne's recommendation. He could see the initial reactions of despair and fatigue in their eyes as they foresaw a tough road ahead. Alternative options (for example, outsourcing and production leveling) were discussed and discarded, and within an hour, the team had concluded that Dwayne was right. The only solution was the LP conversion.

With the team in his office, Charlie made the call to his boss at GMI. Initial shock from the other end of the line was followed by a series of "What can we do?" questions. Fortunately, GMI management maintained confidence in Ameristeel's team because historically they possessed a "get-it-done" attitude. But everyone knew that this would challenge that moniker and reputation.

Following the discussion with GMI, Charlie walked to his whiteboard and wrote a simple goal for the team: "Ameristeel will maintain 100% on-time delivery throughout the natural gas crisis."

"Now that the objective is clear," he told them, "let's figure out how we're going to do it." Everyone agreed that their reputation as a get-it-done team was on the line and that they would find a way to deliver the goods. They knew the goal, they knew they had ten days to make the conversion, and, although they were tired, they were also somewhat excited about the challenge to prove that they had what it took to succeed. Here's how they delegated responsibilities:

- Dwayne would carry the initial load of leading the redesign of the gas plumbing system and finding the right components.
- Charlie would call customers and alert them to the issue and coordinate discussions with the local union leadership to seek their ideas in overcoming the challenge.
- The production manager accepted the challenge of building up an inventory before the gas supply was curtailed.

The next coordination meeting would be in twenty-four hours.

DAY 2: A NEW PROBLEM ARISES, AND THE NEED FOR URGENCY INCREASES

The team reassembled. Dwayne led the discussion, explaining that he had met earlier that day with the engineers from the gas company, who committed to providing technical support for creating the LP system. Dwayne also found that most of the materials required for the system were readily available—with one major exception: an enormous storage tank, normally custom made, would be required to support the system.

The only tank that was currently available was located in Canada. The owner of the tank offered to move quickly, ensuring that they could have it on Ameristeel's property in five weeks. But that was about twenty-five days too late. It seems that customs requirements, shipping factors, and logistics were conspiring to slow the movement of a flammable container across international borders. Suddenly, the focus had narrowed to the tank, and the need for urgency escalated. Once again, Charlie decided to pump up the volume.

DAY 3: INCREASING THE SIZE OF THE TEAM TO MAKE THINGS HAPPEN FASTER

In the morning hours of the third day, all hope of moderating weather vanished, as a Canadian clipper swept in, plunging temperatures to −15 degrees. Charlie and his team became even more determined to beat this frigid nemesis. Over the course of the day, Charlie expanded the team working the issue to include the corporate purchasing people, the automotive customer's Washington D.C. liaison, the company's customs brokers, plus a raft of other minor players.

- The liaison contacted elected government officials, explaining that a delay would result in approximately thirty thousand industry-wide temporary pre-Christmas layoffs. Suddenly, elected officials were anxious to help ignite a fire under the bureaucracy to avoid paperwork delays rather than see layoffs in their districts.
- Purchasing and treasury people reduced approval time for support documents, ensuring that money would flow when needed.
- Shipping people found the proper carriers overnight and ensured that they would be ready to move the tank.

All in all, a process that would have taken five weeks was accomplished in only four days! The tank arrived on Ameristeel's property, ready for installation, on day 6 of the crisis.

DAYS 4–7: ENSURING UNION SUPPORT, INCENTIVIZING THE WORKERS, AND REHEARSING THE CHANGE PROCESS

During the four-day in-transit period, the team's progress continued in Wisconsin. Charlie met with union leaders to explain the critical nature of this initiative, asking their support in identifying a twenty-person team of skilled tradespeople willing to work in shifts around the clock to get the installation job done. Because of the need to keep the tank outdoors, much of the work would be done in subzero weather. The union responded favorably, the team of volunteers was identified, and Charlie met with them to rally them concerning the importance of the task that lay ahead. He also announced that each of them would receive a $500 bonus in addition to normal pay if the job were completed on time. The team was pumped up and ready for action.

Piping routes were created, pumps and regulators installed, and a plan developed for the installation of the tank upon its arrival. Wearing special cold-weather gear procured by the local purchasing team, the installation crew rehearsed the actual installation to ensure that they had the right tools, support equipment, and other necessities. By the time the tank arrived, they were totally focused on the steps needed to hook it up and convert the natural gas to LP. With great pride, Charlie watched as the crew worked their magic to get the process on line.

DAY 8: SUCCESS AND CELEBRATION

The installation was completed. Civil inspectors verified the hookup, and an initial charge of propane was pumped into the tank. Natural gas was shut off to the isolated equipment, burner changes were made, the new system was turned on, and gas began to flow. Minor regulator adjustments were made, and with a loud cheer from the installation crew, the system was declared operational.

A project that normally would have taken eighteen months was completed in *eight days*. In his quarterback role, Charlie was able to focus his leadership team, the corporate people, elected officials, inspectors, and a host of others on maintaining a constant sense of urgency for achieving the goal. The local pub was a place of great celebration that night.

DAY 10: MEETING THE GOAL—AND MAINTAINING IT

As promised, the utility reduced the volume allocation to the plant by 20 percent. And on day 10 (and beyond), Charlie's team met its goal, that "Ameristeel will maintain 100% on-time delivery throughout the natural gas crisis," which lasted the rest of the long winter. Charlie had done an outstanding job of leading his team through this crisis by making sure he stayed focused and kept his team motivated on doing the right things the right way. Charlie also made sure that this success was celebrated, not only at his facility in a variety of forms, but throughout the entire organization.

REAL IMPROVEMENT AND CHANGE REQUIRE FOCUS AND A SENSE OF URGENCY

There are a number of lessons that can be drawn from the Super Bowl play of the New England Patriots and from Charlie Hudak and his team at Ameristeel during the natural gas crisis. In both cases, people had to handle inordinate pressures and maintain their composure so that they could think clearly and do all the things necessary to win. Embedded in these lessons is the simple truth that people and teams can accomplish remarkable feats under the following conditions:

- When they believe they are working on something *important*
- When they are properly *focused*
- When they have a true sense of *urgency* to fuel their performance

The qualities that enabled the people at Ameristeel to solve their natural gas crisis were the very same qualities that enabled the New England Patriots to perform at an exceptional level when they found themselves behind late in the biggest game of their careers.

In the Prologue, we asked you to describe a successful and an unsuccessful change initiative that you have personally experienced. We are very confident that you will see the issues of importance, focus, and a sense of urgency emerge in your descriptions. Previous research by Kotter and by Murray and Richardson has made a strong case that strategic and cultural transformations are frequently driven by a sense of urgency.[1] Our research supports this contention, but not only for large-scale organizational change; a sense of urgency is appropriate for *any serious* organizational change, regardless of the type of change or the level in the organization's hierarchy.

We made it clear in Chapter Four that as a quarterback of change, you must assess your franchise and playing conditions. In our experience, we have found that organizations vary greatly in their attitude concerning change, as illustrated in Exhibit 5.1. Your job as the quarterback of your change team is to create a set

Exhibit 5.1: Organizational Attitudes Concerning Change

Organizational Lethargy	Organizational Urgency	Organizational Panic
• Nothing is important.	• The right things are important.	• Everything is important.
• Lack of focus.	• Focus on desired outcome.	• Lack of focus.
• Inaction.	• Appropriate action.	• Chaotic action.

of playing conditions around the desired change so that it is easy for people on your team to realize the importance of what you are trying to do, properly focus their energies on what you are trying to accomplish, and play out their assignments with a sense of commitment and urgency.

Clearly, one of the key elements of any successful rapid change initiative is the ability of the team to create and sustain a sense of urgency and not lose focus on the results that it hopes to achieve. It's important to use a disciplined *process* of change—but that's not enough. More notably, if it hopes to win, the team must find a way to keep the *intended results* in the crosshairs of the initiative.

TMD MOMENTUM BUILDERS FOR CREATING EXTREME FOCUS AND A SENSE OF URGENCY

Much has been written over the years in journals and books on management practices outlining the need for creating a sense of urgency and focus. In general, when the organization is operating in a normal mode, the approaches discussed in these publications are quite sufficient. But when the stakes are high and time is short, the practice of instilling urgency and focus must be elevated to a new level. At the risk of carrying the sports metaphor too far, we must apply the term *extreme* to both focus and urgency. A team concentrating on winning the Super Bowl with only 4 seconds remaining or a team working to prevent a major business crisis must be *extremely* focused and must experience an *extreme* sense of urgency during those efforts. Elevating personal and group efforts to a level beyond normal represents a challenge and, quite frankly, is not sustainable over long periods of time. It exacts a toll on the resources dedicated to achieving the goal. But in the arena of a TMD, such extremity often is the factor that decides the winner among equally qualified competitors. Creating extreme focus and a sense of urgency can be fueled by the following momentum builders.

MOMENTUM BUILDER 1: DECLARE THE IMPORTANCE OF THE WIN

As we've already discussed, effective quarterbacks start any serious effort at organizational improvement or change by clearly defining what winning means. Once the team knows the definition of winning, it is critically important for everyone to know and understand the importance of this desired outcome. In the Super Bowl, this job is easy. For Charlie Hudak at Ameristeel, it wasn't very hard to do, either, because of the clear ramifications of trying to run the business without enough fuel.

A starting point for understanding how to create a set of playing conditions that motivate people to do their very best is to ask yourself the following question:

> **Key Question**
> What must you do to convince your people of the importance of this initiative?

We have found that when people believe a change is *truly important*, they will act very differently than if they believe the change is something trivial, bureaucratic, meaningless, non-value-added, or disconnected from an important performance variable. People are reluctant to commit themselves to any activity conducted just for its own sake. So how do people know if a change or an improvement effort is truly important? Exhibit 5.2 shows what we've learned—and the list is actually quite short.

Exhibit 5.2: How People Know When a Change Is Truly Important

People know a change is truly important when ...

- A credible leader takes the time to explain how the change affects their future.
- They are made to feel part of the change.
- People's livelihoods, jobs, or careers hang in the balance.
- The change involves retaining or attracting customers.
- Revenue or money is involved.
- The change challenges people's professional pride or problem-solving talents (or both).
- People are held accountable for the success or failure of the effort.

Leadership expert Max DePree is known for his belief, "The first responsibility of a leader is to define reality." Part of that definition includes distinguishing the unimportant from the important. Regardless of terminology, you are going back to the idea of "making the main thing the main thing." With this backdrop, an effective quarterback-leader will prepare a game plan to let his or her people know why the change is truly important and why they must be willing to expend the extra time, effort, and energy to execute the plays necessary to win. If you yourself aren't convinced that the changes you are attempting to make are important, you will not be able to convince your people, and your TMD will more than likely fail.

MOMENTUM BUILDER 2: CREATE EXTREME FOCUS

Patriots quarterback Tom Brady is characterized by an uncanny talent for being able to stay extremely focused in loud and stressful situations, as in Super Bowl XXXVIII. But wait a minute. Tom had the luxury of being able to focus on one simple goal: driving his team down for the winning score. Most business leaders are being asked to focus on a multitude of activities and performance variables on a continuous, unrelenting basis. This demand carries over into their efforts at changing and improving their operations. We can all find ourselves with so many things on our plate that we feel overwhelmed, so no, you are not alone. For example, Charlie Hudak at Ameristeel was already busy with his regular job and a host of other change activities when the gas crisis hit. He had to stop and let go of some of the less important things so that he had the time, energy, and intellectual capacity to focus on the needed changes. This required a tremendous effort on his part, but he did it.

Here is an important research finding that you should remember. We asked managers, "How many major change or improvement efforts can you successfully manage simultaneously?" Their answer (when we compiled all) was an average of 2.4, which means that most business leaders believe that they can effectively manage somewhere between two and three serious change initiatives at the same time.

Now, contrast that finding with their response to this question: "How many serious change or improvement initiatives do you believe the average business leader has on his or her plate?" Their answer (again, when we compiled all) was 5.8.

That leaders have *twice as many* projects as they can handle at one time makes it exceedingly difficult for them to create focus for themselves, let alone for the people they are expected to lead. If a change is truly important and must happen quickly, you as the leader must find a way to focus your energies and the energies of your people on the truly important issues related to the change. You can do a lot to create and maintain focus, including, for example,

- Clarify individual responsibilities
- Prioritize activities
- Measure performance on an ongoing basis
- Provide ongoing feedback
- Conduct update meetings and send e-mails on the progress of the initiative
- Provide visual aids to remind people of critical dates and deadlines and to recognize short-term gains

Instilling focus on any one "play" demands that you

- Limit the number of goals
- Limit the number of action items
- Limit the informational requirements that support the play

Otherwise, in place of focus there will be a blur of activity.

We stated earlier that change is a hardship for people because it takes place on top of their existing heavy workload and makes the issue of focus even more challenging. An effective leader must learn how to take some things off others' plates as well as off their own. When we are behind on the scoreboard, we must prioritize in order to free up time and define winning in a way that really gets people's attention. Our people need to know that we are very serious about making real changes sooner rather than later. This attention must then be translated into focus on the specific plays and individual assignments that will lead to a successful improvement drive. If you are going after real change, ask yourself the following question:

Key Question
What must you, as a quarterback, do to help your team of players focus their efforts and talents on the activities that will lead to a win?

MOMENTUM BUILDER 3: RATCHET UP THE SENSE OF URGENCY

Focus without urgency can lead to a business-as-usual mentality, which is pervasive in far too many change efforts. A consistent factor in successful change is a sense of urgency. In a world dominated by a demand for accelerated results, focus alone is not sufficient. As noted motivational speaker Gary Ryan Blair puts it, "An atmosphere of urgency will create an atmosphere of achievement."

For example, after watching more than 26 minutes of a scoreless game, fans were probably not anticipating a record number of points in the fourth quarter of Super Bowl XXXVIII. They were expecting "business as usual." But the players on the field had an entirely different mind-set. Each team craved victory, and both squads knew they would have to put some serious points on the board to win. Having a sense of urgency cannot simply be an emotional "rah-rah" to get people excited, but must also be a systematic, structural approach to rapid movement and efficiency.

On that Super Bowl Sunday, the structural aspects of urgency entailed doing all of the following:

- Going to the no-huddle offense
- Running plays designed to gain large chunks of yardage in minimal amounts of time
- Using scoreboard information with the utmost care

In the case of Ameristeel, extreme urgency can be seen in its approach to all of the following:

- Working with the union
- Rapidly reengineering its gas-supply process
- Streamlining its procurement process
- Creatively engaging "bureaucracy-busting" officials

All these actions enabled Ameristeel to achieve in days what normally might have taken months.

In both cases, the leaders of these teams knew that their role was to keep the teams moving in the right direction, and success was fueled by a sense of urgency. Or, as Denver Broncos quarterback John Elway has put it, "My job in a two-minute drill is to get the team back to the line of scrimmage and make things happen."

If you think about it, the foundational aspect of urgency is, not surprisingly, *time*. Creating a sense of urgency alludes to the fact that limited time exists for whatever task lies ahead. Going into a TMD situation in football, a quarterback and his team always know how much time they have available to score. The same should be true in the workplace. Accordingly, creating a sense of urgency that is truly productive necessitates the elimination of processes or actions that simply consume time while not moving the team closer to its objective. Essentially, it calls for *the elimination of waste!*

Football teams often waste precious time by doing any or all of the following:

- Returning slowly after a play
- Huddling excessively
- Getting penalized

In the organizational world, time-wasting urgency killers are frequently numerous, obvious, and entrenched:

- Top-heavy approval processes
- Excessive meetings
- Bureaucratic procedures

In addition, however, beneath the surface of most organizations lie other elements that nibble away at the precious commodity of time. These stealth time killers may include

- Unnecessary e-mails
- The inefficient handoff of information throughout the supply chain
- "Pack-ratting" of knowledge
- That age-old time-consuming indulgence, watercooler gossip

Such elements, if unchecked, slow down the team on their march across the field.

As we noted in Chapter Two, our studies of workplace leaders show that the average manager has a little over two hours each day in which to do results-oriented, bottom-line work, regardless of the length of the manager's day. Here's what they say fills up the balance of their day:

"Meetings that are longer than necessary"

"Lengthy and unnecessary phone calls"

"Mountainous paperwork"

"Dealing with incompetence"

"Bureaucratic machinations"

So as a quarterback, you must demonstrate the ability to dedicate your time to the activities that yield the best outcomes, while at the same time controlling the factors that eat all but about two productive hours of your day. You must demonstrate extreme time sensitivity, but, equally important, you must carry this mentality into your interactions with your team, helping them do the same. *Kill the time wasters, before they kill you!*

Remember, creating a sense of urgency is not simply an idea; it is an *action*. And as the quarterback, you must take proactive steps to eliminate these activities that consume time but do not move you closer to the end zone. You simply must create playing conditions that enable everyone on the team to keep his or her eyes open and alert for opportunities to eliminate these organizational drive killers. Therefore, ask yourself the following question.

Key Question
When executing a change initiative, do you and your people feel a sense of urgency around this effort?

MOMENTUM BUILDER 4: RALLY THE TEAM—FAST

In football TMDs, the following familiar phrases conjure up visions of a football team getting ready to play:

- "Getting pumped up"
- "Juicing up the team"
- "Getting their heads in the game"
- "Getting your players to ride the Big Mo[mentum]"
- "Turning up the volume"

In the business world, we tend to use more moderate terms:

- "Motivating the task team"
- "Inspiring the department"
- "Encouraging the staff"

The purpose of these kinds of statements is to get people excited about what lies ahead. For a football team in a big game, this is much easier than getting people at work fired up over reengineering a process or implementing a new human resource management information system. Yet keeping your team motivated throughout the contest is critical.

> **Key Question**
> When you go into a serious change effort, what do you
> do to rally your team members and get them pumped up
> for what lies ahead?

One method leaders often use to rally their team is to deal with a crisis. People frequently say there is nothing like a good, old-fashioned crisis if you want to make things happen. And it has even been said that it is very difficult to create a sense of urgency *without* some kind of crisis.[2] Dealing with a crisis is a legitimate way to rally your team. However, continually using crises as the primary means to create urgency has some serious drawbacks:

- This tactic gets old quickly.
- Using crises reflects poorly on the leader (you), whose effectiveness is judged on his or her ability to *minimize* crises.
- Crises can create panic, which is both stressful and counterproductive.
- When a real crisis comes along, people say, "Yeah, yeah, yeah." In other words, a boy-who-cried-wolf mentality takes over, and people won't take you seriously anymore.

In other cases, when leaders want to rally their team around an improvement effort, they can dip into a thick playbook of what might be described as gimmicks or trick plays to get people's attention:

- Kickoff rallies
- Motivational speakers
- T-shirts
- Retreats
- Pizza parties
- Book signings
- Webcasts
- Banners
- E-mail blasts and blogs
- Raffles and lapel pins

Although people might wrinkle their noses or scoff cynically at these, we have seen all these tools used effectively by credible leaders to let people know that the upcoming effort is worthy of their attention and commitment. The keys here are *the leader's credibility* and coupling these attention-getting practices with the other factors that we have described to let people know this upcoming effort is not business as usual or "change as usual."

One of the best ways to rally your team around a desired change ties back into rallying individuals around the roles that they must play in the change effort. A good quarterback-leader knows the strengths and weaknesses of each person on his or her team on each and every play of an improvement drive, and the quarterback works hard to help people maintain their individual focus and sense of urgency by reminding them of the importance of what they are doing. Recognition, feedback, and "on-the-field" coaching are critical skills for change quarterbacks.

Finally, we have learned that you can generate and sustain this sense of extreme focus and urgency only by addressing both data-driven, *factual* arguments and the needed *emotional* investment of senior management, your customers, and other key players in the change initiative. Essentially, the quarterback must use his or her skills to secure a personal attachment by all parties in the effort. Having a "sideline huddle" at the beginning of the TMD and creating performance metrics to focus groups and individuals are both quite helpful in this quest for success.

CONCLUSION: SIX KEYS TO VICTORY

In a postcrisis interview with Ameristeel's Charlie Hudak, he humbly shared with us several lessons from his experience that we believe are noteworthy; we've summed them up in Exhibit 5.3.

As an addition to point 6 on staying focused, Charlie reported that during the crisis, he met with his coworker and confidant Dwayne, the plant engineer, at least twice a day to make sure Dwayne knew what was going on and that Dwayne was holding him accountable to do the right things. This practice carried over into weekly meetings between these two leaders and has led to an ongoing peer-mentoring relationship that both men believe has improved not only their performance but also the quality of their work life.

Exhibit 5.3: Six Keys to Victory

1. Great lessons can be learned from a crisis, because people discover that things do not always have to take as long to get done as first thought and that a sense of urgency is a friend of change.
2. Real change comes when people are properly focused on exactly what needs to take place, when it needs to take place, and who needs to do it.
3. As the leader, you must stay calm and not panic, regardless of how serious the change or crisis at hand. Remember, people will follow your lead.
4. Make sure that people realize the importance of what you are attempting to accomplish, as not everyone is listening or watching or in a position to fully grasp what is taking place.
5. It's your duty as the leader to get the team excited about what must happen and to help the team maintain their motivation and energy during the change.
6. As the leader, you must stay focused and energized around the changes that you are attempting to make, and you must do the things necessary to properly lead the charge.

These are invaluable lessons that serve as a capstone for this chapter. Charlie and his team did the impossible in ten days.

As we wrap things up, we want to give you one last thing to think about. Two minutes represent one-thirtieth of a 60-minute football game. If we apply the same percentages to an average professional's 2,500-hour work year, one-thirtieth is 83 hours, or between eight and ten work days. We are going out on a limb here, but on the basis of our observations, we believe that the majority of organizational changes that do not require significant transformation in physical, operational, or technological platforms *can be accomplished in eight to ten working days when they are properly staffed, resourced, and executed.*

These days might be spread out or compressed, but time and time again we have witnessed successful change in organizations take place *rapidly*, rather than be drawn out over extended periods of time that have a tendency to suck the momentum and life out of both the change itself and the participants. Haven't we all been guilty of doing the majority of the work on a sixty-day project the night before its due date? Haven't we all been guilty of reiterating project reports multiple times and coming up with the same conclusions after wasting both time and energy? Haven't we all been culpable for spending too much or too little time planning, with negative consequences in both cases? Remember, good quarterbacks remain poised and keep their teams moving with a sense of urgency and focus when they are serious about winning.

Finally, take the time to review your TMD Momentum Builder Checklist, shown in Exhibit 5.4, to think through the items discussed in this chapter.

Exhibit 5.4: TMD Momentum Builder Checklist

Listed below are momentum builders for creating focus and a sense of urgency. Ask yourself the check-off questions to determine how well you stack up to the challenge! ✔

TMD field winner: QB declares the importance of the win.

Your check-off: Are you convincing people of the importance of the win? ❑

TMD field winner: QB creates focus, not chaos, on the field.

Your check-off: Are you distinguishing the important factors from the unimportant, focusing only on those critical to success? ❑

TMD field winner: QB ratchets up the team's sense of urgency to an EXTREME level.

Your check-off: Are you taking commitment, focus, and urgency to a new, higher level? ❑

TMD field winner: QB rallies the team . . . FAST.

Your check-off: Are you creating the needed emotional attachment of team members to achieving the goal? ❑

CHAPTER SIX

DEVELOP YOUR WINNING TWO-MINUTE DRILL PACKAGE

Get the Right Players on the Field and Take Ownership of the Plan

When planning improvement, it seems like more things can go wrong than right. . . . We have to be careful or our change initiatives can become too complicated to execute, too cumbersome to move forward quickly, and we frequently have lots of personnel challenges because we either have too many people involved, too few people involved, or the wrong people involved. . . . It's no wonder execution is tough when we don't always start out with a realistic and strong plan of attack, and we have nobody to blame but ourselves.

—MIDDLE MANAGER, TIER-1 AUTOMOTIVE PARTS SUPPLIER

It's not the will to win but the will to prepare that makes the difference in a big game.

—PAUL "BEAR" BRYANT, LEGENDARY ALABAMA HEAD COACH

WINNING IMPERATIVE: *Plan to Win*

Develop a realistic game plan that you are confident will move the chains and keep the ball in the hands of people who are ready and able to play.

"The Rematch": San Francisco 49ers vs. Cincinnati Bengals, Super Bowl XXIII, January 22, 1989

Super Bowl XXIII has been ranked as the number one Super Bowl of all time according to NFL.com, for a number of interesting reasons, but none of them more important than how this spectacular Super Bowl ended. Super Bowl XXIII was played in Joe Robie Stadium in Miami, Florida, at the completion of the 1988 regular season, pairing the San Francisco 49ers against the Cincinnati Bengals. The two teams had met before in Super Bowl XVI in 1982, when San Francisco won a tight game 26–21. In the five previous Super Bowls, the games had been "blowouts," with the average margin of victory being 27.6 points per game. In many cases, the Super Bowl had become boring by halftime, and the networks were hard pressed to keep their audience tuned into the game to maximize commercial advertising revenue in the second half. Super Bowl XXIII would ease their pain.

Trailing the Cincinnati Bengals 16–13, San Francisco quarterback Joe Montana, the legendary Hall of Famer, brought his 49er offense onto the field in the waning minutes of the fourth quarter. Joe's high-powered offense had been kept in check for most of the game, despite the fact that his team featured All-Pro wide receiver Jerry Rice and NFL Offensive Player of the Year running back Roger Craig. Joe Montana had won his two previous Super Bowl starts and walked away from both contests with MVP honors, so confidence was not a problem. San Francisco moved the ball throughout the game but was unable to put points on the board.

Head coach Bill Walsh had a solid reputation for TMD preparation, and Joe Montana had proven himself time and time again during his career for his ability to prepare and lead his team to a quick score when the chips were down. Joe was legendary for his calm in such situations. To illustrate the point, people often refer to his comment at the start of this game-winning drive: Joe looked up from his huddle, pointed into the crowd, and said, "Hey, isn't that [the comedian] John Candy?" This helped take some of the stress and tension out of this pressure-packed situation.

In the game-winning drive, the 49ers covered 92 yards in eleven plays that culminated in a 10-yard scoring pass to wide receiver John Taylor with 0:34 remaining in the contest. Joe's TMD package was a unique combination of plays intended to keep the chains moving. The package included two running plays designed to keep the defense off balance and two unexpected pass plays to running back Roger Craig in the middle of the field (which caught the defenders off guard, as they were expecting passes to the sidelines to stop the clock). In this drive, Joe Montana completed eight of nine passes, used the scoreboard masterfully, and executed a play package that put the ball in the hands of four different players at various points of the drive.

Further, the scoring play to Taylor had been intentionally designed to exploit the fact that wide receiver Jerry Rice was double covered on several of the previous plays and was viewed as the "go-to guy" in this critical situation. This Super Bowl–winning drive solidified Montana's reputation as "Joe Cool" for his ability to lead game-winning drives in do-or-die game situations. The 49ers brought a winning TMD package of plays and players to the Super Bowl and used it with great success, securing their third Super Bowl win and allowing head coach Bill Walsh to retire from the NFL on a victorious note

An Engineering Firm Creates a Winning Plan for Change

Now let's look at a business example. TMS Engineering was a leading engineering firm that specialized in commercial and industrial building and process design. The organization had a thirty-year track record of providing creative, cutting-edge, and cost-effective engineering solutions to its diversified customer base. TMS had a solid and profitable market share, but recently its competitors had begun using a newer 3-D computer-assisted design (CAD) technology to great effect in selling their services against TMS. This newer technology made it easier, quicker, and more efficient to make changes in engineering designs and was highly effective in cross-functional design activities in the engineering process. No doubt about it: 3-D CAD was the future.

Background: An Engineering Company Is Unwilling to Adopt New Technology

TMS's CEO, Ben Rieman, had been encouraging company leaders to expand the use of the newer CAD technology with limited success over the two previous years. He decided that something must be done quickly to expand the use and application of this technology to their engineering design processes before TMS fell further behind in the market. In Ben's words, "People were talking about using this newer technology, but when it was time to implement the process, our people did not want to take the time, effort, and energy to do so because they were so busy just keeping up with their current workload. At the same time, most people 'in the know' knew in their guts that we had to do this, or our organization would be seriously hurt in the long run."

TMS had a very professional, decentralized organizational culture that tended to move slowly. As a general rule, the company avoided taking risks, and put the onus for change on individual managers. One of its rare examples of using a centralized, team-based approach to improvement took place around the subject of 3-D CAD two years earlier. At that time, a large, cross-functional organizational improvement team developed a rather exhaustive and complicated set of implementation plans and manuals to accelerate the use of 3-D CAD. The plans for this initiative were handed to managers, who were then "encouraged and cajoled" to implement this new technology on their own. Little improvement (or action, for that matter) was generated by this half-hearted effort. Ben viewed it as a failure, and his views were widely shared.

A NEW APPROACH TO CHANGE: PUTTING TOGETHER THE RIGHT TEAM

Ben pledged that things would be different this time around, and he created a six-person senior leadership team to spearhead the initiative. He made sure that the composition of the team included people who had the following attributes that Ben felt were important:

- They were well respected.
- They were already busy and didn't have time to mess around.
- They had a track record for making things happen.

The team was made up of three people who were already using the new technology to some extent and three people who (though they were strong leaders) were initially opposed to this technological change or, at a minimum, were indifferent. Ben assigned the project to the team with a minimum of fanfare and asked that they give him a "serious and straightforward game plan" for expanding this new technology across the entire organization in the next ninety days. The three change-resistant team members were not happy about their assignment, and in very heated discussions told the CEO of their lack of interest in being part of the team, but Ben held firm to both the team membership and the timeline.

A NEW PLAN OF ATTACK: STEP-BY-STEP

In the first meeting, the team reviewed what had been done on the 3-D CAD initiative to date and then outlined the steps that they would take to develop their plan of attack. These leaders all were experienced problem solvers; consequently, at their first meeting, they did a quick analysis of why past change efforts in this organization frequently did not produce the desired results. They also assessed their own strengths and weaknesses going into this effort. Because all of them were now responsible for the success of the initiative, they vowed that this change was going to be different. And it was!

The team's analysis of the organization's prior change efforts revealed that TMS frequently developed improvement plans that were too complicated and did not have the right people involved. At various stages, their plans frequently broke down and were fraught with communication problems that delayed the actions that were to follow. Furthermore, they agreed, most change efforts took more time than necessary.

To create a more successful approach, the leadership team decided on a three-step program that would engage the right people at each phase:

Step 1: Their first order of business was to conduct a *needs assessment* and to analyze the data to determine what percentage of people within the organization were currently using this new technology. They also needed to assess organizational barriers and people's overarching concerns with this new technology.

Step 2: They developed and formalized *specific action steps* that would be used to expand the implementation of this technology. These steps included

• Clarifying leadership responsibilities and roles in the change process
• Developing an effective 3-D training component
• Creating effective project measurement tools
• Developing a system for ongoing performance feedback

The team also integrated a "people plan" into the steps to involve the right people at the right time.

Step 3: The team developed a specific plan so that each action step would advance the overall effort. The steps had specific starting and completion points that could be measured in a timely fashion to help create momentum.

The Result: Success, and Ahead of Schedule

The team completed its task in forty-eight days (forty-two days ahead of schedule) and made a presentation to Ben Rieman. Ben gave the team his blessing and public endorsement, setting the goal that the organization should be using this technology on 60 percent of all projects in the next twelve months, up from the current level of 30 percent. As the senior leadership team implemented their "change package," they made sure that leaders at all levels of the organization were properly trained and convinced of the necessity and urgency of this effort. Measuring devices were put into place that would track the percentage of "usage" of the new technology on each and every project that worked its way through the organization.

To everyone's surprise (including the senior leadership team responsible for the project), within eight months after the organization's launch of this change effort, nearly 80 percent of all projects moving through the organization were employing the new technology. TMS had improved on its conventional approach to change by applying the key TMD principles of having a sense of urgency and of developing an understandable and realistic plan of action that could be executed in the heat of battle and that involved the right players on the project at every phase.

The senior leadership team on this project made it a top priority to keep its plan of attack simple and closely tied to what it was ultimately trying to achieve. In the words of one team member, "Having 'can-do' people on our team made a huge difference. . . . We were all serious about creating a real action plan that could actually drive positive change and it did." The efforts of these leaders created tremendous momentum around this improvement initiative, with outstanding results. Their CEO summarized the success of this project in a very simple yet eloquent statement when he said, "Having the right leaders willing to do the right things at the right time made all the difference in this effort. . . . We learned a lot about ourselves in doing so. . . . It was a great win for our organization."

DEVELOPING YOUR WINNING PACKAGE OF PLAYS

Joe Montana and the 49ers went into Super Bowl XXIII hoping to dominate the game, but they didn't operate on hope alone: they were prepared with a two-minute drill package that would allow them to score if they found themselves in trouble and behind on the scoreboard late in the game. In the waning moments of the game, the 49ers knew they needed a touchdown to win. Similarly, when TMS found itself trailing the competition, the company defined winning as doubling the usage of the 3-D CAD process in its organization within one year. In both cases, winning was clearly defined, there was clear focus, and there was a sense of urgency to make things happen.

Although many organizations spend a great deal of time *talking* about change and improvement, great organizations take great pains to develop effective *game plans* for how to win, and they *get the right people on the field* to carry out those plans.

When football coaches are preparing for the prospect of running a two-minute drill, they frequently use the word "package" to describe the set of plays and players that they will put on the field in their effort to score quickly. Exhibit 6.1 describes the attributes of a winning two-minute drill football package.

Exhibit 6.1: Attributes of a Winning TMD Football Package

Plays

1. Each and every play is designed with a specific outcome in mind and takes the clock into account.
2. Only plays that the team is confident will succeed become part of the package, and they are practiced and rehearsed prior to execution.
3. Each and every play has a clearly defined assignment for every player on the field, and each is known and understood by every other team member.
4. Each and every play starts with the snap count signaling when the play begins.
5. Every play has a measurable outcome that serves as feedback to players on the field.

Players

1. Teams put their most talented players on the field.
2. Players on the field are committed to the success of the team's efforts to win.
3. Players are motivated to perform at their highest level.
4. Every player on the field knows exactly what his assignment is on each and every play.
5. Every player realizes that he must do his part on every play if the team is to be successful.

As you can see from Exhibit 6.1, the plays and players are critical to the success of a TMD in football, but they are even more important to the success of an organizational change effort. As the quarterback of your team, you are responsible for selecting those plays and identifying the proper players to carry them out. The creation of your TMD package is predicated on a very clear and simple principle: as quarterback, you must create a series of specific actions that employ the skills of the right people who will help you achieve the right results in the time you have available.

This is easy to say, but the fact is that acting on this principle can be a real challenge in the harried and stressful game conditions of today's workplace. However, entering any change or

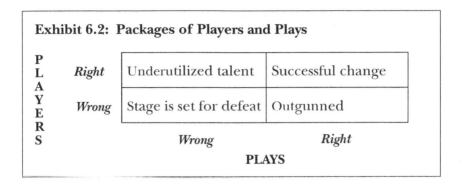

Exhibit 6.2: Packages of Players and Plays

improvement situation without a good combination of plays and players can spell real trouble. Again, your goal as a quarterback is to help your team create a *successful change package* with the right combination of improvement plays and players. Exhibit 6.2 illustrates the consequences, both good and bad, of different combinations of these two critical factors.

As shown in Exhibit 6.2, there are four possible scenarios, and only one is optimal:

1. When an improvement effort involves the right players, but their collection of plays is ineffective, the outcome is an "underutilized talent" package; players cannot maximize their performance. Improvement plays, such as needs assessment, benchmarking, training, problem solving, planning, developing a new computer platform or strategic plan, and the like, must all be deployed in the right set of circumstances if they are to be truly useful. Good players will eventually figure out what to do—but time, effort, and energy will have been wasted.

2. When an organization has the right plays in its improvement game plan but does not engage the right players to make it happen, the improvement package will find itself "outgunned," operating without the talent it needs for success.

3. The worst-case scenario occurs when an organization is attempting to change and uses both the wrong plays and the wrong players. In this scenario, leaders have unintentionally set the stage for the defeat of their own change effort. Although it's easy to say that no one in their right mind would ever do this, we've all seen it happen!

4. The fourth scenario, the optimal one, is to create a successful change package with the right combination of improvement plays and players.

EIGHT TYPICAL PROBLEMS FACING ORGANIZATIONS STRUGGLING TO IMPROVE

In our studies of successful and unsuccessful change efforts, we discerned a pattern of behaviors that cause organizations to develop ineffective packages. In the business world, using an ineffective package can quickly kill an organization's efforts at change, just like bad play calling and individual players'"not getting it done" can kill a scoring drive on the football field.

The following are some of the more frequently occurring problems we have chronicled in our research. We've included football examples to highlight the ineffectiveness of the behaviors we describe.

1. **Organizations design change plans that are not tied to improving specific performance outcomes.**
   Business example: You design and implement a customer satisfaction improvement effort that does not have a way of measuring improved customer satisfaction.
   Football example: You don't know if you need a field goal or a touchdown going into a TMD.
2. **Change initiatives are overly aggressive or optimistic in the outcomes they are trying to achieve.**
   Business example: You need a 3 percent productivity improvement, but you go for a 10 percent improvement.
   Football example: You go for a 2-point conversion when the game is tied, and you only need to kick 1 extra point to win the game.
3. **Organizations design improvement plans that cannot be executed under actual playing conditions.**
   Business example: To improve cycle time, a process improvement team develops an extremely complex twenty-nine-step model—that must be implemented in the next thirty days.
   Football example: On third and 1 on your own 25-yard line, you run a triple-reverse in an attempt to get a first down.

4. **Change efforts do not have the right number of people involved at each of the various stages of the effort.**

   Business example: A twelve-person improvement team is engaged in a needs assessment that could be conducted by five people.

   Football example: Even though you know that the defense is blitzing, you send out running backs on receiving routes, which leaves the quarterback without the needed blocking.

5. **People involved in the improvement process do not have the requisite skills or motivation to do their part to move the effort forward.**

   Business example: A person who is a "political appointee" on a process improvement team does not have good analytical skills or a desire to do any real work to push the improvement forward.

   Football example: An offensive lineman is sent in to be the primary receiver running a quick post pattern down the center of the field on a critical third-down-and-10 play.

6. **Organizations attempt to implement a change without making it "personal" by clarifying each person's roles, goals, and responsibilities that must be fulfilled if the change is to become reality.**

   Business example: The organization rolls out a new inventory control system without making it clear what each person's duties entail and without holding him or her accountable for his or her new actions.

   Football example: The quarterback goes to the line of scrimmage and snaps the ball without first calling a play.

7. **Organizations burn out players who are engaged in multiple change projects.**

   Business example: An organization has a tendency to assign the same people to nearly every improvement initiative, while at the same time expecting them to maintain their performance in their regular job.

   Football example: The quarterback hands the ball off on a fourth-and-goal play to a player who has been on the field for every previous offensive, defensive, and special team play, and expects him to score.

8. **Organizations fail to listen to and take into account the input and feedback of the people responsible for executing the change.**

Business example: A "lean team" designs a cost-cutting program for a department without taking into account the input of the people in the department who will have to live with the changes.

Football example: A quarterback ignores the input of a wide receiver who comes back to the huddle and says that he can beat the opposing cornerback, who is limping badly, on a "deep" route.

Let's be honest: The football examples seem pretty ludicrous, don't they? And yet the workplace equivalents of these play package errors are all too common. What would be easy to see on a football field is not quite so apparent in organizational life when you are trying to make change happen. We cannot overemphasize that if you are serious about winning as a quarterback, you need to take great care in ensuring that you use the *right plays* and the *right players* to get the *right results.* So let's talk about how to create your own winning TMD package.

DEVELOPING YOUR TMD PACKAGE

One of the cornerstones of any successful TMD is a select set of plays that are designed to keep the chains moving and that can be executed with great precision to produce desired results. Some plays are designed to get 10 yards and stop the clock. Others are designed to move the ball deep down the center of the field, where the team can use a time-out to set up a score. For example, both Joe Montana in Super Bowl XXIII and the CEO of TMS demonstrated that every play in a successful TMD is designed with a specific outcome in mind, an outcome that can be achieved when the play is properly executed by players who have both the skill and the desire to win.

For purposes of discussion of the TMD in the workplace, we define a play as a *specific action step or activity that must be successfully executed to move the improvement or change effort forward.* In our definition, improvement plays include

- Needs assessment
- Brainstorming
- Gap analysis

- Process mapping
- Benchmarking
- Procedure redesign
- Training
- Restructuring
- Implementation planning
- Measurement and follow-up

Each of these actions is part of the improvement process and should be viewed as an individual play that is designed to advance the change initiative (the ball) with the sole purpose of helping the team achieve the overall desired change or improvement when the drive is complete.

You can avoid the eight problems we discussed earlier by ensuring that your plays address the following factors:

1. Each and every play is designed with a *specific outcome* in mind (to advance the ball and, ultimately, score).
2. Every play has *clearly defined roles* for every participant on the field, and each player has a *specific assignment* that he or she must execute for the play to be successful.
3. Successful plays are driven by *teamwork,* and every player knows what every other player on the field is supposed to do on that play.
4. Every play is driven by *a sense of urgency,* and it has a starting and stopping point that is known and understood by every player on the field (the snap of the ball and the blowing of the whistle).
5. The effectiveness of plays *can be measured immediately.*
6. When one play is complete, the team quickly moves to the next play to keep *momentum* in the drive.

These factors are as crucial to organizational improvement initiatives as they are to football TMDs. Here's a key question for any leader quarterbacking a change initiative:

> **Key Question**
> When you are embarking on an improvement initiative, do your action steps (plays) meet the six criteria we have just outlined?

So where does a TMD package come from? There are two possibilities:

1. In one scenario, your improvement package is *handed to you by other people*, and you as a leader are given the charge to implement it. (For example, you might be asked to implement at your site a software package chosen by the corporation.) In this situation, your job is to prepare your team to properly execute plays that other people have already determined will work to improve performance. This is not as easy as we are frequently led to believe.
2. In the second scenario, you as the leader must *create your own change package* of improvement plays based on your problem-solving and opportunity-creating talents.

The next sections discuss these two different scenarios in more detail.

SCENARIO 1: IMPLEMENTING A PREPACKAGED IMPROVEMENT PLAN IMPOSED ON YOU BY OTHERS

Our research tells us that more and more often, organizations go to their managers with "prepackaged" change or improvement initiatives and solutions. In these cases, organizations expect leaders to implement a change initiative that was developed by someone other than the individuals who have to implement the change. Rather than have every leader in the organization address a problem or needed change on his or her own, the organization comes up with a standardized set of steps.

Prepackaged improvement initiatives can come from your superiors; corporate headquarters; consultants; formal problem-solving teams; Lean, Kaizen, or Six Sigma initiatives; or even a customer. Prepackaged plans are frequently turned over to business leaders by a wide variety of methods, ranging from e-mailed instructions to full-blown rollout retreats and everything in between. In the case of the Constar distribution center described in Chapter Two, the distribution manager was handed the TPMS improvement plan and told to "make it happen." (As a quarterback, the manager failed to lead his team and properly implement this improvement plan, and he was sacked—literally.)

The potential advantages of the prepackaged approach are numerous; they can include greater efficiency of effort, faster speed to implementation, all the advantages of benchmarking, benefiting from the expertise of others, and not having to reinvent the wheel.[1] From an organizational perspective, prepackaged improvement initiatives are tempting because they look very attractive on paper and are presented nicely, they allow for large-scale improvement activity across an organization, and the creators of these improvement plans have convinced top management of their benefits.

However, the prepackaged approach has its downside. The disadvantages can include solutions that are not realistic, plans that are not applicable to unique situations, and action plans that are too cumbersome or complicated to implement in the field or in the "heat of battle." Although all these factors can cause problems in implementing a prepackaged change plan, the greatest threat to the effectiveness of these efforts is this: they frequently have *limited buy-in* and *fail to create a sense of ownership* among the people being asked to implement them.

On a football field, using a prepackaged plan would be the equivalent of handing a team another team's playbook and saying, "Now go and run these plays in a game." The outcome would be problematic at best for both the authors of the playbook and the team attempting to implement it, but this is what happens in far too many organizations in the scramble for improvement and change.

It is interesting to note that when we ask managers to describe unsuccessful change initiatives, nearly 75 percent of those described as failures fell into the category of prepackaged change. These failures included

- Process improvement initiatives
- Customer service programs
- Cost-cutting endeavors
- Quality improvement efforts
- Work-force productivity procedures
- Both technical and operational practices

All these efforts began with the best of intentions and with the belief that if properly implemented, they would have a positive effect on the organization. Yet, again and again, managers reported that these efforts are prime candidates for failure. Consider what leaders say can go wrong:

"We were told by corporate that this change effort would make a real difference in our performance if we executed it according to their plan. We did—and it didn't."

"The MAS (Measurement Audit System) showed great promise on paper, but after we put it in and worked to support it, it really didn't help us make any kind of real improvement."

"When we try to take somebody else's plan and implement it in this operation, things rarely turn out as promised. . . . In all sincerity, we do our very best to make things happen, but we come up short when compared to the expectations of the people above us—and they remind us of that pretty regularly."

"I won't say that we don't have good improvement initiatives across our organization, but I will say that when you take somebody else's ideas and try to apply them to your own operation, it's easier said than done."

"People in our parent company are constantly dropping 'flavor-of-the-month' programs on our laps, and it happens so often, we are never quite sure which ones to take seriously and which ones to hold out on."

"Any time you try to implement a change without taking ownership of the actions and making people feel like they are driving the change, it's like pushing rope uphill."

Having said all this, most business leaders do have to implement prepackaged improvement initiatives as part of their jobs; this is the reality of today's workplace. If you as a leader are asked to implement a prepackaged change initiative and you are serious about making it happen, consider this: *you must take this prepackaged plan for change and transform it into a set of plays using the right players: it must become your TMD package.*

Here is a great place to interject the power of TMD thinking with a question.

Key Question
What do you need to do as your team's quarterback to ensure that this change plan becomes *your* playbook that can be executed in the reality of *your* workplace?

Without effective leadership to drive them, prepackaged change initiatives stand a great chance of failure, and failure erodes your credibility as a leader. We will return shortly to the topic of what you can do as a leader to effectively execute prepackaged change efforts. But now let's look at what has to be done when you have to develop *your own* improvement plan.

SCENARIO 2: CREATING YOUR OWN IMPROVEMENT PLAN

Let's say that you realize that your work group's performance is not where it needs to be; you know you are behind on the scoreboard. Using that information, you define what winning means; now it's time to develop your own TMD package to drive improvement. Most managers have experience with problem-solving and opportunity analysis, but when a leader has to create his or her own action plan for improvement, these skills become extremely critical. The basic steps in creating your own TMD play set are not really different from what you might use in Six Sigma, Lean, Toyota Production Systems, TQM, or other organization development models. The difference lies in your approach: you will design and develop each step with a "play package" mentality. If you are like most of us, after you have defined winning and determined what needs to improve, you will most likely go through a process that includes

- Needs assessment, data collection, and gap analysis
- Generation of alternate courses of action to create improvement
- Selection of the most desirable set of actions
- Development of your plan of attack for implementation

Each of these activities represents a play in a TMD. The same principles of an effective play discussed earlier in the chapter apply to creating your action plan (TMD package). In this case, you are using diagnostic plays to create your actual improvement plays. You must design each step in this process so as to achieve a specific outcome that you believe has the greatest chance for success as you move to the next step of the process. Time is critically important, as you and your team can easily get bogged down at various stages of developing your own improvement plan. You can become fatigued, distracted, or demotivated by the time it is necessary to implement your game plan. It is imperative that the end result of this effort is a specific collection of actions that when properly executed will help your team improve performance.

Developing your own improvement plan can have its disadvantages, including lack of experience on your part or on the part of your team, lack of time and resources, and a potential lack of support from other members of the organization. Conversely, the advantages of creating your own improvement plan include tailor-made solutions to meet your improvement needs, commitment to your efforts among team members, excellent developmental experience for your players, and ownership of both the process and outcome. And ownership is key.[2]

Please remember that even if you choose to create your own TMD package, you still face the same challenge that exists with implementing a prepackaged improvement plan: *you must engage the right people at each phase of the process, and your people must be ready to play.*

Key Question
Once again, what do you need to do as your team's quarterback to ensure that this change plan becomes *your* playbook that can be executed in the reality of *your* workplace?

TMD PACKAGE MOMENTUM BUILDERS

As the quarterback of your improvement effort, you must draw on all the QB leadership imperatives we discussed in Chapter Two. When you properly apply those momentum builders to the ones we describe here, you increase the likelihood of creating a winning plan.

Momentum Builder 1: Choose the Right People to Have on the Field and Get Them Ready to Play

Legendary Ohio State head coach Woody Hayes said it best when he stated, "You win with people." These simple and elegant words are critically important in developing your TMD package and for the overall success of your change initiative. Whether you are asked to implement a prepackaged improvement plan or you are creating your own, as quarterback-leader you must control the players whom you choose to bring onto the playing field. Time and time again, we have found that one of the real keys to successful improvement is getting the right players on the field. For example, the success of the TMS technology expansion was driven by CEO Ben Rieman's putting the right leaders on the team, who were both able and ready to perform the job that they had been asked to do. Note, however, that although all of them started out as able participants because of their talents, not all of them were immediately ready to play. It took the CEO's selling and arm twisting to get all the team members ready.

Choosing the right individuals to involve in developing and executing your TMD package is quite possibly the most important decision that you will make as a quarterback. Whether you are dealing with a prepackaged improvement plan or an improvement initiative that you create yourself, getting the right players involved is the cornerstone of successful change. The right player has the talent and skills that match up with the demands of the improvement play, and is motivated to perform at his or her highest level. For example, if you are creating a web-based solution, the team must include someone with networking design skills and another who is great at graphics.

> **Key Question**
> Do you take great care in getting the right people involved with each and every phase of your improvement effort and ensure that they have the talent and motivation to play?

MOMENTUM BUILDER 2: TAKE OWNERSHIP OF EVERY PLAY IN THE TMD PACKAGE AND COME READY TO PLAY

In the words of Missouri head football coach Gary Pinkel, "The quarterback and the ten other players on the field must own the drive if they are to truly be successful." As the quarterback of your team, you must take the action steps that are critical for success and turn those action steps into plays that your team knows, understands, and has the confidence to properly execute. You and your team must "own" the improvement drive—you can't just go through the motions or simply try to execute someone else's plan of attack. Whether you are conducting a needs assessment to determine the next step in your package or conducting the training necessary to implement your organization's new compliance software system, you must help the members of your team take ownership of the change.

Without ownership of the package and accountability for action, your team will have a hard time getting to the improvement end zone. Here are just a few of the tools you as the quarterback-leader can use to help create ownership of whatever improvement you are attempting to make:

- Effective communications
- Team-based problem-solving and planning
- Empowerment
- Effective feedback mechanisms
- Open-book management

Choose any and all that you think will work best for your team.

> **Key Question**
> Do you take the necessary steps to engage and empower your team so that they take ownership of the activities and outcomes of your change process?

MOMENTUM BUILDER 3: USE THE RIGHT PLAYS THAT WILL KEEP THE CHAINS MOVING AND PUT YOU IN A POSITION TO SCORE QUICKLY

In the words of legendary Dallas Cowboys head coach Tom Landry, "Setting a goal is not the main thing; it's deciding how you'll go about achieving it." When an organization wants real improvement or real change, the starting point is to define what the goal really is, or as we have said, to *define winning*. Developing the action plan to achieve the win is when the real work starts. Regardless of the improvement model you and your organization presently employ, each step you take *must* be directly tied to the outcome you are attempting to achieve.

As the quarterback, you must execute each play in an effective and time sensitive fashion to keep your team moving toward the end zone. Thinking of action steps in your improvement process as plays helps people develop a more effective mind-set concerning both the purpose of each action and the key issue of time sensitivity.

Teams lose momentum when they use the wrong plays or when a particular play gets bogged down or stalemated. Effective quarterbacks never use a play in a TMD without knowing exactly what outcome they expect. The same should be true of a business leader attempting to improve performance. Further, good quarterbacks and organizational leaders are adept at modifying the overall package as plays unfold and circumstances change, to keep the chains moving.

> **Key Question**
> Do you make sure that each activity in your change effort is value-added and moving your team toward the overarching desired outcome?

MOMENTUM BUILDER 4: ENSURE THAT EACH PLAY HAS A STARTING AND STOPPING POINT, AND MEASURE PERFORMANCE ON EACH PLAY

"Blue 29. Blue 29. Hut. Hut. Hut." Although these words might seem like gibberish to a regular person, to a football player, these few words might remind a player of both the play and the fact that it is time for action. It is an important point to remember that every improvement play in your TMD package needs to have a starting point—a point when specific action takes place, with a specific desired outcome in mind. When a quarterback does not do a good job of clarifying the starting point for a play or when players are not paying attention at the moment action is to commence, there are usually penalty flags in the air or blown assignments. In many organizational improvement efforts, people will say things like

"When is the kickoff?"
"When do we throw the switch?"
"So what is happening?"
"Where are we now?"
"Is there a report due sometime soon?"

These questions signify that people are not cognizant of the starting and stopping points for a given action step in the improvement plan.

Starting points let people know that the time for action is *now*. The stopping point, or whistle, lets people know it's time to look at what has taken place, to measure performance, and to get ready for the next play. When plays have starting and stopping points, they create momentum because they reinforce the sense of urgency that is necessary for successful change to take place. As the quarterback of your improvement team, you must call plays that meet these criteria and communicate the snap count to each and every player on your team.

Key Question
Do you monitor the starting point, the activity, and the stopping point of each and every phase of your improvement process and measure your progress in a time-sensitive fashion?

Momentum Builder 5: Clearly Define Individual Assignments on Each Play

It is not uncommon to hear sportscasters say things like

"That blown assignment nearly cost them the game."
"That receiver should have made that catch."
"That quarterback was sacked because the running back didn't pick up the blitzing linebacker."

These comments indicate that for any improvement effort to be successful, individual players *must do their job on each and every play*. From this perspective, all change efforts are personal; each player must fully understand his or her assignment.

In our previous research, we have found that when change is required, individual employees' roles, goals, and responsibilities frequently are poorly defined.[3] The bigger the change, the greater the likelihood that this fuzziness occurs. In a TMD situation, every person on the field is there because he or she is the most talented player available for that position. Equally important, they are there because they know their assignments and know what must be done for the team to be successful on that play.

On a football field, blown assignments are very obvious to everyone and very humiliating for the player who let his team down. It may not be so obvious in the workplace. Effective leaders always work hard to ensure that every player avoids this potentially embarrassing and momentum-stifling situation. For example, as described at the beginning of this chapter, one of the key success factors at TMS was that each step of the change effort was staffed by people who knew exactly what must be done, how it must be done, and by when.

Key Question
Are you critically aware of the importance of clarifying individual roles, goals, and responsibilities for each and every member of your team on each and every play in your TMD?

MOMENTUM BUILDER 6: VIRTUAL PRACTICE MAKES PERFECT

Legendary NFL coach Joe Gibbs had a reputation for having his team ready to play on game day, and was often known to say, "A winning effort begins with preparation." Football teams have the luxury of practicing their TMD plays *before* the game, but businesses usually don't—at least not physically. Before a play begins, successful leaders will engage the members of their team in visualizing and discussing what they will do and how they will do it.

Exhibit 6.3: Attributes of a Winning TMD Improvement Package

Plays

1. Have you clearly identified the set of plays (actions) that will enable you to achieve the win you have defined?
2. Are you confident that the plays you have identified are capable of being executed under actual game conditions?
3. Does each play clearly define assignments for every player on the field?
4. Do team members mutually understand each other's roles and responsibilities on each and every play?
5. Does each play have a measurable outcome?

Players

1. Does each player on the field have the requisite talent for carrying out his or her assignment on a given play?
2. Are the players on the field committed to the success of the team's effort to win?
3. Is every player motivated to do his or her very best, or are they just going through the motions?
4. Does each player on the field know exactly what his or her assignment is on each and every play?
5. Does each player understand how his or her assignment fits in with the overall success of each play?

This approach is an excellent way to get the team to rehearse what each person is going to do, how he or she is going to do it, and when he or she is going to do it. We suggest that you and your team discuss the questions in Exhibit 6.3 for what we call "virtual practice." Doing so can help your team think through the issues that might interfere with or increase the likelihood of a successful play, whether that play is training, benchmarking, gap analysis, or the like.

> **Key Question**
> Prior to snapping the ball, do you discuss and review what must take place for each play in your TMD to be successful?

CONCLUSION: PLAN TO WIN!

In your efforts to do everything you can to develop a game-winning TMD package, review the questions in Exhibit 6.3 to assess yourself on the key factors that we have discussed in this chapter. It is imperative that you use your skills as a quarterback to create a winning TMD package and to make sure that you and your team are ready to go when you move into your next serious change game.

CHAPTER SEVEN

SNAP THE BALL AND EXECUTE THE RIGHT PLAYS

Execution Is Critical to Improvement

It is not surprising that so many change efforts fail when it is time to execute. . . . Sometimes we have exhausted ourselves getting to the point of implementation. Other times, we go from a good idea right to implementation, and we are not ready to throw the switch. And other times, we throw the switch and find that our plans need quick adjustments if they are to succeed. . . . Implementation is where leadership rises to the top.
—GENERAL MANAGER, FORTUNE 500 MANUFACTURING COMPANY

A lifetime contract for a coach means if you're ahead in the third quarter and moving the ball, they can't fire you.
—LOU HOLTZ, LEGENDARY FOOTBALL COACH AND COMMENTATOR

WINNING IMPERATIVE: *Execute for Results*

You have set the stage for a successful change; now you must snap the ball and execute.

"The Stop": Tennessee Titans vs. St. Louis Rams,
Super Bowl XXXIV, January 30, 2000

Super Bowl XXXIV featured two marquee quarterbacks: the
St. Louis Rams' Kurt Warner and the Tennessee Titans' Steve
McNair. Both of these quarterbacks had reputations for high-
powered offense, gutsy play calling, and strong on-the-field
leadership. Surprisingly, the halftime score was St. Louis 9,
Tennessee 0, in a game that featured great defensive play. At
the end of the third quarter, St. Louis led 16–6, which was cut
to 16–13 after the Titans executed an effective thirteen-play,
79-yard touchdown scoring drive that consumed 7:39.

On the next possession, Tennessee forced the Rams to punt, and
quarterback Steve McNair took possession of the ball. The Titans
drove to the St. Louis 25-yard line, where Al Del Greco kicked a
43-yard field goal to knot the game at 16, leading up to one of the
most exciting Super Bowl finishes of all time. The St. Louis Rams
took possession with 2:12 left on the clock at their own 27-yard line.
Kurt Warner connected with Isaac Bruce at the Titans' 38-yard line;
in a one-play scoring drive, Bruce outran the Titans defense for
a 73-yard touchdown as Kurt Warner showed no fear in throwing a
risky pass in front of a crowd of 72,625 and another 88 million
television viewers. The extra point was good. Score: Rams 23,
Titans 16.

Now Tennessee would have the opportunity to take control of its destiny if the team could execute a TMD. The Titans started the drive
on their own 12-yard line. They needed to gain 88 yards in 1:48.
QB Steve McNair systematically moved his team down the field and
executed what appeared to many to be a textbook TMD by controlling the clock and moving the chains. On the second-to-last play of
the game, McNair scrambled, hitting wide receiver Kevin Dyson for
a 16-yard gain and putting the ball on the St. Louis 10-yard line with
0:05 remaining. McNair then used the Titans' last time-out, which he
had managed to save for this very situation, as the Titans selected the
best potential scoring play from their play package.

Tennessee now had the ball on its opponent's 10-yard line with an
opportunity to execute one more play in the hopes of tying
St. Louis and going into overtime—or even playing for the win on
a 2-point conversion. McNair lined up in a shotgun, dropped back
to pass, and once again threw the ball to Kevin Dyson, who made a
solid catch but was immediately hit by Rams defender Mike Jones.
Dyson attempted to spin out of the tackle and lunged for the end

zone, but he was stopped just a couple feet short of the goal line. The Titans had covered 87 yards in their drive, only to end up just short of their 88-yard goal.

Even to this day, sports pundits ask why Dyson didn't run his pass route one yard deeper, which would have allowed him to score. This particular play shows up continuously on highlight films because of the drama and disappointment of that Super Bowl moment. The ineffective execution of the final play of this impressive drive had nullified all the great work that the team had done in their attempt to win Super Bowl XXXIV. Final score: St. Louis Rams 23, Tennessee Titans 16.

A Time for Lean Action at CTSK Industries, LLC

Executing the right plays is critical in business too, as we'll see in this business case study. Sara Payne was no rookie when it came to leading change initiatives. She had been the operations manager for two CTSK Industries manufacturing facilities in the past three years, and she was recently given a special assignment to promote Lean initiatives at a third facility in as many years. Sara viewed this as a great opportunity to hone her improvement skills and make a real difference in the performance of this facility, which had fallen on hard times. Sara was well aware that it was easy for a manufacturing team to get caught up in the planning and training aspects of a change initiative without ever achieving real results and improvement, so she went in to this assignment with her eyes wide open.

Background: Declining Profits Require Cost-Cutting Initiatives

Sara's new assignment was at the CTSK Industries production facility just south of Houston, Texas. The facility had a long track record of excellent customer satisfaction and quality performance, resulting in several industry awards and recognitions. But recently the facility had been squeezed by the economic conditions of the hi-tech hydraulic pump market, and the facility was struggling to adjust accordingly. The plant had seen declining profits for eight consecutive quarters and had been operating in the red for the past eighteen months. The facility was currently losing more than

$100,000 per month, and it had been determined by "Corporate" that it would need to improve significantly in the next quarter, or a number of the product lines from this facility would be pulled out and taken offshore.

Corporate management had targeted three areas for significant cost improvement, which is where Sara Payne came in. These troublesome areas were (1) excessive overtime, (2) the use of three outside warehouses for excessive finished goods storage, and (3) a habit of constantly carrying a large work-in-process inventory.

Just two years prior, the corporate engineering and logistics group had begun a Lean initiative to champion the necessary cost reduction efforts as part of an organization-wide improvement strategy. Plant management at this facility had been engaged in several appropriate planning activities for the improvement initiatives, including conducting plantwide training classes and issuing certifications, using colorful banners throughout the plant, creating the full-time position of continuous improvement coordinator, and developing process maps and prominently displaying them in the front office lobby. To date, however, the plant had not achieved any significant improvement in the targeted areas.

THE REAL PROBLEM: FAILURE TO IMPLEMENT THE COST-CUTTING METHODS

Sara was given an eight-week assignment as the acting plant manager. She was assigned to the plant specifically in an effort to move the facility beyond the planning and training stages of their improvement efforts toward achieving real results. It was Sara's job, in the words of her boss, "to go in and make real improvement happen."

Sara made a detailed assessment of the situation before she hit the ground, and continued her analysis on her first day in the facility. It was obvious to her that the plant had good people in place who could ensure that the current operations met the ongoing service and quality requirements during the proposed cost-cutting initiatives. Each of the managers had a history of achievement and an understanding of their roles in all aspects of the operation. Every team member understood the dire situation the plant was in and had a vested interest in the plant's turnaround. It was Sara's assessment that the team was just failing to use the tools they had developed. Sara was determined to succeed in this assignment, and she realized that the opportunities for improvement were definitely achievable. She felt very optimistic going into this incredibly trying situation.

THE SOLUTION: THREE TEAMS WITH CLEAR GOALS AND SPECIFIC RESPONSIBILITIES

Sara called a staff meeting on the afternoon of her first day at the plant. Clarifying roles, goals, and the current state of the operation, she established three cross-functional teams to attack each of the targeted improvement areas. She also defined clear, specific goals for each of the three teams:

Team 1: Eliminate all overtime for the entire plant in eight weeks. The targeted savings were to be $650,000 annually.

Team 2: Eliminate all three outside warehouses and associated logistics and perform all necessary warehousing functions in the company's own attached warehouse in eight weeks. The targeted savings were to be $1,600,000 annually.

Team 3: Reduce finished goods and work-in-process inventory by 50 percent. The targeted improvement was a one-time savings of $900,000 and an annual savings in material handling of $460,000.

The Lean initiatives and training had prepared her team to take on these challenges, but it was now time to execute. These changes would take place quickly, and the plant still had to maintain both its production and shipping schedules, making the challenge even greater.

Each team was given the following five assignments and timeline for action:

Week 1: Measure the current situation and identify the specific reasons for waste, using process mapping, layout analysis, work sampling, and historical analysis.

Week 2: Analyze and assess the specific opportunities for improvement and develop appropriate buy-in from plant personnel.

Week 3: Redesign the current operation, create an action plan, and present the proposed improvement plan to the entire plant staff.

Week 4: Develop a detailed implementation plan that ensures team buy-in, clearly defines roles and responsibilities, achieves goals, and includes appropriate measurement and a plan for execution.

Weeks 5 through 8: Implement the proposed improvement plan and measure improvements toward attaining the goals, making ongoing adjustments as the situation changes.

CREATING A SCOREBOARD AND SCHEDULING WEEKLY MEETINGS TO TRACK THE THREE TEAMS' PROGRESS

Sara created a single four-by-eight-foot whiteboard that depicted the plant's current financial performance in the three problem areas. The board would also display information on the progress and timing for all three teams, goals, and attainment. Finally, the board had a daily countdown for the eight weeks that was to be continuously updated. The whiteboard was strategically located between the front office and the employee break room so that every team member had a constant reminder of the current status of his or her project. The board also kept all the plant's personnel informed and updated.

A weekly meeting was scheduled for every Thursday morning to review each team's progress. At these update meetings, each team was to provide a fifteen-minute status report, comment on the project status board, identify issues that needed decisions, and open up to group discussion for an additional five minutes of problem solving. Each team was then given the weekend to adjust its activities if that week's goals and project timing were not where they needed to be. This adjusted plan was shared with Sara on Monday for her input and blessing.

Week 1: Uncertainty About Timing and Support

At the end of the first week, the improvement reviews were made with cautious enthusiasm. Each team knew what needed to be done, was confident that it could be achieved, but was uncertain about the timing and support. Each team presented its findings, and it was clear that the targets for improvement were achievable (to everyone's relief). Sara assured the teams that their training, ability, and focus could make it happen.

Week 2: Making Sure Everyone Involved Is Informed About Changes

The second week was critical because each of the changes affected a significant number of other employees throughout the plant. Each team held daily meetings to review its findings, obtain team input, and ensure that everyone affected by the change understood the necessity for the action. Each team learned from the other teams as they presented their weekly assessments. Week 2 was filled with concerns, suggestions, resistance, and even some enthusiasm for what was going on. The leaders of each team showed eagerness to advance to the detailed designs of their game plan for improvement, making sure that their people were informed and involved. The team members knew their assignments and were performing their individual roles effectively.

Week 3: Facing a Roadblock—but Quickly Overcoming It

Week 3 saw the detailed designs developed and again presented daily to the people affected by these changes. By Thursday of that week, the teams had nearly completed their designs, with the exception of the team charged with eliminating the outside warehouses. It had reached a roadblock: two of the three warehouses could be eliminated, but the third was still needed for space in the interim. Investigation and discussion by the entire group led to the idea of improving the racking and storage in the existing facility. Sara adjusted this team's plan by providing immediate corporate support to redesign the in-house racking system. This redesign effort would dip into Week 4 of the timeline, but it appeared to offer the solution necessary to achieve the original goals.

Week 4: Quick Review and Approvals—Ready to Move Forward

Week 4 witnessed the development of a detailed implementation plan for each of the three teams, as well as a continued redesign of their detailed proposals. By Thursday of that week, each team saw its implementation plans thoroughly reviewed and approved by Sara. In only four weeks, these teams had executed all the steps necessary to develop game plans in each of the three designated cost reduction areas. Now it was time to execute the actual changes to the plant's operation; these would begin that weekend. Sara's three teams had moved quickly, worked together effectively, and set the stage for the change effort, but now it was time to see if they could score.

Weeks 5–8: Team 1 Solves the Overtime Problem

The next four weeks provided a stage for a wide variety of emotions: enthusiasm, frustration, excitement, stress, passion, apprehension, and even glee. Team 1 was focused on its issue and managed to avoid scheduling overtime for week 6. Changes to achieve this reduction included reorganizing maintenance activities into the production teams, concentrating on product completion rather than on just keeping people busy, and developing an understanding that overtime could not continue with a business-as-usual attitude. Eight weeks after the beginning of this specific change initiative, the plant was running zero overtime.

Weeks 5–8: Team 2 Solves the Warehouse Problem

Team 2 was on a tear by their second week of implementation, as they targeted "obsolescence" in the facility: dealing with material without a purpose and poor storage habits. This housekeeping endeavor, combined with the efforts of the third team to reduce inventories, resulted in the elimination of the first two warehouses. "It was like spring cleaning, and all the junk needed to go," was a comment made by the leader of team 2. The new racking systems, allocation methods, aisles, and traffic patterns were implemented in the in-house warehouse, and the lights of the third warehouse were turned off by the end of week 8. Two of the warehouses had month-to-month leases, and their expenses were eliminated immediately. The third warehouse was subleased to a neighboring organization (this idea was a brainchild of a team member) and within two months was generating income.

Weeks 5–8: Team 3 Solves the Inventory Problem

Team 3 saw their finished goods inventory reduced significantly by redesigning their production process and ultimately reducing production lead time. This was achieved by the elimination of work-in-process (WIP) at two critical processing steps. The WIP had always been deemed important in the production process at this facility until team 3 challenged those processing requirements and implemented experiments to prove that they were unnecessary. Rethinking these two processing steps accounted for nearly 80 percent of the WIP throughout the entire facility. This activity created a reduction in production lead time, which led to the opportunity to "produce to order" many of the lower-volume products that had previously accounted for a high percentage of finished goods stock.

WHY THIS EXECUTION WAS SUCCESSFUL

Although the earlier "Lean effort" at CTSK had laid the foundation for improved performance, it did not by itself create the momentum necessary to drive real change. Going in, Sara created a clear focus on what had to take place for real improvement to occur. She also created a sense of urgency about implementing the initiative by conveying the importance and necessity of the changes. Sara spent the majority of her time supporting each team's activities throughout the eight-week rapid improvement period. Here are a few comments that team members offered about Sara's performance as a change leader when they were asked to evaluate her as part of a post-project assessment:

"Sara created the vision for what improvements were needed, but more importantly, what we needed to systematically do to get there."

"She was always reminding us that we could pull this off and was encouraging people to stay on task."

"Sara helped our team solve problems fast, and she was on the phone getting quick answers from the corporate people . . . which was no small thing."

"She was constantly communicating with all of us and asking what we needed from her to get the job done."

"She was good at answering questions and encouraging people to be innovative in all that they were doing."

"Ms. Payne was quick to compliment people and give praise, but she was also not afraid to let people know what they needed to do to improve and move faster."

Sara had helped her team achieve real performance improvement because of her confident, calm, and caring style of leadership using a disciplined approach to change. At the conclusion of this chapter, we will share the outcome of the CTSK initiative and offer several additional observations.

A TIME FOR ACTION

When the Tennessee Titans used their last time-out in Super Bowl XXXIV with 5 seconds remaining in the contest, they dipped into their play package and pulled out a play that they believed would get them a touchdown if properly executed. In theory, if everyone on the team did his part, the play would result in a score, but as we know, theory and reality frequently collide, as they did on that final play. Wide receiver Kevin Dyson did *not* run his pass route deep enough, and when he caught the ball, he was tackled just short of the goal line. Despite the fact that the team discussed what to do and planned for this moment, *ineffective execution* meant that the entire team lost.

Similarly, previous plant management at CTSK had fallen short in their halfhearted efforts to improve the organization's performance. There was a lot of talk and training and planning associated with their so-called Lean initiative, and they worked to get their team into a position to score. But their efforts did not translate into the actual execution of plays that would get them into the cost-savings end zone. In other words, the leaders at CTSK gave the *appearance* of running an improvement effort, but they did not execute *all* the plays necessary to score.

Execution is receiving increasing attention as a topic in both business research and the popular press because it focuses on the ability of organizations to make vision and plans reality.[1] In the words of Jim Collins and Jerry Porras, "The ability to translate vision into consistent and concrete reality separates those who build substantial, lasting companies from mere visionaries." Although a great deal is known about how to create vision and to plan at the strategic, business unit, and operational levels, business analysts are not quite so well versed and researched on the topic of execution.[2] And for leaders, execution is really the name of the change game.

Before we discuss how to execute change initiatives more effectively, let's briefly outline the difference between leaders who know how to do it and those who do not, based on a large sample of leaders whom we have chronicled in our research inquiries. We'll discuss some of the challenges leaders face in quarterbacking change efforts and the importance of their skills at executing change.

A variety of factors influences how a leader approaches change. In Exhibit 7.1, we have classified three different approaches that leaders frequently take when executing improvement initiatives.

Exhibit 7.1: Various Leadership Approaches to Executing Change

KEY FACTORS	DO NOTHING	DO SOMETHING!	REAL CHANGE
Attitude about change	Avoidance	Gimmicks and fads	Ongoing change is necessary
Leadership style	Hands-off	Dictatorial	Results-oriented
Goals	Unclear goals	Unrealistic or incorrect goals	Clearly defined outcomes
Actions	Talk about change	Chaotic action	Controlled and synergistic activity
Planning	Piecemeal	Hurried and harried	Systematic and disciplined
Preparation	Does not know what to prepare for	Ineffective	On a play-by-play basis
Communication	Rumors and gossip	One-way	Results-oriented, situation-driven
Time	All the time in the world	Unrealistic time frames	Effective clock management
Teamwork	Nonexistent	Patronizing and disingenuous	Accelerator of change

Do Nothing Leaders

As shown in Exhibit 7.1, we reluctantly classify some leaders as Do Nothing leaders on the issue of change. In football terms, these leaders are quarterbacks who like the attention, uniform, prestige, and title that come with the position, but they do not like stepping onto the playing field, sweating, getting dirty, or risking injury. Do Nothing leaders typically have an avoidance attitude about change and operate in a business-as-usual mind-set. When change is required, their leadership style is very hands-off and frequently results in situations where no one or everyone is ultimately in charge of change. These leaders go into change efforts with unclear goals, frequently talking more about change than taking specific tangible action.

Their approach to change planning is frequently piecemeal and disjointed, and their preparation is marked by their not knowing what to specifically prepare for because their game plan is unclear. The activities of Do Nothing leaders are usually shrouded by rumors and gossip, and their people are frequently in the dark about what is really going on. Finally, Do Nothing leaders typically embody an attitude of having all the time in the world to make any changes, and the very thought of teamwork is nonexistent. In a nutshell, Do Nothing leaders have little, if any, credibility with their people and are sitting on a job-ending time bomb if they are operating in a rapidly changing environment. They are quite simply the worst kind of quarterback for a team, unless getting nothing done is the goal of the game!

Do Something! Leaders

The opposite of a Do Nothing leader of change is a DO SOMETHING! leader. DO SOMETHING! leaders are leaders who aren't always sure what they want to do in the way of change, but they know they've got to do *something*, so they do. As a change quarterback, they are always looking for the Hail Mary pass when they find themselves behind in the game. These leaders simply drop back and throw the ball down the field, hoping someone catches it and that the team scores. They are always looking for the quick, easy, and painless score so that they can say, "See, I'm doing something." They want to be seen trying to change and as going on record as being associated with a change, so that they can go back to their normal activity.

Although Hail Mary passes do work on occasion, they have a low probability of success, require virtually no discipline, and are almost always born out of pure desperation. These types of leaders frequently fall prey to improvement gimmicks and fads or have the unique ability to take a proven improvement practice and turn it into a gimmick, fad, or flavor of the month. They frequently approach change in a dictatorial fashion, set unrealistic or incorrect goals, and demand rapid activity around whatever change they are currently "doing something with," which can easily turn into chaos.

DO SOMETHING! leaders approach planning in a hurried and harried fashion, which frequently results in ineffective analysis and little or no discussion or thought about the real issues. These leaders often throw themselves and their people into a change with little or no thought or preparation, and the communications surrounding change initiatives are more often than not truncated and one-way. These leaders talk and assume that their people are listening, but real communication is not a priority. Further, these leaders are prone to setting unrealistic time frames for whatever change they are currently wedded to, thus stimulating even more chaos and uncertainty.

Finally, these leaders take a patronizing or disingenuous approach to teamwork, and they usually don't even know it. They talk about teamwork, remind their people that there is no "I" in team, and then go on and do little, if anything, to promote cooperation and effective interaction. Sadly, we have observed a growing number of leaders who fall into this category and who damage their own credibility and breed cynicism and demotivation among the people they are supposedly leading.

Many organizations actually encourage, breed, and even reward DO SOMETHING! leaders in their quest to produce quick hits and overnight improvements. DO SOMETHING! leaders go out on the playing field with a TMD package of four Hail Mary passes. Once in a while they do score a touchdown, but their completion percentage is woefully inadequate for the current change game required of leaders today.

Real Change Leaders

In our final category are Real Change leaders. We hope this doesn't sound too obvious, but they are leaders who take change very seriously, as they would any other part of their job. As quarterbacks of change, these are the leaders who practice the momentum builders discussed in Chapter Two. They are willing to step onto the playing field, "get strapped up," "put their game face on," and do all the things necessary to make meaningful change a reality. Any leader can pull off a quick change or two; Real Change leaders can execute change on an ongoing basis without demoralizing their people and losing their own credibility in the process. They are people who accept change as an ongoing business necessity that must be handled with great care. And their leadership style in approaching change tends to be very results-oriented instead of simply driven by a need for activity.

These leaders establish clearly defined outcomes for whatever change they are attempting to make, and they approach these efforts with controlled and synergistic activities on their part and on the part of their team members. They take a very systematic and disciplined approach to the change process, which allows people to work together and build a plan of attack that everyone knows, understands, and supports. These leaders are also known for their great communication skills that are contingent on the demands of every situation. They know how to run meetings and communicate in large group settings; they possess good listening skills; they know how to probe for more information; and they are effective in one-on-one interactions with their people.

Finally, Real Change leaders realize that their most important resource in the change process is actually *time*, and they take great care to manage the clock. Real Change leaders understand that teamwork, when properly applied, can be the ultimate change accelerator, and they take great care to ensure that their team works together and rallies around whatever change is on the playing field. Reading this, you might erroneously conclude that Real Change leaders have some mythical or larger-than-life stature, but the truth of the matter is that Real Change leaders can be found all around us, executing change effectively and doing so without a great deal of fanfare or hoopla.

HOW TO EXECUTE THE RIGHT PLAYS IN YOUR ORGANIZATION

You might be thinking to yourself, the focus of this chapter is execution—why this lengthy discussion about leadership? The answer is simple: without effective leadership and great quarterbacking, very few, if any, real change initiatives are executed in an optimal and rapid fashion. Thus far we have discussed the importance of knowing the score and clearly defining what winning means in each specific effort. We have talked about the importance of creating extreme focus and a clear sense of urgency around your change efforts. We have also reviewed the critical nature of creating a "play" mentality around each step in your change initiative and ensuring that you have the proper people on the field, ready to play. Now we would like to offer some specific recommendations to help you more effectively execute or put into action the steps in your change game plan. These recommendations are based on some of the best practices of Real Change leaders with whom we have had the privilege of studying and working.

MOMENTUM BUILDER 1: ESTABLISH YOUR TMD SCOREBOARD

As you have seen throughout our discussions of football in this book, scoreboards play a critical role in helping a team execute an effective scoring drive when time is of the essence. In our discussion of knowing the score and defining winning in Chapter Three, scoreboards play a critical role in triggering your recognition that change is needed. *It is essential at the start of any rapid improvement effort that you, as the quarterback, and your team set up a scoreboard to help manage the change process and keep the team informed of the information that is most critical to success.*

When their team has the opportunity to run a TMD to win a game, football coaches will frequently tell their teams that "the scoreboard has been reset for a two-minute football game," and that is what we are suggesting here. One of the key characteristics of successful change initiatives is that you and your team know exactly the status of your change effort at every point during the change process. A TMD scoreboard can help make that happen when used properly.

A *TMD scoreboard* is a specific visual aid that contains the most pertinent performance measurements and information for a given improvement initiative. A critical component for effective execution is having all the team players know exactly where they are on the playing field, what the score is, and how much time remains in the game.

The *visibility* of the scoreboard is paramount to its usefulness, and the change scoreboard should be located such that every team member has a clear view of the critical game statistics. To that end, many organizations use electronic and even web-based scoreboards with great effect to supplement physical work-place scoreboards. It is also important that every team member clearly *understands* every indicator of the game status that is presented on the scoreboard. This may at times require both explanation and training for team members. Finally, to ensure that every member of the team understands the scoreboard, the scoreboard must be *kept simple.*

Recall that Tennessee Titans QB Steve McNair called time-out with 5 seconds left in the Super Bowl because he knew he had a time-out left, he knew how much time remained in the game, and he knew the ball was on the 10-yard line. The information was readily available on the stadium scoreboard for him and his team to use. In the workplace, scoreboards can serve the exact same purpose. For example, recall that setting up her change score-board was one of the first things Sara did when she entered the CTSK facility after meeting with the team and defining winning. Sara's scoreboard kept the specific performance details of the cost-cutting initiatives in the forefront of team members' thoughts and provided critical information to guide their actions.

We are frequently asked about what information should be on a TMD scoreboard. Our answer is usually rhetorical:

Key Question

What information do you and your team members need to have in front of you on an ongoing basis to best execute each and every play in your TMD package in a timely fashion?

This information frequently includes key measures of improvement and the status of the change initiative. Here are some of the key components we frequently see on TMD scoreboards:

1. The **current score** is the status of an improvement effort compared to the ultimate goal that indicates a victory for the team. For example, CTSK's monthly plant financial losses represented the "current score." Tracking this score helped ensure a clear focus and understanding of the changes that would drive the daily decisions and necessary adjustments toward the ultimate goal.

2. The **current field position** provides an opportunity for the team to focus on progress after each play in their TMD package. For example, in the case of CTSK, the field position drove the daily progression of the three teams and created some friendly competition. Rather than report on every aspect of the project against the ultimate goal, the current field position can help benchmark progress for various teams, thereby determining the timing of the next play that will be called and clarifying necessary adjustments.

3. The **game clock** is a clear indicator of the urgency of the situation and ultimately identifies the drop-dead date for victory. It also serves as a gauge of the progress of the various plays in your game plan. For example, in the case of CTSK, the game time was the eight-week countdown, and the time remaining on the scoreboard drove the priorities and play calling for the team.

4. **Time-outs** are often the preestablished and mutually agreed-on schedule of team meetings, when team members come together to review and discuss the performance on the play that has just been completed and to determine the next set of actions that will be necessary for the team to score. These time-outs ensure that the team understands the current score on the scoreboard and has the next plays that must be run to keep the drive moving forward. Time-outs can also be called extemporaneously when the leader sees that discussion is needed. In CTSK's case, the time-outs occurred at very specific milestones; critical team assessments were used to make necessary adjustments and to call the next appropriate play from the TMD package.

As a quarterback who is serious about executing your TMD package, are you prepared to answer the following questions as they pertain to your current change initiative? Doing so will ensure that your team always knows the score and is always armed with the information necessary to make good calls and move quickly.

Key Questions
1. Has your team established a TMD scoreboard for the specific change initiative—one that everyone can see and understand?
2. Does the scoreboard reflect the current status of your change effort, thus helping the team maintain focus and a sense of urgency?
3. Is the TMD scoreboard updated in a timely manner?

MOMENTUM BUILDER 2: SNAP THE BALL AND MOVE THE CHAINS

One of the most notable aspects of a TMD in football is that teams cannot afford to waste time and plays. Waste loses games. Each play in a TMD must be executed in a time-sensitive fashion to achieve a specific desired outcome (as discussed in Chapter Six). When people talk about execution in the context of organizational change, they frequently target their discussions around the actual implementation phase of the change process. In reality, successful change requires that *each* phase of an improvement process be properly executed in a time-sensitive fashion. That is why we describe phases of a change initiative as *plays*. They start with the snap of the ball, generate organized activity, have a clear stopping point, and have an outcome that is measurable.

In Chapter Six, we discussed two scenarios that frequently confront leaders when change is necessary: in one scenario, the organization hands you a prepackaged improvement plan of plays created by someone else; in the other scenario, you have to create your own game plan for improving performance. In either case, each activity in your change effort should be viewed as a specific play to achieve a specific desired outcome. In the case of CTSK, Sara asked her team to run these five plays:

Play 1: Needs assessment (1 week)
Play 2: Analysis of options (1 week)
Play 3: Designing the change (1 week)
Play 4: Implementation planning (1 week)
Play 5: Implementation of the actual change initiative (4 weeks)

Sara was highly effective at "keeping the chains moving." That is, she took steps to ensure that each play was properly executed and measured to determine the outcome before calling the next play. On Monday of each week during the first month, the ball was snapped on four different plays, and the players on each of the three improvement teams executed their individual assignments. In one month, her teams ran four specific plays designed to move the facility to a position on the field where they could actually experience real improvement in cost savings. At the completion of each play during this month, the team measured performance and made appropriate adjustments to keep the overall improvement initiative on track. Members of her teams constantly reviewed the cost reduction scoreboard that had been set up to monitor the performance of each of the teams on each of the plays it was running during that first month.

At the start of the second month, Sara's teams executed play 5 in their improvement drive: implementing the actual changes, which took place during the rest of the month. Again, the scoreboard tracked both time and performance so that everybody could see how his or her individual team was doing. It is important to note that Sara's successful effort included three critical factors:

1. Clear starting points for each improvement play
2. A performance tracking device for each play in her play package
3. A completion date and stopping point for each play

Sara, as quarterback, snapped the ball five times for each of the specific plays in her play package, and although she did not use a whistle to signify the end of each play, the completion dates for each activity served the same purpose. On each play in her play package, different players came out onto the field to fulfill their individual assignments, each of which was deemed necessary for the success of that play.

Sara encouraged all three teams to execute their individual plays and each team member to execute his or her individual assignment. She provided the necessary support to keep the teams progressing toward the ultimate goal of real cost savings. Sara also ensured that every team had ownership and control of each of its improvement drives. As we've noted, ownership is a fundamental characteristic of successful change initiatives.

Every player on the field for this change initiative had a specific contribution to each play. Although Sara led the team, she knew that it was up to the individual players to seize control of the factors that affected the outcome of the change. Sara had the courage to take a few hits when resistance to change occurred, but she avoided unnecessary mistakes and sacks. Thinking along these lines, are you prepared to answer the following questions when it is time to execute a change effort?

Key Questions
1. Does each play have a clearly defined starting and stopping point that builds on the activity of the previous play?
2. Is your team prepared to execute each of the necessary plays for this specific initiative?
3. Has each player come to the change initiative ready to play at a higher level in performing his or her individual assignments on every play?
4. Are you, as the quarterback, measuring your team's performance on each play and using the scoreboard effectively?

CTSK had spent two years working on Lean initiatives that resulted in no significant improvement to the plant's bottom line.

The company spent more time on following protocols and planning than it did on addressing the problems that were sucking the life out of the plant, and out of the managers too, for that matter. Plant leadership possessed a potentially useful tool (the Lean initiatives), yet failed to execute the activities that move the chains toward real improvement. From this perspective, they had taken a useful tool and turned it into a major distraction from real, bottom-line improvement. And they are not alone!

Momentum Builder 3: Make Necessary Adjustments Fast

In reality, most TMDs, both in football and in the workplace, require some adjustments between and even during the plays. As a quarterback, you must keep your finger on the pulse of the game and always know what is going on during each play during your improvement effort. In a football game, a wide variety of things can occur that require a quarterback to make rapid adjustments on the playing field: a penalty, a dropped pass, failing to get out of bounds to stop the clock, an injury to a key player, or an unanticipated defensive formation, to name a few. In these situations, the quarterback has only seconds to call an "audible" and make the decisions necessary to keep the "drive alive." When he doesn't, the team frequently loses.

In the workplace, the same thing happens and requires change leaders to make adjustments quickly to keep the drive alive. Here are just a few of the things that we have seen go wrong in some organizations:

- A needs assessment took longer than necessary to secure accurate data.
- Team members could not meet because they were pulled out of meetings to handle a crisis with a customer.
- A team could not agree on an appropriate set of action steps for a needed change because they were stuck in analysis paralysis.
- Information technology people said that they could not provide the necessary software to support a needed change by the agreed-on due date.
- A current department budget could not support the training needs for the implementation of a new customized work procedure.

All these problems have two things in common:

1. They were unanticipated.
2. They require immediate attention on the part of the change leader to keep the change initiative on track.

Adjustments are usually required whether you are implementing someone else's "foolproof" improvement plan or creating your own. Titans quarterback Steve McNair had to make several adjustments during the final drive to get his team into the red zone in Super Bowl XXXIV, and so did Sara Payne.

Sara made several key adjustments throughout the improvement drive to ensure success:

- She provided time on the weekends for each team to fine-tune assignments that took longer than planned.
- She adjusted personnel to support the racking designs in the warehouse during the third week of the effort.
- She adjusted the implementation phase for several of the teams to allow them earlier starts to meet time requirements.

Making adjustments *quickly* requires that change leaders always know what is going on around them, constantly monitor the progress and performance of each team, act quickly when barriers to progress emerge, and have the courage to do what it takes to get the team back on track. To that end, ask yourself this question:

> **Key Question**
> When quarterbacking a change initiative, are you quick to take action and make the necessary adjustments to ensure that your team stays on track?

Your answer to this question will determine how effectively your team can execute each change play in a timely fashion. You'll need to use your peripheral vision to see things that are coming that require adjustment and to anticipate obstacles that will stop your improvement drive dead in its tracks if ignored. *Remember: to keep a change effort on track, you must make adjustments quickly.*

Momentum Builder 4: Manage the Clock and Keep Your Team Hustling

One of the primary reasons that TMDs are successful is that quarterbacks and their teams are extremely sensitive to the issue of time. Fans and analysts are frequently amazed when a team runs a seven-play scoring drive in less than a minute. How is this possible? The answer to that question is quite simple:

- Every activity in the team's TMD play package is designed not only to advance the ball but also to do so in the least possible amount of time.
- Every player on the team has to "dig deep" and hustle on every play.

Manage the Clock

We have noted throughout the book that change in the workplace represents a hardship for the people involved. This is primarily a time issue. People who are already busy with their regular jobs now have to find time to take on additional responsibilities. Keeping this in mind, effective change quarterbacks look for creative ways to manage the clock and minimize nonproductive change activities at all costs. They remain ever aware of two old axioms that lie at either end of a continuum: *haste makes waste* at one end, and *work expands to fill the time allotted to it* at the other. Change initiatives with an aggressively short time frame can yield unsustainable, ineffective change—a waste of effort. Conversely, allotting six months to implement a change that could be achieved in two is a poor use of everyone's limited time.

Managing the clock is the practice of ensuring that the team and individual players are running each play in a time-sensitive fashion. As we stated in Chapter Five, time needs to be handled with the utmost care. Here is what you as an effective change leader need to do to manage the clock:

- Know how much time you really have to work with and ensure that every player understands the overall game clock and the associated actions required.
- Set and maintain aggressive yet realistic timelines and deadlines for plays in your improvement package, with the input and ownership of your people who have to execute them.
- Ensure that both individuals and teams complete assignments on schedule, which might require periodic one-on-one meetings with you as the quarterback.
- Seek out ways to speed up activity during the various phases of your improvement efforts and remove all time wasters—such as unneeded conference calls, bureaucratic barriers, lengthy reports, unnecessary paperwork, and so on.
- View meetings as time-outs, demonstrating extreme care in scheduling and running them, and working to minimize non-productive activity associated with them, including travel time, involving too many people, failing to have an agenda, and so on.
- Track the progress on every play or action, and measure the outcome with the chains that you have established on your scoreboard.

Keep Your Team Hustling

In addition to managing the clock, effective change leaders *keep their team hustling* during the entire improvement effort, which is no easy task. In a football game, quarterbacks hurry their players to the line of scrimmage, high-five a receiver for making a big play, and back-slap their offensive linemen to tell them that they appreciate their efforts. All these things can take place on the playing field and during the game. As a change quarterback you need to do the same kind of things to keep your team motivated and hustling. To that end, you should

- Monitor the performance of individual players and encourage successful performance
- Hold the team to established deadlines and look for ways to create friendly competition in completing assignments

- Offer ongoing feedback and praise when individual assignments are performed effectively and when the team successfully completes a play
- Address any performance breakdowns immediately and be willing to remove nonproductive members from the team who are damaging team performance
- Keep your scoreboard in front of your people and remind them that there will be an end to this change game when the team achieves its goal
- Look for ways to free up time to allow individuals to complete important assignments that are critical to the success of the overall team effort

Sara did an excellent job of monitoring the clock for the three teams' initiatives. She provided a public scoreboard with constant measures of each team's performance and a countdown for the eight weeks. Thursday meetings created ongoing pressure to achieve that week's assignments, and friendly competition was used to keep people excited about the time frame. The implementation began on time, and four weeks later, the CTSK facility was on its way to real improvement.

As the quarterback of your team, ask yourself the following questions:

Key Questions
1. Is the timing of your change initiative appropriate to the time required to achieve real and sustainable results?
2. Are you managing the clock and making the best possible use of the time you have available to complete this change initiative?
3. Are you doing the things that are necessary to keep your team motivated and hustling?

MOMENTUM BUILDER 5: EXECUTE IN THE RED ZONE AND SCORE

Football devotees will tell you that it is performance in the red zone that determines their favorite team's ultimate success.

A team is in the red zone when the offense has used the various plays in its play package to move the team to within 20 yards of its primary objective: the end zone. The team is in a position to score either a touchdown or a field goal. In the workplace, the final play of the drive is to execute the implementation of the actual change flawlessly so that real improvement takes place. We call this the *scoring play*.

This is often the most difficult play and often requires a time-out just before the ball is actually snapped. It is during this time-out, with little time on the clock and the team in position to score, that the team leader ensures one last time that the team is prepared for the change implementation and ready to score. Everyone understands his or her role, eyes are on the scoreboard, the quarterback has control of the game, and the ball is snapped one last time. It is at this point that each individual carries out his or her assignment(s) in support of the actual change in operation.

The CTSK teams did a great job of running the first four plays to set the stage for them to execute their actual improvement plans in weeks 5 through 8. All three teams executed in the red zone and achieved their desired cost-saving scores. Prior to Sara's arrival, they had executed planning plays and training plays and the like, but they had not created or executed a scoring play. The true mark of Real Change leaders is their ability to get their team into the improvement end zone, which is exactly what Sara did. To that end, are you and your team prepared to answer the following questions? Doing so will allow you, as the quarterback, to ensure that you are a Real Change leader in getting your team into the end zone.

Key Questions
1. Is the team in the red zone when they actually implement the change initiative? In other words, are they in position to score?
2. Have you called one last time-out to ensure that every member is prepared and clearly understands his or her responsibilities?
3. As the quarterback, are you in control of the scoring play?
4. Does everyone understand his or her assignment on the scoring play?

CTSK Industries: The Outcome

CTSK Industries achieved tremendous improvements in just eight weeks of concentrated and focused effort. The proper execution of this organization's Lean initiative achieved savings of over $2.5 million annually. This plant continued to see additional improvements and was actually performing in the black by the end of the following quarter, in great part because of success in executing the three cost-saving initiatives with the utmost precision. Today, this plant is one of the best performers in the company and has shown its ability to respond to new market opportunities and other organizational changes.

Although Sara received a great deal of recognition for her efforts in leading this potentially plant-saving improvement initiative, she was quick to give credit to the people on her improvement team and everyone in the plant for all their hard and noble work. Sara did a great job of quarterbacking her team down the field and into the end zone, executing each of the plays in her team's improvement play package with great precision. Every team member knew what to do, but more important, he or she did it. During weeks 1 through 4, Sara created the necessary momentum for her team to get into the red zone. She then took the appropriate steps to ensure that the team scored by actually executing the improvement plan that had been designed and mapped out during those four weeks. When asked what the secret to her success was, Sara offered this simple axiom: "If you really want your organization to change, you have to help your people change, so be ready to put your heart and soul in the effort, because they are worth it."

Conclusion: What Can Go Wrong in Executing

In closing this chapter, we thought it would be appropriate to share our research findings on the subject of the challenges that Real Change leaders must address for effective execution to take place. Exhibit 7.2 is our top ten list of the factors that damage the execution of a TMD improvement package; these factors will keep your team from getting near its goal and, ultimately, out of the end zone. Please review this list with great care, noting that 7.5 of the 10 factors listed here are *within your control as a leader*.

Exhibit 7.2: The Top Ten Factors That Damage the Execution of a TMD Improvement Package

1. Communication breakdowns and confusion
2. Ineffective individual performance on the part of leaders and team members
3. Wasting time and not making adjustments quickly
4. Unclear performance goals and assignments during various phases of the change process
5. Ineffective measurement, feedback, and accountability for performance
6. Lack of preparation and planning for the needed changes
7. Lack of top management support
8. Losing track of timelines and timing issues
9. Lack of resources and infrastructure
10. Organizational barriers and lack of teamwork

Your actions have a great influence on getting your team into the end zone, so don't underestimate the importance of your role in helping your team execute! And failing to execute is very painful, as the 2000 Tennessee Titans team will tell you. The words of Harvey Mackay, author of *Swim with the Sharks Without Being Eaten Alive,* seem very appropriate as we close this chapter on the issue of execution: "Take control of your destiny before somebody else does it for you."

Finally, take the time to review Exhibit 7.3, your TMD Momentum Builder Checklist, to think through the items discussed in this chapter that can help you execute.

Exhibit 7.3: TMD Momentum Builder Checklist

Listed below are momentum builders for snapping the ball and executing the right plays. Ask yourself the check-off questions to determine how well you stack up to the challenge!   ✔

TMD field winner: A TMD scoreboard is established for the change initiative.

Your check-off: Is every team member monitoring the scoreboard for this change initiative?   ❑

TMD field winner: QB takes a clean snap, executes the play, and keeps the chains moving.

Your check-off: Is the team prepped, and are the plays being executed to move the team into the red zone?   ❑

TMD field winner: QB calls an audible when circumstances change.

Your check-off: Are you making midcourse adjustments, creating new plays as circumstances warrant?   ❑

TMD field winner: QB manages the clock and the hustle to ensure that the team has time to score.

Your check-off: Are you motivating your team and eliminating time wasters to keep the initiative on track?   ❑

TMD field winner: QB calls and executes the scoring play, creating the win.

Your check-off: Are you moving your team into position and initiating the final set of actions to win?   ❑

CHAPTER EIGHT

CLOSE OUT THE GAME, THEN CELEBRATE

Don't Reward "Victory" Until You See Truly Lasting Success

One of the top four reasons for failure is claiming victory before the war is over.
—JOHN KOTTER

Most people give up just when they're about to achieve success. They quit on the one-yard line. They give up at the last minute of the game, one foot from a winning touchdown.
—ROSS PEROT

WINNING IMPERATIVE: *Finish the Game*
Take the necessary actions to ensure that your change game is complete before you declare victory; then make sure you celebrate!

"The Bluegrass Miracle": Kentucky Wildcats vs. LSU Tigers, November 9, 2002

When fans filed into the University of Kentucky's Commonwealth Stadium, they had no idea that they were about to become part of one of the wildest finishes in the history of NCAA football, which has simply become known as

"The Bluegrass Miracle." The Kentucky Wildcats found themselves trailing the LSU Tigers for most of the first three quarters of this contest, until their quarterback, Jared Lorenzen, engineered a 14-point comeback to tie the game 27–27 in the fourth quarter. The Kentucky defense got the ball back for its offense, which successfully completed a short drive that culminated in a 29-yard field goal by kicker Taylor Begley to give the Wildcats a 30–27 lead, with only 11 seconds left on the clock.

Kentucky fans erupted and began pouring out of the stands in anticipation of rushing onto the playing field. Jubilant Kentucky players on the sidelines and on the field began their victory celebration as the ball split the uprights. This game-winning drive and score would finally give the Wildcats a win over their rival LSU. This would be especially sweet, a little bit of payback from the previous year, when Kentucky had overcome a 12-point halftime deficit only to lose 29–25 on a touchdown pass with 13 seconds left.

But hold on! There were still 11 seconds left on the clock, and the Tigers would have a chance for at least a couple of plays before the students could rush onto the field in celebration and tear down the goalposts.

Kentucky kicked off, and the Tigers started the drive on their own 8-yard line after a delay-of-game penalty. LSU had 92 yards to cover in 11 seconds. On their very first play, LSU quarterback Marcus Randall passed the ball to wide receiver Michael Clayton for a 17-yard gain, putting the ball at their own 25-yard line. LSU called a time-out with 2 seconds left on the game clock and huddled their team on the sidelines with their coaching staff. During the time-out, jubilant Kentucky players on the sidelines, caught up in the celebration, gave head coach Guy Morriss a celebratory "Gatorade dunk" as TV cameras moved in for a close-up of the rather touching moment. The Tigers approached the line of scrimmage for the final play of the contest as the Kentucky players lined up in a "deep prevent defense," and the stadium roared in anticipation of the win. LSU quarterback Randall took the snap, dropped back to his own 18-yard line, and threw the ball as hard as he could to a host of LSU wide receivers streaking down the field, attempting a Hail Mary play. But the ball came down well short of the end zone and was tipped by a Kentucky defensive back between the 20- and 25-yard lines, as fans stormed out onto the field and engulfed the LSU quarterback who had just thrown the ball.

But Kentucky's victory celebration was short lived as LSU wide receiver Devery Henderson snatched the ball from the air with one hand just short of the 15-yard line, broke a shoestring tackle, and ran into the end zone with 0:00 on the scoreboard. The game-winning play was "Dash 93 Right Berlin" (which has become permanently known as the "Bluegrass Miracle" in the LSU playbook). There was pandemonium in the stadium and in the press box, as numerous press organizations posted the game final as Kentucky 30, LSU 27, when in truth LSU had just won the contest 33–30.

The Kentucky Wildcats had lost to LSU for the second consecutive year in the final seconds of the contest, but this time they had no one to blame but themselves. They had begun their celebration before the game was complete, assuming that a 3-point lead was enough to guarantee victory. In the final 11 seconds of this game, their opponent had reversed their fortunes and put Kentucky behind yet again, only this time there was no opportunity to come back because time had expired.

What made this loss particularly painful was the fact that a Kentucky player mistakenly called time-out with 11 seconds in the game prior to Kentucky's "game-winning" field goal. The clock should have been allowed to wind down to 2 or 3 seconds before this time-out, which would have denied LSU an opportunity to come back, because time would have expired during the kick. But in all the excitement and celebration associated with kicking the supposedly game-winning field goal, the team had not been thinking ahead about closing out the game. LSU head coach Nick Saban took a very humble approach to this amazing win when he stated, "Truth be told, we probably should not have won." But the record book still recorded an "L" for the Wildcats and a "W" for the Tigers.

KINGSWOOD VALLEY HEALTHCARE ALMOST RUINED ITS REPUTATION

The same mistake of celebrating success before it really is achieved also takes place in many business settings, as we'll see in this case example. Carla Lopez was an experienced health care entrepreneur enjoying the career ride of her life. Carla had founded Kingswood Valley Healthcare (KVH) twelve years earlier and had managed its growth to a regional enterprise with more than twenty locations in several large cities along the eastern seaboard.

KVH offered a full line of care for the aging baby-boomer population; residential assisted living, advanced nursing care, and a wing for individuals with dementia rounded out the services provided at each location.

BACKGROUND: A COMPANY EARNS ITS TERRIFIC REPUTATION FOR QUALITY CARE

Supported by an experienced group of health care leaders, Carla had created a business model that focused on a high level of quality care in attractive facilities that appealed to an upper-middle-class professional resident population. The three thousand or so residents throughout the system seemed quite willing to pay an above-average rate to enjoy the superior quality of living and care at KVH. Consequently, KVH was very profitable and could afford to employ a higher-caliber staff that enjoyed salaries and benefits well above industry average.

THE PROBLEM: EXPANSION ALMOST BACKFIRES

KVH was selected on numerous occasions to be honored as both a great business and as a contributor to the needs of the communities in which it was located, and Carla had received several individual awards for entrepreneurship as well. The outstanding reputation of KVH resulted in word-of-mouth marketing that led to lengthy waiting lists of individuals seeking to enjoy their later years at KVH. Two years earlier, Carla and her top leadership team, knowing that KVH needed to continue growing, had embarked on a shift in strategy that would add a dozen facilities in smaller towns and rural areas. They had determined that the national health care companies would soon put extensive pressure on the large-city market, squeezing their margins and forcing them to change their business model. Their analysis led them to believe that those same organizations would not be as active in the smaller towns and rural markets, allowing KVH more flexibility and greater opportunity.

To paraphrase an old adage, KVH's reputation preceded it. Over the next two years, twelve attractive facilities were built, and the KVH annual shareholder report and trade publications heralded the coming success that the company would enjoy because of its new strategy. As expected, the management team was excited, and it began celebrating its decision to pursue this strategy. Over an aggressive four-month grand-opening phase, the twelve facilities welcomed more than eight hundred new residents, and the facilities were rapidly moving toward capacity. Overall, things were looking good at all the new locations, and the staff members at the KVH corporate office were "high-fiving" each other over the achievement. Members of the strategy and implementation teams received significant bonuses, recognizing their accomplishments to date and the public praise for the anticipated success of the new locations.

But then it appeared that the celebration may have been a bit premature, as the number of resident complaints (a quality tracking metric) at the new locations began to increase rapidly, becoming significantly higher than similar metrics at the older, large-city facilities. In addition, staff turnover shot up within the first three months of operations. When management benchmarked these numbers against the start-up periods of the older facilities, the disturbing news was confirmed to be a threat to achieving the overall goals of the initiative. Further, the word-of-mouth communications that helped build the company's envied reputation over the previous twelve years began to backfire as these problems, which eroded the confidence of residents and industry watchdogs, began to surface. The fact that KVH was viewed as a company that could do no wrong exacerbated its problems.

What had gone wrong? KVH had a great business model, and the industry lauded the company at every opportunity. Rapid growth seemed to be an appropriate strategy. Facilities were built on time and within budget. Everyone was excited. KVH was winning. Management, with great fanfare, had gone on record with the press and shareholders that they had created a system that would fulfill the needs of these new markets and that they were bringing their track record of success with them. But it was all coming apart within four months of start-up as residents were leaving facilities, costs were rising, and a host of "people issues" were damaging performance.

MOVING QUICKLY TO SOLVE THE PROBLEM BY WORKING TO UNDERSTAND WHAT CAUSED IT

Carla, knowing that she and her management team needed to move quickly to regain lost momentum, initiated an immediate assessment of both the resident complaint data and the exit interview feedback from former staff members. She stressed the urgency of the situation, defining winning of this turnaround initiative to be regaining the outstanding reputation of KVH, even at the expense of profit margin.

The assessment led the team to conclude that the business model, originally created for the big-city environment, was not directly transferable to a rural, smaller-town market. Providing great care was fine. The model broke down, however, in assuming that sufficient high-caliber staff would be plentiful in these same areas. Unfortunately, it was not. In reality, many of the young professionals who had moved to the larger cities to attend health care schools had stayed in the larger cities, creating a dearth of qualified people to support the smaller communities. Although KVH had originally identified sufficient numbers of personnel to staff the facilities, it soon found that the employees' experience level and attitude were well below what was needed to provide the type of care that KVH and the residents demanded. Accordingly, complaints rose, pressure ensued, and staff turnover ballooned.

It very quickly became obvious to Carla and her management that they had celebrated a bit prematurely and that, in fact, they had not put the right players in key positions in staffing their new operations. They had also failed to monitor their quality metrics closely enough during the start-up. Essentially, they had not finished the game, and their premature celebration caused them to fail to see the problems that were coming. Could they recover? Did they? We will discuss this in further detail later in the chapter.

DON'T CELEBRATE VICTORY PREMATURELY

The world is replete with examples in business, in politics, in sports, and, yes, in genuine wars where a supposed victory fell short of the mark and the apparent victors became the vanquished. Few things in life are as difficult to watch as wins becoming losses, for three essential reasons:

1. Tasting victory is a very pleasant experience; it reinforces your confidence that you are good and can compete. Slipping backwards damages, and can even shatter, that confidence.
2. Winning allows you to conclude that your preparation and hard work were worth it. Losing can cause people to draw the exact opposite conclusion, with detrimental motivational and attitudinal consequences.
3. Losing feels bad especially when you were on the brink of victory. When success is in your grasp, it is painful to see it pried from your hand or even dropped.

In all three of these cases, losing a game that was won causes participants to second-guess themselves or play Monday-morning quarterback with a "coulda, shoulda, woulda" mentality. How many times have you heard these sorts of comments:

"We were almost there, but we didn't finish the job."
"Our initial gains were very promising, but we couldn't get over the hump."
"There was light at the end of the tunnel, but it turned out to be a train."
"Every time it seemed like we were there, something would push us backwards."
"Whenever we took our eye off the ball, things went back to where we started."

These sobering comments reflect the frustrations that can come from not making changes stick. Closing out a game is critically important for leaders who wish to avoid these frustrations and the experiences of Kentucky football coach Guy Morriss or health care executive Carla Lopez.

By *closing out the game*, we mean that once an improvement effort has been implemented and real progress has been made, it is imperative for leaders and team members to continue to perform the specific assignments, activities, and behaviors that led to this improvement. True victory occurs when desired practices become part of a team's modus operandi or daily habits that produce better results on a sustainable basis.

WHAT HAPPENS WHEN VICTORY IS CELEBRATED TOO EARLY

We have seen countless change efforts relapse or deteriorate when teams and leaders failed to close out their change game. Here are some painful examples that we have personally witnessed:

- A transportation company using self-directive work teams sees a 15 percent increase in freight-handling productivity, only to see it vanish when frontline supervisors are threatened by empowered unionized workers and revert back to their traditional hard-core approach to supervision.
- A multinational food processing enterprise automated a sandwich meat production line with the intent of increasing output and reducing costs in this 24/7 operation. When the new high-tech line was brought online, output shot up, and direct labor costs fell dramatically. Four months later, however, the opposite was true, as the organization did not have the talent for ongoing production line maintenance and machine balancing. This created a continuous production nightmare, causing output to dip back to original levels.
- A nonprofit organization put an organization-wide cost containment program in place to better manage nonessential spending, under the close scrutiny of top leadership. The first four months of the program witnessed dramatic cost savings, but by the end of the next quarter, costs were right back where they started because top leadership failed to maintain both its focus and the monitoring program.
- A Midwest furniture manufacturing organization went through an ISO certification process because it had quality problems and was experiencing market pressures for the credential. The company did a terrific job of focusing its efforts in the ISO mapping and documentation process, and it resolved a number of serious quality problems as a consequence. Once the company

was formally ISO certified, however, it slipped back to business as usual, and the quality problems were right back on the table.

- An insurance company restructured its claims handling department to reduce supervisory overhead. Work groups were combined and supervisors were eliminated, and claims handling output actually improved slightly as work groups took more ownership of daily activities. Several months into these changes, the organization implemented a totally new procedure for automated claims handling that completely changed how work was processed. The change was like a car accident, and the teams struggled to cope, with only limited planning and input from their already stretched supervisors. Productivity fell, and quality was a disaster.

WHY ORGANIZATIONS CELEBRATE VICTORY TOO EARLY

Why do smart, hard-working, and progressive leaders and teams allow these sorts of things to happen? Truth be told, one of the greatest challenges associated with any change or improvement process is *getting the changes to stick* and ensuring that performance improvement is *sustainable.* If you and your team fight hard to make serious changes, as all the organizations we listed did, why would you sit back and watch your victory go down the tubes? In our interviews and research with a diverse group of leaders, we have found several universal patterns of behavior relative to closing out change efforts that shed light on the challenge of making change stick:

1. There is a tendency to confuse *progress* with *victory* on the part of leaders, because they are frequently looking for information that tells them that what they are doing is working and that they have won. Leaders have a tendency to declare victory prematurely.
2. Because of the overwhelming number of activities on their schedules, managers can easily "take their eyes off the ball" once improvement begins, which results in a loss of focus and causes slippage or a relapse to former ways of doing things.

3. For any improvement to be a real and lasting victory, members of work groups have to change their individual behaviors and habits and stick with those changes. This requires ongoing focus, attention, and discipline on their part, which is frequently lost because of the barrage of ongoing work challenges and the practice of multi- or hypertasking.

4. Managers must reinforce appropriate performance and behavior at both individual and work group levels, on an ongoing basis, until desired practices become habits. If this reinforcement and attention are withdrawn too soon, old habits return, and sustained performance improvement (victory) is in jeopardy.

5. Organizations typically have a wide variety of nonfinancial and financial rewards that can be used to celebrate success and to keep the memory of victory alive in the minds of people on the team. Yet these rewards are frequently not effectively or strategically used by leaders to celebrate success.

All these challenges make it tough getting change to stick. Anxious to show results in a demanding world, where time is short and better performance is constantly expected, many leaders often declare victory, trash-talk their opponents, dump the water cooler on their own heads, schedule the victory dance, and quit playing before the game is actually over. Because of this tendency, the improvement they were seeking does not become a permanent reality. And, as would be expected, they frequently lose after victory was in their grasp. If you cannot relate to this discussion, count your blessings. But for most leaders, closing out the game of change can be a career maker or a career breaker.

CLOSE OUT THE GAME BEFORE YOU CELEBRATE

Frequently, the tyranny of the crowded plate and crazy schedules causes leaders and organizations to take their eyes off the ball. This is especially true when they score big during a change initiative and everyone is excited about initial improvements. This interim success feels good personally and organizationally; people feel relieved that an objective has been achieved and that the changes are working. Unfortunately, in many cases those same busy people involved in the change then divert their energies to other activities and tasks, thus thwarting the momentum needed to ensure a true completion of the initiative at hand. There is a tendency to declare victory too soon!

We've looked at some of the challenges and consequences of declaring victory too soon. In everything we've said, we have not intended to imply that celebration after closing out a victorious game was uncalled for. On the contrary, celebration after a big win is critical to future success. Leaders can sometimes fail to celebrate victory with all the tools they have available at their disposal, thus throwing away the opportunity to reward desired behavior and motivate people to do more of the same in the future. Closing out the game is vital, and so is enthusiastic celebration. Here are some of the things that can help you do both.

MOMENTUM BUILDER 1: CHECK OUT YOUR SCOREBOARD AND MAKE SURE YOU ARE REALLY SCORING

Time is running out, and the ball carrier is tackled at the edge of the goal line, but it looks like he got in; the clock expires, the stands go wild, and the game is won. But wait a minute—the officials have not yet signaled touchdown. Although it looked as though the player had scored, several things might stand in the way. Did his knee hit the ground before he crossed the goal line? Did he step out of bounds? What is the reason for that small piece of yellow cloth lying on the playing field? Football couch potatoes have spilled their drinks and popcorn over harrowing moments like this; in the business arena, similar scenarios play out as well, though often without such drama.

As the quarterback of any change effort, you must know whether your team actually achieved the results that your improvement drive had been designed to achieve. On the football field, success or failure is easy to measure and apparent to everyone (at least with instant replay). Off the field, it is usually not quite so easy or obvious. To determine if you scored and indeed won the game, it is critical to go back and review how you defined winning and success at the start of your improvement effort. You need to use your scoreboard metrics to declare victory as well as recognize the parties that were most critical in achieving the win. To understand and evaluate how successful an initiative has been, you must

- **Check the scoreboard.** How do the metrics you used to measure your results compare to your initial goals and definition of winning?
- **Consult your customer(s).** How have they benefited from what you have done?
- **Monitor your competitors.** What is their reaction and response to your change initiative?

Did the Kentucky Wildcats interpret the scoreboard correctly? With 2 seconds remaining, they doused the coach with Gatorade to celebrate the upset. However, the scoreboard didn't say they had *won;* it simply said they were *winning.*

How about Kingswood Valley Heathcare? Following the company's series of grand openings, did its scoreboard say it had won? No, it said that KVH had built and opened a dozen new facilities and that these facilities were now in the game. The real business goals of profitable, effective growth in new markets and of maintaining the company's reputation as a quality health care provider were far from being achieved. Yet the CEO and management were already celebrating.

In reality, the scoreboard would soon show that they were rapidly falling behind. KVH employed several metrics that in time alerted the management to a serious issue, calling for a change in their business model. One may legitimately question, however, whether KVH should have had different metrics in place during its planning process that would have highlighted the shortage of qualified staff in the development phase.

Consulting with your customers and monitoring your competitors are also two vital aspects to knowing whether or not you are really scoring and that your changes have prevailed. Most of us realize that ultimately, the customer's response on most initiatives is the true measure of success. One lesson to learn from KVH is that *customer satisfaction must constantly be monitored and measured.*

Your competitors' responses to changes can also be handy indicators of success. From the competitors' standpoint, your good news is often their bad news. Typically they react or respond, and what they do just might let you know that you really did score and that you should be ready to respond in kind.

In Chapter Three we quoted the inimitable Vince Lombardi: "If winning isn't everything, why do they keep score?" We suggest here that you alter his words a bit to ask yourself the following question:

Key Question
If you don't keep the right score, how do you know you really won?

MOMENTUM BUILDER 2: DON'T CELEBRATE PREMATURELY

Football play-by-play broadcasters will frequently use phrases like these:

"Don't anybody leave their seats just yet."
"You'd better wait before you put the 'W' in the win column."
"It ain't over till it's over."
"It's not over till the fat lady sings."

All these sayings are warning reminders to fans that even though their team might be ahead, they shouldn't celebrate prematurely. In both football and business, a premature celebration causes teams and leaders alike to lose focus and the motivation to keep doing the things that are necessary for their scoring advantage to hold up. We have a hard time believing that the Kentucky head football coach was concentrating and communicating in an optimal fashion on the final play of the game against LSU. He had just been soaked to the bone with ice cold Gatorade, was standing outside in frigid weather, and was surrounded by players screaming in his ear, with fans going wild all around him. In retrospect, there just may have been instructions that he could have communicated to his players or defensive coordinator that would have changed the outcome on that last play. Talk about coulda, shoulda, woulda! The Kentucky fans spilled onto the field ready to celebrate the upset, only to find *themselves* driving home upset.

A premature celebration of success also got in the way of effective leadership at KVH. Carla and her management team went into full celebration mode once the facilities were built and open on time and on budget. Unfortunately, they too were soon to discover that their celebration was a bit early. The temptation to declare victory and celebrate our achievements can get in the way of making the necessary adjustments and providing the leadership and reinforcement necessary to make changes stick. This is truly a challenge for most leaders: to fight the urge to claim the victory of a change initiative prematurely. The costs of doing so, as we have seen, can be high. So ask yourself this question:

Key Question
In your organization, do you and your senior management team have a tendency to claim success in a change effort before the game is complete?

MOMENTUM BUILDER 3: MAKE SURE THE SCORE HOLDS UP

Coaches will tell you that when a team gets in the end zone late in the game and it's ahead on the scoreboard, it is critically important that the team do the things necessary to ensure that the score holds up until the game is officially over. These might include taking time off the clock whenever possible, executing excellent special teams play, and running an effective prevent defense. In organizational TMDs, making sure that the score holds up means doing the things necessary to ensure that everyone maintains whatever changes you and your team have made to produce improvements. Leaders and team members must maintain their focus and discipline so that the improvement practices become habits.

There is an extensive amount of research about the challenges we all face in attempting to adopt new behaviors (personal or professional) and turn them into habits that become part of our lifestyle.[1] None of us have to look too far to see how difficult it is for people to break old habits and replace them with new ones. To illustrate just how hard it can be to change, one research study recently reported that only one out of nine people who had undergone coronary bypass surgery had stuck with the comprehensive lifestyle changes, including diet, exercise, and stress reduction, that would be necessary to sustain their life over the long term. The researcher went on to say, "Even though they know they have a very bad disease and they should improve their lifestyle, for whatever reason, they don't."[2]

In response to the challenges people face in their attempts to change, we have learned a great deal through our own research and that of others about how to help people stick with changes when it is in their best interest to do so.[3] These principles apply to changes in both their personal and professional lives, although the mechanisms might be somewhat different. Suppose for the moment that your team has just executed an effective TMD, and the performance outcomes you were hoping for have been realized. Your team has scored, and you want to declare victory, but you are holding off until you are sure that the score will hold. If you are serious about helping your team develop their new, effective behaviors and practices into the work habits that will maintain these improvements, you can refer to Exhibit 8.1, which lists some of the very specific things you can do.

Exhibit 8.1: How to Transform New Behaviors into Habits

- **If you want change to stick, start with yourself.** As quarterback you must demonstrate and role-model the behaviors that are necessary to maintain the performance of your team. Create a system for yourself that will encourage you to do this, and consider using a mentor or personal coach to help you stick with your personal game plan.
- **Keep people focused on the positive aspects** and outcomes of the changes that you are making. This allows people to see that their hard work is making a difference and is linked to something good that is worth the extra effort required.
- **Do not use fear as the *primary* motivator for a change effort.** Fear gets old quickly and keeps people in a negative frame of mind, which makes it easier for them *not* to want to think about the change. Look for ways to inject excitement, healthy competition, and even fun into the change, so that people equate positive feelings and events with the change effort.

- **Train and retrain people to perform their new tasks and behaviors** so that they have both the confidence and skill necessary to perform with great proficiency, while at the same time experiencing the advantages and motivation associated with personal development.
- **Find support groups of people who are going through, or who have gone through, a similar experience.** This is critical for creating ongoing awareness, camaraderie, focus, counsel, and accountability for maintaining new behaviors. Look for opportunities to bring team members together to discuss what they are experiencing and to encourage each other.
- **Develop and foster individual accountability for the new behaviors** in a meaningful way, so that people know that their actions are being critiqued and assessed on an ongoing basis. Increasing both informal and formal performance appraisals during periods of change can help create this accountability.
- **Continually reinforce the positive outcomes of successful behavior.** At the same time, address inappropriate or undesirable actions at both the individual and group levels. The ratio of positive to negative feedback should be a minimum of 4:1 if the change is to be long term and meaningful and if people are to perceive the change as a personally favorable experience.
- **Make sure team members have ready access to visual aids illustrating appropriate actions and behaviors.** This helps them keep appropriate behaviors in the forefront of their thinking.

Exhibit 8.1 lists just a few of the things that effective quarterback-leaders do to help the members of their teams get ahead and stay ahead on the scoreboard. Don't assume that your scoring drive will be victorious without leadership that helps these practices stick. Maintain the same focus and sense of urgency that enabled the offense to put points on the board in the first place, and the Las Vegas odds makers will bet that your score will hold and turn into victory.

> **Key Question**
> What do you need to do to make your improvement score hold up?

MOMENTUM BUILDER 4: CELEBRATE BOTH THE SCORING DRIVE AND THE WIN

In a football game, what happens when a team scores at the end of a TMD and appears to have won the game? The crowd roars, hard-core fans go crazy, the scoreboard flashes, cannons fire, fireworks go off, and the band plays. What is particularly interesting is to watch the reaction of the players on the field. They celebrate! They really celebrate! This celebration is dramatic, energized, enthusiastic, exciting, motivating, and high powered.

What is it like at your organization when a team makes a terrific improvement or scores a big touchdown?

A college offensive lineman falls on a fumble in the end zone. Touchdown! And although no one in the universe would have missed recovering the ball, he jumps up, belly-bumps several players on his team, holds the ball in the air, and runs around the field screaming and carrying the souvenir ball, as if he had just exhibited a combination of talents and skills never before seen in the world of football. Truth be told, he just happened to be at the right place at the right time, but because of that, his team strains under his three-hundred-pound frame to carry him off the field on their shoulders, and he is assured that his name will be on tomorrow's sports page. This is a defining moment in his life, and he feels like he is ready to take on the world.

Contrast that scenario with our organizational world. A market analyst completes an intense two-month study of new business opportunities, outlining several prospective initiatives (including a portfolio of detailed action plans, risks, funding requirements, and so on) that could double the sales potential of this entire business unit. The analyst proudly hands the study to her boss, who glances up from his computer terminal with a glazed look in his eye, grunts a low-decibel thank you, and motions for her to toss it in his in-box, indicating that he hopes to get to it in a couple of weeks. She turns and walks out of his office discouraged, demotivated, and unappreciated, asking herself if all the twelve-hour days were really worth it. She feels defeated.

Is there a problem here?

In football, celebrating success is a huge deal. In fact, it is such a huge deal that both the NFL and NCAA have had to develop strict guidelines to *restrict* celebrations! If you happen to play in the NFL, 12.3.1 is an important set of numbers that governs your life. No, it's not a snap cadence or a trick play. It's rule 12, section 3, article 1 of the Official NFL Rule Book, which places limits on scoring celebrations. Even if a player scores what may prove to be the game-winning touchdown, he is prohibited from excessive celebration. Prohibited acts include dancing while on the ground and collaborating with team members in group ballets that are premeditated, prolonged, excessive, or choreographed, among others. The list of banned celebratory activities is lengthy and well defined, with the set purpose of limiting or governing the enthusiastic outbursts associated with successful performance.

So let's get this straight. In a football game, players need rules and enforcement to control the celebrations associated with great performance. In the workplace, great performance all too often *takes place in a motivational vacuum,* with little or no response from the beneficiaries and fans of that great performance. Does this make sense?

As noted author Tom Peters said, "Celebrate what you want to see more of." When your team completes a successful TMD, and their efforts lead to performance improvement, it is imperative that you, as their leader, practice the art of celebration. If you want to see more of this kind of behavior, *you must celebrate it.* You have two things to celebrate, and you must be careful to delineate between them:

1. You need to celebrate the scoring drive, the change effort that led to performance improvement. You need to celebrate both the team and individual efforts that took place during this drive.

2. You need to celebrate victory when the improvement efforts stick and the score holds. If you celebrate the improvement effort prematurely, you may be damaging the opportunity for the win.

If you celebrate only the win without celebrating the process and the people who got you that win, you are throwing away a motivational opportunity to give credit to those who deserve it. These performers need to be high-fived and carried off the field. Celebration is important. Numerous studies have revealed the obvious: people perform better when they enjoy what they are doing.[4] Celebrations fuel that enjoyment.

Successful change leaders make celebrating a key component in closing out the game and getting change to stick. Celebrations can include a range of events and practices, from formal awards ceremonies to dinners to meetings with the board of directors and everything in between. Celebration encourages repetition of performance, publicizes achievement, gathers and strengthens organizational support, and injects excitement into the lives of organizational players, who are desperately seeking recognition and a sense of achievement.

Key Question
When your people score and improve performance, how do you help them celebrate?

MOMENTUM BUILDER 5: HAND OUT THE RIGHT TROPHIES

Some of our fondest memories of big wins for our favorite team include pictures and posters of team members holding the game trophy high over their heads in celebration. Celebrating a championship game or a successful change initiative should always include giving out trophies to the winners. Trophies can be any type of reward that reinforces high performance.

Over the last couple of decades, a great deal has been written and discussed about the need to recognize and reward people in the workplace. In fact, employee recognition is frequently mentioned as a key cultural component in the success of some of America's best-run companies.[5] Although winning brings with it the intrinsic satisfaction of a job well done, organizations have a responsibility to recognize and reward the achievements of people involved in successful change efforts.

One of the key findings associated with our study of successful change efforts is that the leaders of these winning initiatives create a change effort that is intrinsically motivating to team members. That is, the team members perform well because they are driven from within to do so. Yet these same leaders also find meaningful and creative ways to reward their people for doing a great job. (If you need help coming up with ideas, Bob Nelson's much acclaimed book *1001 Ways to Reward Employees* is replete with practical and useful ways of rewarding employees and teams who have been "difference makers.")

A key principle to remember when it comes to passing out trophies is to ensure that the trophies and rewards *match up* with the contribution of the players and the size of the win. In one case analysis, we chronicled the activities of a five-person front-office cost reduction team in which members creatively worked extra hours every week for one year and generated more than $200,000 of cost savings for the company. They scored a big win with a great deal of pride, blood, sweat, and tears. Their trophy: a pizza party, a nicely engraved pen-and-pencil set with the company's logo on it, and their picture on the company's website for a couple of weeks. The talk in the locker room after the celebration: NEVER AGAIN!

Team members had gone into this change effort with the intention of helping their organization improve during some rather challenging times. Once they realized what they had accomplished, how big a win they had generated, and all that they had sacrificed, the absence of meaningful recognition for their efforts caused them to conclude that the effort wasn't worthwhile. One team member stated, "We went into this effort expecting little, but we did a whole lot. . . . We won a big one, and the pizza party and pen were almost laughable—no, they *were* laughable. So little for so few for so much . . . I hate it!" This is a classic example of a reward system failing to give meaningful recognition when the team made a real change that worked.

Conversely, at the Kingswood Valley headquarters, the trophies appeared to be commensurate with the achievement: bonuses were liberally distributed and large-scale celebrations took place following the grand openings. But even though the expansion teams had worked long hours to bring their vision to fruition, the profitability and reputation of the company were now at risk. One should question the wisdom of passing out these trophies while the players were still on the field and the contest was in question.

Just as a football team plans for the celebration and the style of trophies and awards they will distribute in anticipation of a win, effective change quarterbacks do the same. We have identified three questions that should be part of your decision making as you plan how to reward team members for their success. Addressing these issues will go a long way in helping you pass out the right trophies to the right players at the right time for the right reasons.

Key Questions

1. Do your rewards appropriately recognize the skill, commitment, and efforts of the team in relation to the impact of the outcome on the organization?
2. Is the timing of your rewards coordinated with the completion of the initiative and closing out the game?
3. Are all the contributors to the success recognized and rewarded appropriately?

CLOSING OUT THE GAME AT KINGSWOOD VALLEY HEALTHCARE

So was Kingswood Valley Healthcare able to get its act together? Was it able to close out the game and celebrate a true victory? Let's take a look:

- Carla took personal command of the corrective initiative, realizing that she had to make durable changes quickly.
- She created a five-person response team of her key managers and demonstrated the same passionate leadership in turning

this situation around that she did in the founding of the enterprise twelve years earlier.

- Carla set the timeline, insisting that changes would be planned and implemented within thirty days.
- She personally visited each of the twelve facilities, informing the staff and the residents that change would be happening—and soon.
- The team quickly concluded that they would be able to cut the turnover at the new facilities through staff training, shift adjustments, and recruiting a few key people in key areas. That same training was seen as a way of reducing the number of complaints and preventing a relapse of the original problem.
- Acknowledging the emotional dimension of reputation building, the response team also created somewhat unique local groups composed of resident volunteers, who were encouraged to meet monthly and provide feedback to local administrators.
- Stepping further out of the box, Carla invited industry analysts to review her game plan, informing the analysts that KVH would set the pace as a model for change within the industry.

Carla knew that repairing a reputation required focus and discipline. She and her team focused their efforts and rebuilt damaged relationships. Within six months, complaint levels fell below those at the big-city sites, and staff turnover dropped to normal levels for the industry. Residents were in high spirits, the staff was encouraged, and the people at KVH headquarters could be seen "high-fiving" once again. This time, however, they had something durable to celebrate, and those individuals who had received their bonuses a bit prematurely nine months earlier now knew they had earned them.

As a final step, Carla enlisted individuals from the locations and the response team and asked them to analyze the change effort and understand why it had worked so well. In doing so, she was able to embed organizational learning throughout KVH to be ready for other opportunities that undoubtedly would be coming. In addition, they would need a good story to tell. Other health care companies were now lining up to benchmark KVH's recovery, because Carla's team was once again smiling on the cover of industry publications. Carla was almost quoting the words of Woody Hayes when she said, "We turned this around and won because of our people!"

CONCLUSION: THE POWER OF CELEBRATION

Please note that we all believe winning is important. It's up to you as the quarterback-leader to ensure that your team keeps moving until success is certain and the win is locked in. Then you, along with everyone else, can enjoy high-fiving and celebrating as a reward for staying the course until the game was complete and the "W" was truly in the win column. As we wrap up this chapter, assess yourself using Exhibit 8.2 and make sure that you are practicing the things necessary to close out your change game and celebrate the big win. In doing so, remember the words of Vince Lombardi when he said, "Some of us will do our jobs well and some will not, but we will be judged by only one thing—THE RESULT!"

Exhibit 8.2: TMD Momentum Builder Checklist

Do you keep track of the scoreboard to make sure that you are truly scoring? ❏

Do you resist the urge to claim victory and celebrate prematurely? ❏

Do you take the appropriate steps to ensure that your improvement efforts hold up? ❏

Do you celebrate both the scoring drive and the win? ❏

Do you hand out the right trophies to the right people at the right time for the right reasons? ❏

CHAPTER NINE

CONDUCT A POSTGAME PRESS CONFERENCE AND ANALYSIS

Review Your Successes So That You and Others Can Do Even Better in the Future

It's a sanity check to stop and look back at what has just taken place.... If you win with your change, you absolutely want to do it again, and if you lose, you want to know what went wrong so you can avoid it.... In my twenty-five years of experience, most companies and leaders for that matter do not take the time for this type of debriefing or introspection.

—SENIOR EXECUTIVE, FORTUNE 500 MANUFACTURING ORGANIZATION

We are taking the same approach, win or lose. We are looking to be consistent, learn from the things we didn't do very well yesterday, and build on the things that we did positive. We'll put that stuff in the bank and move on . . .

—ERIC MANGINI, HEAD COACH, NEW YORK JETS

WINNING IMPERATIVE: *Learn from Each Game*

Once the game is over, take the time to analyze the reasons for victory or defeat, and share the lessons.

"The Comeback Redo": Indianapolis Colts vs.
New York Jets, October 1, 2006

"Well, I told my team in the locker room, we're obviously very fortunate to win. The one good thing I do like about our team is we do know how to win, and we play hard for 60 minutes, and we seem to find ways to win these games."

These calm and calculated words came from Indianapolis Colts head coach Tony Dungy in a postgame press conference after his team had just had a big win. The Colts had just defeated the New York Jets at the Meadowlands 31–28 after coming back from defeat twice late in the fourth quarter. His star quarterback, Peyton Manning, led his team in a hurry-up offense on a twelve-play, 68-yard scoring drive to put his team up 24–21 with 2:34 left. The Colts had taken control of a "seesaw" game that had seen the lead change hands five times. However, on the ensuing kickoff, New York kick returner Justin Miller dashed 103 yards for a touchdown, giving the Jets a 28–24 lead with 2:20 left in the contest. Peyton Manning and his offense had just made their way to the bench when they were called on again to score, as the lead changed hands for the sixth time.

The Colts returned the ensuing kickoff out to their own 32-yard line, and their offense took to the field. The Colts knew exactly what they needed to win the game (a touchdown), how far they had to go to do it (68 yards), and how much time they had to work with (2:20). Despite the fact that this game was early in the season, the team's AFC rivalry with the Jets gave the Colts a true sense of the importance of this win. Peyton Manning demonstrated extreme poise as he led his team in a textbook two-minute drill, with the drive culminating in a 1-yard plunge by the All-Pro quarterback for the winning touchdown. The normally composed QB uncharacteristically spiked the ball into the end zone turf in celebration of the big score. On this drive, Manning completed six of eight passes for 67 yards. Now it was up to the defense to close out the game.

The Jets offense ran five plays in the final seconds of the game in their desperate efforts to score, all of which were stopped by the Colts defense. The most bizarre play of the game was the final play. The Colts defense had to scramble when a pass from the Jets QB Chad Pennington to rookie wide receiver Leon Washington began a series of five laterals, which included two fumbles and subsequent recoveries by Jets players, who advanced the ball to the Indianapolis 27-yard line, where they were finally stopped for a 41-yard gain as time expired.

After the game, Jets first-year head coach Eric Mangini commented on the play of his own team, but was quick to praise his opponent. Reflecting on the loss, Mangini stated, "They are a very good team. It shows us we need to keep working, keep focusing, keep coming back with the same consistent approach, and we'll keep making progress. . . . It's a disappointing loss, but the Colts have won a lot of games over the last six years for a very good reason."

The Colts' postgame press conference brought to light a number of reasons for the team's success. In the Colts' locker room, Manning said, "There never truly was really any panic . . . we didn't have time. . . . It can be deflating to see, you know, Miller run that kick-off [back], but only if that's the last play of the game. . . . You know you have time to go back out there and do something about it. . . . The offense said . . . let's go down and get it in the end zone." Manning went on to highlight the play of his offensive line, how their running game opened up their passing game during the final two drives, the great catches his receivers made, and how patient his team was in their two-minute drill.

During the rest of the press conference, Tony Dungy praised his quarterback, but he was also careful to give credit to the entire team. He also noted that the team practices for these game situations every Thursday. He went on to say that his team ran the ball well and that better tackling was needed, and he also reiterated the themes from his opening quotation (cited above) and seemed politely proud that his team played hard and found ways to win.

Other members of the team answered a wide variety of questions from the media. Locker room security was tight, as "unauthorized personnel" pressed to gain access to players and coaches alike. Players offered their unique insight and reflection on every facet of the victory over the Jets, ranging from big catches to key plays to the Colts' stopping the bizarre final play of the game. To summarize the game, Colts linebacker Gary Brackett said, "I think it's a never-give-up type of team. I thought that to the very end of the game, we had a chance to win, and that's what we did."

Segments of the postgame press conference made it to the national and local sports newscasts that evening, and segments also showed up on the sports pages of local and national newspapers, which caused Colts fans to feel the warm glow of victory and Jets fans to think, "Please, not again." And while all this was going on in the public eye, it was the postgame analysis taking place behind the scenes at the Colts complex that would help the team continue its winning ways—but more on that later in this chapter.

TRI-X CORPORATION'S BIG WIN

Now let's look at a business example of how a "postgame analysis" and "press conference" might help an organization. BJ Titman had been hired twenty-two months ago as the vice president of sales for Tri-X Corporation, a very successful regional office equipment distributor that served as a broker for all the major office equipment manufacturers. Tri-X had prided itself on a seasoned sales force that was quick to help their customers replace and service old, ineffective equipment in the blink of an eye. Three years ago, though, the sales at Tri-X had been flatlining, and eventually BJ had been brought on board to turn things around.

BACKGROUND: A NEW VP DOES AN "AMAZING JOB" TO REVIVE SALES

BJ had arrived at Tri-X with a reputation for being a principled, progressive, and high-energy leader who "loved to sell," but he was equally passionate about developing people and processes. Now BJ and his sales group had just completed another excellent quarter, and he was sitting at his desk reading a letter that the president had just written to him. The letter congratulated him and the sales group on all that they had achieved during the past year.

The last part of the letter read,

BJ, I can speak for everyone on the Board in telling you that you have done an amazing job with our sales group since your arrival. Even with the market being more competitive today than ever, our sales have grown, our sales people are developing in ways that I had not considered, and our customers are happier than ever.

I would like to give you an opportunity to come to the next Board of Directors meeting and walk us through how you pulled this off. I've filled Board members in on some of the reasons for your success from my vantage point, but they want to hear it directly from the race horse's mouth. You will have their undivided attention, as several Board members have stated that they would love to see this type of transformation take place in their own organizations. I strongly believe that everybody in our organization knows that our sales have improved significantly in the past year, but they may not know how and why all of this has taken place. Maybe this meeting should be used to create an opportunity to share some of that experience with the rest of our people as well. Please think about that as well.

BJ was simultaneously flattered and humbled by the invitation. He opened his top desk drawer and pulled out the sales improvement game plan they had implemented sixteen months ago. He opened the comb-bound document, took out a pen, and began writing on the inside front cover. BJ created two headings, "Why we won" and "What we learned," and began jotting down his thoughts.

REVIEWING "WHY WE WON"

1. *Everyone was convinced that we had to change* and that we could no longer continue with our traditional approach to sales.
2. *We defined winning as increasing overall sales* by 5 percent per quarter over the next six quarters, which benefited the company, *but also as increasing the financial benefits* to individual salespeople so that they could win too. We cascaded this overall definition down to specific definitions for each of the five sales group leaders and then to each salesperson.
3. *We got the right people involved* to lead the change and created a lot of enthusiasm around the effort. Our sales leaders were responsible for moving our improvement plan forward and for making adjustments and removing performance barriers quickly to reduce "drag" and resistance to the effort.

4. *We made intense communication a key priority* for our leadership team, so that everyone knew what was going on and what was coming at all times.

5. *We tried to move quickly and not waste time* at every phase of the effort. We developed and implemented guidelines for meetings, paperwork, and e-mails to emphasize the importance of not wasting time.

6. *We came up with a new sales model and support system* with the input of a lot of our most talented people that would help differentiate us from our competitors and help our salespeople better meet our customers' needs.

7. *We created peer mentors* for our sales teams that were responsible for helping each other enact the right behaviors, solve problems (both ours and the customers'), and control each person's time usage.

8. *We reframed everyone's job* as a salesperson and *retrained everyone* to increase their talents and confidence so that they could provide not just products, but rather business solutions to our customers' growing needs.

9. *We measured performance on an ongoing basis* and gave everyone meaningful feedback and coaching and made sure that our incentive system supported the new Tri-X sales model (and especially during the ramp-up).

10. *We shared performance data* with both sales teams and individuals on an ongoing basis so that everyone knew the real score.

11. *We tried hard to celebrate success* using a wide variety of methods that would be meaningful to the various personalities in our sales group.

12. *We made sure that if we said we were going to do something, we did it.* So we executed each phase of this plan with energy.

REVIEWING "WHAT WE LEARNED"

1. *I wasted time trying to build consensus* around the fact that we needed to change when everyone already knew that we had to change. I could have defined what we were trying to accomplish without a lot of meetings, discussion, and debate in the early stages of this effort, and we could have jump-started our progress.

2. We started out with the assumption that the more people involved in the process, the better. I learned, though, that

I needed to be more careful in how many people were involved at different stages of our change effort. Although we tried not to, we wasted some people's time when they could have been selling or been involved with more "value-added" activity. In retrospect, we had busy people sitting through too many meetings with too many people, with too few tangible outcomes.

3. *We could have sped up our needs assessment* if we had used web-based questionnaires instead of pencil and paper, which would have given us information much more quickly, which we needed for our redesign.

4. Our training was pretty effective overall, but *we should have trained in teams,* and *we should have spread the training days out* instead of "cramming and jamming"—which helped us get the training done quickly but had a somewhat detrimental effect on real learning.

5. There was no substitute for each and every salesperson to know not just what to do but how to do it with great confidence. A lot of our salespeople had to either build on their old habits or break their old habits altogether. *I needed to do a better job of reinforcing the right behaviors and creating more accountability* to encourage people to do what we all agreed were the keys to a more successful approach to sales.

6. Without my five sales group leaders, this change would have been impossible because they were the ones who made things happen with their people. *I should have spent more time with them as a group and one on one.* I learned a great deal about them individually, and I watched them develop through this process. They deserve special recognition from the board, as each one of them used their talents at different stages of the process to make this effort a success:

- Dave Carpenter—a great analytical thinker
- Mike McCartney—a terrific motivator
- Vicky Black—the strategic thinker
- Tom Gutteridge—a leader of leaders
- Don Warner—a great developer of people

After forty-five minutes of thinking and taking notes, BJ closed the notebook and knew that he had clarified the things that he wanted to share with his boss and the board. He felt good not only about the recognition that he was experiencing but also about being able to help his team feel good about what they were doing and about having an opportunity to help others learn from his team's effort. He also realized that

- He would have to continue to do the right things if success was to continue.
- He had learned a great many things through this effort that would serve him well on "the back nine" of his career, if he hung onto them.

The Importance of the Postgame Press Conference and Analysis

BJ and the Colts' Coach Dungy both have something in common: they are attempting to learn from their recent challenging experience. The concept of the learning organization is by no means new to business leaders. Peter Senge's 1990 best-selling book *The Fifth Discipline* made an extremely strong case for the importance of organizations' learning from their previous experiences, good, bad, and ugly.[1] Although there are many definitions for the term *learning organization,* here is one that we have adapted that works for us: "The organizational practice of continually generating, sharing, and leveraging individual and collective learning experiences to improve organizational performance."[2] And although this definition may sound somewhat arcane and academic, the lesson here is a simple one:

> **Key Lesson**
> Leaders and their organizations must not only constantly *do* but also make a practice of taking time to *reflect* and to *learn* from what they have done. This important and often overlooked practice can help fuel future success both for individual leaders and for the organizations they lead.

Real change leaders know that once this reflection and analysis have taken place and lessons have been drawn out from their experience, it is incumbent on them to share those lessons in a fashion that benefits other people in their organization. The military is known for its great proficiency, discipline, and thoroughness in conducting "post-action reports" and "mission debriefs" so that leaders and their people are forced to reflect on, document, and *share* what they learned from a given experience, whether real or simulated.[3] Why? Because sharing these lessons can save missions and lives, and the cost of not sharing these lessons can be very high. This level of seriousness makes post-action analysis a top priority when the stakes are high.

But if you as a business leader are not careful, the learning opportunities that accompany attempts at rapid organizational improvement can easily be lost in the heat of battle. In our research, we have observed a number of tendencies that can short-circuit true organizational learning:

1. When change initiatives are successful, there is very little analysis of the cause. The win is "chalked up," and the team moves on, without fully understanding the root causes of success and, equally important, what could have been done to accelerate or improve the effort further.

2. When change initiatives are unsuccessful, people are quick to point out that the effort was not a complete failure because of what was learned. Yet all too often there is virtually no serious analysis to understand *why* the effort failed; thus learning from the experience is neutralized if not nonexistent.

3. Whether a change effort is successful or unsuccessful, there can be an organizational tendency to allow politics to enter the equation. The influence of political factors can easily cause the success of an effort to be overstated and dramatized and the failings of an effort to be swept under the rug and minimized. Both of these practices create credibility problems for the leader(s) in charge of the change.

In football, the purpose of postgame press conferences is to provide members of the media an opportunity to ask questions about the outcome of the game; the answers will then become part of the media's story. When members of the Indianapolis Colts were engaged in the obligatory postgame press conference after their big win over the Jets, they shared the obvious facts that had led to their victory. But although the Colts gave members of the media quotable quotes and sound bites, overall these discussions dwelt on the obvious and superficial facts surrounding the win.

The Colts made it clear that they had won because of an effective two-minute drill (which we already knew) and that there had been some "big plays" (which we also already knew). But in terms of discussing the finer points and real factors that led to victory, very little was actually said or shared. In press conferences, coaches and players alike will say things like, "Our defense played big today," "Our QB was in the zone," "Big Nick's interception turned the game around," and "Our running backs could not be stopped." These statements are obvious, but they do not dig very deep in explaining what actually caused the team to perform so well. It is rare and highly unlikely to hear players and coaches discuss the deep-rooted factors that caused the game's actual outcome. This is a critical point to remember: in football, the *postgame press conference precedes the actual analysis of the game (which is where real, in-depth analysis and learning take place)*.

Serious discussions about the real causes of a team's success are frequently reserved for more private venues where a candid discussion of these issues can take place without revealing information that will aid the team's competitors. It is important to note that while all this public activity is going on in a press conference in front of the cameras and microphones, assistant coaches and analysts are working diligently behind the scenes, breaking down game film and game statistics in great detail. They work late into the night after the game and early into the next morning to see what can be learned from the game and applied to their future efforts. This information will then be shared with their teams in great detail to expand the learning process from the experience (win, lose, or draw).

BJ Titman of Tri-X was really asked to conduct a postgame press conference with his president and the board of directors. He was also asked to consider sharing that same information with the rest of the organization. But BJ had it in the right order. Before going in and stating the obvious keys to the sales victory, he took the time to conduct his own in-depth postgame analysis, and in doing so, he learned some things about his change initiative that he would not otherwise have realized. Taking the time to reflect was critically important to his being able to learn from the successful change he and his people had just experienced. In doing so, he also put himself in a position to share those lessons with others. It is interesting to note that he identified not only the things that could have *improved* the overall effectiveness of the effort but also a number of factors that could have *accelerated* the change process. He was doing his part in helping Tri-X become a learning organization, and he continues his great work today.

The Importance of Assessing Both Success and Speed

From our experience in working with hundreds of organizations that were seeking improvement, we have learned, as BJ Titman did, that there are two critical, bottom-line outcomes that must be appraised in a postgame analysis—success and speed:

- A *successful change* is one that is effective in producing a desired, sustainable outcome; in other words, it is one that achieves the objectives that you have defined as winning (per our discussion in Chapter Three).
- The *speed of the change* relates to whether the actual change is carried out in a timely fashion to help create or maintain competitiveness.

Real Change leaders, regardless of their position in an organization, seek to learn from whatever change they are leading; assessing both effectiveness and the speed of the effort are part and parcel of that analysis. Exhibit 9.1 is a matrix that identifies the potential outcomes of the different combinations of these two critical factors.

As shown in Exhibit 9.1, there are four possible scenarios:

1. A worst-case scenario for any improvement initiative is a slow and drawn-out change initiative that is ineffective in producing real improvement. In this situation, change efforts

Exhibit 9.1: Postgame Outcome Matrix

Effective	Questionable impact on competitiveness, as change may arrive too late (Win-loss?)	Rapidly improved competitiveness and an energized enterprise (Win)
SUCCESS		
Ineffective	Loss of competitiveness, wasting valuable energy and resources (Big loss)	Rapidly damaged competitiveness (Loss)
	Slow	**SPEED** *Fast*

consume valuable resources and energy with no positive outcomes, resulting in a net loss of competitiveness for the business unit and the organization. We have all seen these during our careers, and they are painful to watch—and even more painful to be a part of.

2. Change that happens fast but is ineffective represents a loss or defeat to the organization as well. In this scenario, resources have been expended with no tangible positive outcome(s). If there is any good news in this scenario, it's that the failure took place quickly so that losses could be minimized and action could be taken to right the wrong. In the end, however, the effort was not a success—and your team lost.

3. Some change initiatives are successful in producing desired results, but are too slow in doing so. In today's global marketplace, slowness spells big trouble. The effectiveness of the change or improvement is called into question because of the amount of time it took for the change to take place. Is the change a winner in helping improve the organization's competitiveness? Is it a loser? The issue of time will determine that answer.

4. In an optimal change scenario, success is achieved quickly, both improving an organization's competitiveness and conserving scarce organizational resources. This outcome is a win for the organization; it improves competitiveness and has an energizing effect on the people engaged in the process. This type of outcome makes people feel like winners. Our

research strongly suggests that if you as a leader practice the TMD principles discussed in this book, you greatly increase the likelihood of a more successful and rapid change than might otherwise be the case.

TAKE THE TIME TO REFLECT AND LEARN

If you are willing to take the time and effort to conduct a post game analysis of your change effort, you are a long way toward learning from the experience. Once learning has taken place, you can share these lessons with other members of the organization to help them in their efforts at improvement. Although the subject of learning can be very complex, we believe that the best lessons in both life and work are the simple ones that are drawn from our experience and the experience of others. If you as a leader are prepared to "dig deep" and better understand what you and your team can learn from a change, we suggest that you follow the three momentum builders in this chapter to accelerate learning for yourself and for your organization.

MOMENTUM BUILDER 1: KNOW WHAT WENT RIGHT AND WHAT COULD HAVE BEEN DONE BETTER

As stated earlier, postgame press conferences discuss the more obvious highlights of the game because detailed analysis has not yet been conducted. Teams know that they won or that they lost, but the game films and statistics will reveal an abundance of information that can be put to use to improve future performance. Football has a lot to teach business about postgame analysis. Let's start by considering what goes into such an analysis in football. On average, a college or professional football game will have at least 150 plays, which last around six seconds per play, for a total of about fifteen minutes of actual playing time. This is for a game that lasts nearly four hours from start to finish, excluding drive time and tailgating activities.

In their postgame analysis, coaches and players will review each and every one of those plays at least five times and will grade each play for its effectiveness. After that initial assessment, each player's performance on each play is also assessed and graded.

After postgame film study, the players and teams will typically review the statistics from the game to determine the level of offensive and defensive productivity. If you take into account the total amount of time that a ten-person coaching staff, a ten-person support staff, and an entire football team (eighty-five scholarship players for a college team and fifty-three roster spots for a professional team) put into analysis, you will find that teams can easily spend more than *six hundred man-hours critiquing only fifteen minutes of total playing time from the previous game!*

Why do they spend so much time trying to learn from past performance? The answer is easy. Teams and individuals hate to lose, and understanding past performance is the key to improving future performance, whether you are on the football field or the organizational playing field. Yet in today's workplace, it is easy to find business leaders who don't spend *fifteen minutes of postgame analysis on a change initiative that took six hundred hours of performance!* As we said, football has something to teach business: maybe we have our priorities wrong when it comes to learning from our past performance in the game of change.

We would like to challenge you to improve your proficiency at postgame analysis. Exhibit 9.2 is a postgame analysis matrix that we

---

Exhibit 9.2: Postgame Analysis Matrix

Factors Affecting Outcome	What Went Right	What Could Have Been Done Better	Lessons Learned
Yourself			
Team			
Individual Players			
Organization			

What will you do with this information to help you and your team learn from this experience and help prepare you for your next TMD?

have developed to help business leaders assess the factors that have had a significant impact on both the speed and success of their change efforts. You can use this matrix as a tool for conducting *your* postgame analyses—assessing what went right, what could have been done better, and what lessons were learned during a change process, from start to finish.

Start by *grading yourself* on your personal effectiveness in quarterbacking your team through the various plays in your improvement process. Have you been effective in executing each of the plays in your improvement drive? Remember: learning from your mistakes as leader, or failing to, is tied directly to your long-term career success and survival.[4]

Second, *grade the overall performance of your team* in planning and executing the change from start to finish. It is imperative to assess how well your team played as a team and what could have been done to improve team performance on each play of your improvement drive.

Third, *grade the performance of individual players* on your team for their effectiveness throughout the change process and how well they performed their individual assignments. Post-change analyses frequently reveal that individuals made big plays that led to success and that they at times did not perform their assignments as needed (the business equivalents of fumbles, interceptions, missed blocks, and so on), which caused the improvement effort to bog down or even fail. It is important to note that in many organizations, individuals assigned to improvement teams or change initiatives operate in both obscurity and anonymity (despite the importance of their assignment). Remember that people perform differently when they know they will receive an individual grade for their performance, so make sure that individual assessment is part of your postgame analysis.[5]

Finally, it is important to *evaluate your organization* and how it supported or hindered your efforts at improvement. Much can be learned about your own enterprise and fellow leaders in this critique, as some franchises help accelerate change and others create inordinate drag on your efforts.

This assessment should ensure that each of these key performance pieces is graded across all the plays that you used in conducting your TMD improvement initiative. Your postgame analysis can become a valuable learning tool when you ask each member of your team to complete the same matrix, drawing on his or her experience in the same change initiative. Time and time again, we have seen this type of postgame analysis help solidify team performance and help create meaningful discussions and lessons that can be applied to future change initiatives so that they yield outstanding outcomes. Leaders frequently tell us that they do not have the time for such activities, yet we argue that much can be accomplished in a quick postgame analysis: in addition to helping everyone learn and improve, such analysis helps close out the game and reinforce the changes you and your team have made.

In the words of one manager, "While reflection and introspection take time, and we don't always like what we see, they almost always cause people to learn, which can help us all improve." You can use this same information in developing your scouting report to help you prepare when you are called on to conduct your next change initiative. In summary, when completing a change initiative, always ask the following question—and be brave enough to seek out the real answer.

> **Key Question**
> What have you and your organization really learned through this experience?

MOMENTUM BUILDER 2: ADOPT A PRESS CONFERENCE MENTALITY, AND SHARE YOUR GAME FILMS

The purpose of the Colts' postgame press conference was to share what just took place on the football field with parties interested in their win over the Jets. As stated earlier, the statements made in these postgame press conferences typically do not include a lot of detail, but rather represent a summary of the key points of the game from the people who made it happen. To support this contention, we suggest you go back and read the comments made by the coaches Dungy and Mangini and the players. The parties truly interested in their press conference included their fans, owners, analysts, pundits, networks, sports writers, and even competitors, among others. It is interesting to note that at both the professional and college levels, Monday press conferences are now becoming part of the postgame landscape as well. Coaches and players are asked to meet with the press yet again to provide further reflection and commentary on the game after calming down and objectively looking at game films and statistics in detail.

Why are football teams being asked to do more postgame press conferences? What is it about a press conference that makes people so eager to be a part of them that guards have to be posted at the locker room or team meeting room door to keep unauthorized people out? *It's because people want to know what is really going on. People like to be "in the know."* They like to feel that they have the inside track or scoop on any new information that other people do not have. This is especially true when they have a vested interest. Thus interested parties frequently clamor to be a part of the press conference experience, and this is especially true when things go exceedingly well, as when there is a big win (or a blowout), and in organizations when there are lots of changes afoot.

In organizational life, press conferences are nothing new. Organizations use press conferences to announce expansions, significant earnings, major changes in leadership, new breakthrough products, mergers, acquisitions, and public relations gambits. Yet when an individual manager pulls off a big win with a significant organizational change that helps the enterprise make or save money, increases customer loyalty and satisfaction, or greatly improves workforce productivity and satisfaction, there is typically no press conference, announcement, or platform to share this good news with interested parties. If you go back and look at our definition of organizational learning earlier in this chapter, you'll see just how important it is for leaders to let other leaders know what they are working on and the outcomes of their efforts. To "generate, share, and leverage learning" requires managers who are committed to communicating the change lessons they have learned. This simple point is true regardless of a leader's position or level in his or her organization.

Our experience has shown that organizations and leaders need to adopt a press conference mentality: they need to share what changes people are working on, the processes they are using to get there, and the lessons they learned along the way. This practice can be informal or formalized, but it should address one straightforward question.

> **Key Question**
> How do you go about sharing what you've learned from what you are doing to help others in your organization?

Case Example: How One Company's Leaders Did Their Press Conference Right

One of our clients recently conducted a highly effective change in its operations, which resulted in significant cost savings through the use of empowered work teams. After the leaders of this change found that the results were sustainable and even getting better, they called a "press conference" to share what they had learned with other interested parties in their organization.

They started with a congratulatory meeting and information-sharing session with all the team members at their facility, to walk through what had just taken place and what had been learned. This meeting included their front-office personnel, who were not actually part of the operational change but were deemed "part of the team." (A large facility-wide celebration followed closely behind.) This meeting created a lot of buzz and excitement at their facility. Improvement team leaders then invited all the senior and midlevel managers in their organization to attend a simultaneous podcast during which leaders and team members discussed the changes that they had just planned and executed and the benefits that they were experiencing. There was not a great deal of hoopla, fanfare, or political posturing in the podcast, but rather a genuine attempt to share some of their best practices with other leaders in the organization, all of whom were desperately seeking improvement.

Some of the leaders who sat in on the podcast did nothing with what they heard, whereas others were stimulated and decided to learn more. Still others came to the facility for a visit to find out in more detail how to make similar changes in their own operations. Had this facility not adopted a press conference mind-set, several of these leaders at other facilities would not have implemented these practices—with the same strong results—because they never would have known about them.

In the past, this organization would have just mandated this improvement practice, but they learned that the initiative for real change had to come from the facility leaders. The podcast press conference and follow-up story posted on the company's website stimulated even more buzz. The press conference stirred most managers' interest in the improvement initiative and made them *want* to learn more. And the press conference approach caught on across the organization in various formats for sharing improvement initiatives, best practices, and organizational wins. Research has shown that creating this type of sharing is the real key to long-term organizational success and survival.[6]

How to Conduct Effective "Press Conferences" to Help Others Benefit from Your Successes

The case study just described is a perfect example of an organization really becoming a learning organization. Here are three things you should consider in developing your own postgame press conference mentality.

1. When you've closed out the game on a change effort and conducted your postgame analysis, *hold a press conference for your team* to share with them what you learned in your analysis. This allows them an opportunity for additional learning, and it can help strengthen your credibility, because your team will know that you truly know and understand what *really* went on during the change process.

2. *Hold a press conference for other people in your organization* to let them know the basics and the outcome of the change effort you have just completed. This allows other people working on parallel or similar initiatives to know that they are not alone, and can help prevent reinventing the wheel. They will find it comforting to know that they may be able to learn from the experience of other people in their own organization. Press conferences can be either formal or informal, written or oral, but the important point is to *hold them*—don't allow your change efforts to take place in a vacuum.

3. *Provide interested parties in your organization with access to information.* Press conferences inevitably stimulate people to seek more detailed information about the nature of your change efforts. Although you may not have game films that other people can watch to see how you made your changes and the opponents whom you faced, you should be willing to share your change game plan and materials with other people in your organization who are serious about getting better. These details and support materials can both energize and accelerate other people's efforts at improvement and can stimulate serious learning in your organization.

These three practices may seem simple, but they work—and they don't require a formal organizational edict or the expenditure of significant resources (including excessive time) to be implemented. We have seen this practice work with great consistency when taken seriously by leaders at all levels of an enterprise. So when you have completed your postgame analysis and summarized the lessons you learned in the process, ask yourself the following questions:

Key Questions
1. Are you willing to share the change lessons that you've learned?
2. With whom will you share them, and how will you do it?

High-performance leaders hold press conferences with great proficiency and reap the benefits for their organization and themselves.[7] And although there are lots of reasons for not sharing this type of information—such as ignorance, poor working relationships, resource constraints, internal competition, and personal agendas—all of them are just the sort of thing that your competitors truly enjoy.[8]

Please note: organizations must weigh the need to share organizational improvement success stories against the possible consequences of the organization's making these activities mandatory and highly formalized, which opens the door to activity for the sake of activity and to political posturing.

MOMENTUM BUILDER 3: AVOID POLITICAL PRESS CONFERENCES

We would be naive to think or insinuate that politics do not play a major role in the change process in most organizations. The word *politics* has a wide variety of definitions, but this one works for us: "any action designed to protect or enhance a person's power or influence in an organization."[9]

Politics can determine which changes are priorities, who is in charge of what change, who is on what team, and what change initiatives get resourced. And political activity is frequently used to gain support for making the right changes in an organization's mission and agenda.

Politics, however, can also create real problems if you are not careful when you share postgame information with other organizational leaders and members. When you have effectively quarterbacked your team to a successful improvement and wish to share with others what you learned from your postgame analysis, you may be sorely tempted to use this opportunity to enhance or protect your organizational power or influence in an unproductive fashion. Don't give in!

Our experience has taught us that "political press conferences" must be avoided at all costs. By political press conferences, we mean information sharing with other interested parties that is done with the intent of grandstanding, career posturing, and self-promotion, rather than for the purposes of bettering the organization. In reality, most political press conferences are simply opportunities to put a spin on whatever has just taken place. That approach may have a purpose in politics, but it damages true organizational learning, among other things. We have a strong feeling that you have seen this sort of behavior before at least once or twice in your career. How does it make you feel when you witness grandstanding or headline stealing on the part of a leader? If you were to succumb to this sort of behavior, how do you think others would react?

Politics rears its ugly head in several ways surrounding the completion of change initiatives. More often than we want to think about, we have witnessed moderately successful change efforts presented in an overblown fashion by leaders seeking to expand their reputation and position in their organizations, with problematic results. Overstating the success of a change initiative distorts the truth and creates unrealistic expectations for those who follow. In addition, for the people who were actually part of the change process (and who had to help pay the price for the improvement), such overblown statements damage the credibility of the leader.

Another political maneuver that leaders attempt is to take a less than effective change effort, or a defeat for that matter, and spin it into a victory. Again, the leader's credibility in the eyes of the people involved is called into question. Making excuses, blaming others, and changing the facts are all "credibility busters" for a change leader. People know when a change or improvement is real, and leaders undermine their own efforts and shoot themselves in the foot when they attempt to overstate success.

Finally, political press conferences can be unwise efforts on the part of leaders to take too much of the credit for success. When it is time for your press conference, make sure that you give credit for the success to *everyone on the team* and that you as leader do not use it as a vehicle purely for self-promotion. In the long run, you are damaging your long-term effectiveness as a leader and making the next change effort tougher on everyone. Conversely, when you use a press conference to praise your team members and give them the kudos they deserve, you actually enhance your own stature.

Dilbert author Scott Adams provides daily examples in his cartoons of leaders who talk about change but who don't deal in reality and who take credit for everything good while jettisoning any and all failures. His cartoons drip with cynicism, pessimism, sarcasm, and ill-will, but, sad to say, they are frequently right on the money. Do not allow yourself to become a living Dilbert cartoon character.

Instead, work hard to be like Coach Dungy. Be humble, be thoughtful in what you say, and allow your players to have access to the "press" and have the freedom to share their own opinions on the game. Give credit where credit is due, and make sure that your team members are properly celebrated for their success. Ask yourself this next important question. Your response will tell you a lot about yourself as a leader.

Key Question
Are you willing to accurately share what was accomplished and what you and your team have learned through the change process, and allow others to take credit for their efforts?

CONCLUSION: LEARNING FROM YOUR TMD

Look at what Tony Dungy said about his team after a big win: "The one good thing I do like about our team is we do know how to win, and we play hard for 60 minutes, and we seem to find ways to win these games." He learned this about his team during the game, he shared these views in the postgame press conference with all of those in attendance, and, most important, he reiterated these sentiments after the detailed postgame analysis at his press conference the day after the game. During the actual postgame analysis, he and his staff learned how to get better by closely analyzing the game films and statistics and reviewing in detail what was learned about their performance with the entire team. These are football lessons that we can take right to work, with very positive outcomes, if we are serious about being the best we can be at the game of change.

BJ Titman conducted this same analysis in his press conference with the Tri X board of directors, it was very well received, as board members were looking for ways to improve their own organizations. And BJ gave them some very specific things that they could use to do so. He did the same with all of the senior and midlevel managers at Tri-X, touching off at least four successful large-scale organizational improvements that took place in the next six months. BJ, a real leader, began a positive chain reaction with wide-reaching effects, because he was encouraged by a progressive president to share what he had learned in a meaningful, nonpolitical fashion. BJ reminds us that the best lessons in life are indeed the simple ones. He was, in Coach Dungy's words, simply helping his team find ways to win these games.

In closing, as you assess yourself, your team, and your franchise to ensure that winning becomes a consistent attribute, you may wish to ask yourself the questions posed in Exhibit 9.3. We suggest that you adopt BJ's approach and ask yourself the questions in the following checklist.

Exhibit 9.3: TMD Momentum Builder Checklist

Do you know what went really well with this change initiative?　❑

Do you know what could have gone better?　❑

Can you summarize the things that went right and wrong in a list of lessons learned?　❑

Have you held a congratulatory meeting or appropriate celebration?　❑

Have you shared your appropriate lessons to ensure organizational learning?　❑

WINNING IS BETTER THAN LOSING

The difference between a successful person and others is not a lack of strength, not a lack of knowledge, but rather a lack of will.
—VINCE LOMBARDI

Losers live in the past. Winners learn from the past and enjoy working in the present toward the future.
—DENIS WAITLEY, MOTIVATIONAL SPEAKER AND AUTHOR

WINNING AT LEADING CHANGE

Let's be honest: nobody likes to lose. It doesn't matter whether we're talking sports or business. In our society, we place a tremendous amount of emphasis and energy on winning sports contests, and teams will do everything in their power to avoid losing. In the workplace, we like to win as well, but do we always do what is necessary to win? Do we do everything in our power to avoid losing? In this book, we have discussed using a TMD mind-set in approaching and leading organizational change and improvement. We have emphasized the importance of TMD thinking in making change happen faster by employing the same fundamentals that drive success on the football field. We have asked you to carefully review eight key factors that play a critical role in creating successful and rapid change.

In sports, it's easy to measure winning, but in the workplace, winning means different things to different people. Where change and improvement are concerned, however, winning is the successful execution of a plan that improves performance and produces desired results. In the change game, losing is attempting change and not creating real change. To close this book, we would like to share two examples of how the ability of leaders to lead change had a profound impact on their careers and the lives of people around them.

THE AGONY OF DEFEAT: A LEADER WHO FAILED AND WAS FIRED

We thought that it would be instructive to share with you an e-mail we received from a former MBA student; it provides great insight into the challenge of leading change, getting results, and keeping one's career on track. This business leader was thirty-nine years old and had thus far been extremely successful. He was hard working, motivated, and focused, and he had good people skills. His very progressive leadership style had served him well—up to his most recent promotion. He was accustomed to winning and experiencing all the trappings that accompanied operating in the stratosphere. He had received numerous promotions, hefty pay raises and bonuses, and two awards from his employers for outstanding performance, and he commanded the respect of his coworkers and peers.

With this background in mind, please read the following excerpts from the e-mail he sent the day after he was terminated from a Fortune 500 enterprise. As you read, look carefully at his words and try to sense what he was feeling and why he was feeling that way.

> I simply did not see being let go coming, and it was like being punched in the stomach. . . . I have been extremely busy at work for the past 18 months since starting this new VP position in charge of the improvement process in our division. I mistakenly thought that my boss and I were on the same page in terms of both what I was doing and how well I was doing it. I was wrong, dead wrong! As you know, we started a new performance improvement integration process with high hopes as a division. It was a major activity, aimed at improving performance across all of our various facilities. It sounded like a worthwhile initiative, and I was

very excited to take the lead. But in retrospect, we never really articulated what we were trying to accomplish in realistic, measurable terms, and we struggled with buy-in from the start.

We quickly created an improvement process and tools that everybody should have been able to use in their operations. It all looked good on paper, but when it was time to make real changes, we had no real power to make things happen. . . . There was no sense of urgency or commitment, and leadership in the field was nonexistent. My General Manager had made improvement commitments with our CEO that could not be kept. He oversold what we were able to actually deliver. People all had their own ideas about what we were ultimately trying to accomplish, but the leadership above us let us hang out to twist in the wind. After 18 months, the CEO looked at the costs and the limited return and said 'enough,' and that was it.

A couple of people were reassigned, but I along with one other guy was turned out on the street. I was the highest-ranked person to lose his job. I remember us talking about the importance of never losing sight of what results the organization needs from you, making sure that you and your boss are on the same page, and doing the things that lead to results with diligence. Well, I really dropped the ball on this one, and I am very angry at myself, my boss, and the CEO as well. If I had done a better job of forcing the issue of what we were trying to accomplish, developing a more realistic game plan for our field leaders, and measuring actual changes more effectively, things might have turned out differently.

My biggest mistake is that I failed to practice what I knew to be true. I was in charge of change, and the change never happened. I really screwed up, and I know it, and I have no one to blame for this mess but myself. This is the sickest feeling that I have ever had, and it has been both humiliating and humbling. My faith has helped me greatly, and I truly appreciate the love and support of my wife, but I feel like I have really let her down too. . . . But know this, I will learn from this defeat and I will be back.

Over the course of the next several months, we worked closely with this business leader as friends, confidants, and mentors to help him learn from this experience and restart his career. He was an extremely apt and willing participant in getting his career back on track.

What did you learn by reading this excerpt from this very personal e-mail? A careful analysis of the content will reveal that

- This professional was excited to take on the challenge of being a change leader.
- He started out with great enthusiasm and passion.
- He thought that he and his boss were on the same page.
- In theory, everything he was working on made sense and sounded good.
- In practice, there was no real change and thus no real improvement, which is why he lost his job.
- Losing his job made him feel like he had been punched in the stomach and triggered feelings of anger, frustration, stupidity, and disbelief.
- What made this situation even more painful for this leader was that he knew what he needed to do to prevent this situation from occurring, yet he did not do it.

Socrates once said, "The ongoing challenges of life mandate applying all our wisdom to daily situations lest we fall prey to our own folly." This business leader faced the ongoing challenges of change, yet he failed to apply the wisdom he had already accumulated from earlier in his career. In doing so, he fell prey to his own foolishness. We say this not to be judgmental but rather to speak to the importance of applying the principles that we know will work. Although Socrates' words are very eloquent, the great American actor John Wayne shared exactly the same sentiment in terms we might remember more easily when he said, "Life is tough, but it's tougher if you're stupid."

A person is ignorant when he or she does not know what to do. A person is stupid when he or she *knows* what to do, but for whatever reason just does not do it. In our research on organizational change, we are regularly saddened that we frequently see smart, hard-working, principled business leaders making stupid decisions, for a wide variety of reasons, with similar negative outcomes. Doing the right thing is always important, but not making stupid mistakes might be equally important. When leaders responsible for change know what to do but do not do it, bad things happen.

This leader suffered the agony of defeat because in his role as a leader of change he did not apply many of the principles we have discussed in this book. But remember, in retrospect he knew what he should have done.

THE THRILL OF VICTORY: A LEADER WHO SUCCEEDED THROUGHOUT A LONG CAREER

Whereas failing to lead change effectively can be a career buster, mastering the ability to create ongoing and rapid organizational improvement can be a terrific career enhancer. We recently had the privilege of attending the retirement party of an executive who was being honored at the completion of a thirty-five-year career with a Fortune 1000 pharmaceutical company. This executive had been part of the growth of this organization from a small entrepreneurial research enterprise to a well-established niche player in the ultracompetitive pharmaceutical industry. At the high point of the festivities, this executive received numerous accolades, but the CEO of the organization concluded his remarks about this individual with the following statement: "Ted is a man who has been a difference maker in our organization because he continually developed himself, he led his people through good times and bad, and he was willing to take on the numerous challenges necessary to make good things happen. . . . He has been and always will be a difference maker to all of us who had the privilege of working with him."

Ted then made his way to the podium amid boisterous applause, back-slapping, and cheers. He gave a brief, moving, and heartfelt review of his career, his life, and his family. There wasn't a dry eye in the banquet hall. During Ted's remarks, he made a very poignant statement that is a good lesson for all of us:

> As we all know, our organization has done well over the years. And to a great extent, this is because all of us have done our part to help this great company keep up with all of the changes that are going on around us every single day. People say that when you stop changing, you start dying, and I believe that this is so very true. . . . If there is one thing I think I am pretty good at, it's doing the things

necessary to change and adapt both personally and professionally. And while it's not always easy, it is necessary if we are going to be able to enjoy life and work and be successful at both. . . . Now I'm going to have the opportunity to apply these same principles to my retirement, and I'm looking forward to it with great relish.

Had you had the opportunity to be at this moving event, you would have heard numerous testimonials about what a great leader Ted was. However, embedded in all the comments was the simple fact that Ted was a leader who knew how to lead change. This talent had served him well over the course of his entire career and had led to numerous promotions and commensurate awards. It is interesting to note that hanging on the wall of Ted's office was the following quotation from Vince Lombardi: "The measure of who we are is what we do with what we have." Obviously, Ted applied this nugget of wisdom in all areas of his life.

Hearing what Ted's boss said about his career, we took the opportunity to explore his talents in more depth with a number of his associates. Here is what they said about Ted:

"Ted has an uncanny ability to always know what we needed to be doing to stay ahead of the competition, and he kept us in that loop."

"He is a great motivator and communicator, and he always made sure that you knew exactly what you should be working on and how well you were doing."

"Ted was always quick to knock down roadblocks and eliminate barriers that got in the way of us doing our jobs."

"Even in wild times, Ted always stayed calm and gave you a sense that if we pulled together and worked as a team, we were going to come out ahead."

"With his leadership style, he got us to believe that we could take on any challenge, fix any problem, and hit almost any goal, and I've learned a great deal just by watching Ted over the years."

Essentially, in their own way, Ted's coworkers described him as being a great quarterback. He was an effective leader who was able to motivate his team so that they could accomplish great things in a rapidly changing industry. In essence, Ted's effectiveness in leading his people through ongoing change allowed him, and the people who followed him, to experience the thrill of victory during his career. Ted did great things with what he had!

Late in the Fourth Quarter, with Time Running Out

In closing, we encourage you to do great things with what *you* have. Listed in Exhibit E.1 are the eight key principles from this book in their simplest form. Accompanying them are not the *momentum*

Exhibit E.1: Eight Principles Required for a Change Initiative to Be Successful

1. **Control the game—you are the quarterback.**
   Momentum buster: Placing your success, career, and future in the hands of trainers and "water boys" is a big mistake.
2. **Clearly define winning.**
   Momentum buster: Not using a scoreboard to let everyone know what you need to win creates confusion.
3. **Know your opponents.**
   Momentum buster: Lack of knowledge of your opponents can put you in a risky and even dangerous situation.
4. **Create focus and a sense of urgency.**
   Momentum buster: Supporting a business-as-usual mentality encourages the status quo.
5. **Use the right plays and right players.**
   Momentum buster: Expecting improvement without a real game plan is simply wishful thinking.
6. **Execute and adjust.**
   Momentum buster: Accepting poor performance and not making the necessary corrections quickly can short-circuit improvement.
7. **Ensure the win and celebrate.**
   Momentum buster: Allowing improvement to slip and not rewarding success increase the likelihood of failure.
8. **Learn from game experience.**
   Momentum buster: Moving ahead into the next game without learning from the game you just played creates a lost opportunity.

---

builders that we described throughout the book, but rather the *momentum busters* that will destroy an initiative if these practices are either ignored or not properly incorporated. We share the momentum busters with you to remind you of the factors that can cause you and your team to experience the agony of defeat. But we also want to remind you that the key practices of the TMD are things *within your control,* which should serve as encouragement for you as a leader who is serious about making real change happen.

As a leader, you can greatly enhance your organization's ability to win by making a habit of incorporating these eight practices into all your change efforts. Each practice alone may seem simple, but when you bring them together, they can create a powerful tool for change. To illustrate this, let's look at a few final football case studies.

Why the Dallas Cowboys Lost to the Seattle Seahawks, January 6, 2007

On January 6, 2007, the Dallas Cowboys played the Seattle Seahawks in an NFL playoff game. After executing a successful drive that moved them deep into the red zone in the waning moments of the game, the Cowboys lined up to kick a game-winning field goal from the 2-yard line, down 21–20. On the attempt, Dallas QB Tony Romo bobbled the snap and was forced to attempt a run into the end zone, where he was stopped on the 2-yard line. His error in handling the perfect snap prevented his kicker from winning the game for the Cowboys and abruptly ended their season.

Sports pages and postgame shows repeatedly showed Tony Romo sitting on the artificial turf near the goal line with his hands cupped over his face, with jubilant Seattle Seahawk players celebrating all around him. He knew, as did everyone else, that his mistake had cost his team the game. In his sports column, commenting on Tony Romo's error, *Sports Illustrated* writer Don Banks made an extremely telling observation when he said, "Sometimes it's the littlest things done well that wind up mattering the most." As a leader of change, you may not have a stadium full of people or TV audiences watching your performance, but you must know that your team is depending on you to be successful in executing your role as a change leader so that they can win. Tony Romo wanted to win, had trained to win, and needed to win, but he failed to do a very basic thing that mattered the most to help his team win—and he suffered the agony of defeat.

Why the Underdog Won: Boise State Broncos vs. Oklahoma Sooners, 2007 Fiesta Bowl

After leading the Oklahoma Sooners for almost the entire game, the undefeated Boise State Broncos found themselves in a tie game 28–28 with 1:26 left in the 2007 Fiesta Bowl. Their senior quarterback, Jared Zabransky, led his offense onto the field with 1:10 remaining in the contest to try to execute a two-minute drill to win the game. On the first play from scrimmage, Zabransky threw an interception, which Oklahoma cornerback Marcus Walker returned for a touchdown. Zabransky had made a critical mistake.

Boise State came back on the field, now down 35–28 with 1:02 left in the contest, and executed a successful two-minute drill to tie the game with 7 seconds remaining. Zabransky had maintained his poise in leading his team, executing a perfect 50-yard hook-and-ladder play for the score on fourth down. The extra point tied the game 35–35, taking it into overtime. After Oklahoma scored first, making the score 42–35, the Broncos scored on a fourth-down-and-2 play, setting the stage for the big finish.

Broncos head coach Chris Peterson decided to go for 2 points and the win, and his quarterback executed a picture-perfect "Statue of Liberty" play to running back Ian Johnson for the win. Mid-major underdog Boise State had defeated perennial football powerhouse Oklahoma with great team play led by quarterback Jared Zabransky, who shook off his mistakes, remained poised and confident in the face of adversity, and led his team to an undefeated season (13–0) and a Fiesta Bowl MVP trophy. Jared and his teammates experienced the thrill of victory because they not only knew what to do but also had the will to win.

CONCLUSION: A CALL FOR GREAT QUARTERBACKING

We shared this last football game example with you to remind you that we can all find ourselves behind at times and guilty of making mistakes, but as long as there is still time on the clock, you have an opportunity to win *when you know what to do and have the will to do it.*

Exhibit 1.2: The Two-Minute Drill Self-Assessment

Answer each of the following questions as they pertain to your approach to making change happen in your organization:

When approaching change do I...	Never	Rarely	Sometimes	Usually	Always
1. Take control of the change process and lead by example?	❑	❑	❑	❑	❑
2. Do all the things necessary to lead change so as to drive better results and performance?	❑	❑	❑	❑	❑
3. Know when change is required by using an accurate scoreboard?	❑	❑	❑	❑	❑
4. Clearly define what success means when entering a change initiative?	❑	❑	❑	❑	❑
5. Know and understand the opponents we face when entering a change initiative?	❑	❑	❑	❑	❑
6. Know the strengths and weaknesses of my team so as to create favorable match-ups in a change effort?	❑	❑	❑	❑	❑
7. Create and communicate a clear sense of focus on what we are trying to change and how we are going to do it?	❑	❑	❑	❑	❑
8. Create a sense of importance and urgency around the change initiative?	❑	❑	❑	❑	❑
9. Have a clearly developed set of "plays" that advance the improvement effort and lead to improved performance and success when properly executed?	❑	❑	❑	❑	❑

10. Have the right players on the field equipped and ready to play at an optimal level on each and every play? ❏ ❏ ❏ ❏ ❏

11. Make sure we move the ball down the field, and take corrective action to make adjustments when performance is not where it needs to be? ❏ ❏ ❏ ❏ ❏

12. Ensure that our players are doing the right things the right way at the right time so as to execute change? ❏ ❏ ❏ ❏ ❏

13. Do the things necessary to ensure that the change or improvement sticks? ❏ ❏ ❏ ❏ ❏

14. Let my team members know when we have won the game, and celebrate success? ❏ ❏ ❏ ❏ ❏

15. Review and analyze change efforts when they are completed? ❏ ❏ ❏ ❏ ❏

16. Share the lessons learned from an improvement initiative with others? ❏ ❏ ❏ ❏ ❏

To remind yourself of the specific things that your team needs from you to execute a game-winning TMD at work, reevaluate yourself using the TMD self-assessment in Exhibit E.2. (This is the same self-assessment that you first did in Chapter One.) Having worked with CEOs, entrepreneurs, division vice presidents, general managers, middle managers, and frontline supervisors, we are confident that the practices identified in this book can help you in your quest to become more successful at executing rapid change and improvement. To do this requires a willingness on your part to focus on the basics and give them the extra attention they deserve. In the words of former Dallas Cowboys head coach Jimmy Johnson, "The difference between ordinary and extraordinary is that little extra." We encourage you to give a little extra in running your next improvement initiative, so that you and your people will be winners in the game of change.

ENDNOTES

Prologue
1. *Rutgers University—The Birthplace of College Football.* http://touchdownclub.rutgers.edu/history.htm.
2. "Leading Indicators." *Fortune*, Aug. 7, 2006, p. 15.
3. Longenecker, C. O., and Ariss, S. "Who Goes and Who Stays." *Industrial Management*, May–June 2004, pp. 8–13.
4. Longenecker, C. O., and Simonetti, J. L. *Getting Results: Five Absolutes for High Performance.* San Francisco: Jossey-Bass, 2001.
5. Longenecker, C. O., Neubert, M. J., and Fink, L. S. "Causes and Consequences of Managerial Failure in Rapidly Changing Organizations." *Business Horizons*, 2007, *50*(2), 145–155.
6. Hesselbein, F. "Leading Change: An Imperative of Leadership." In M. Losey, S. Meisinger, and D. Ulrich (eds.), *The Future of Human Resource Management: 64 Thought Leaders Explore the Critical HR Issues of Today and Tomorrow.* Hoboken, N.J.: Wiley, 2005.
7. Chandler, A. D., Jr. *Strategy and Structure.* Cambridge, Mass.: MIT Press, 1962.

Chapter One
1. Kihn, M. "Six Sigma Stigma?" *Fast Company*, Sept. 2005, p. 40.
2. Caproni, P. J. *The Practical Coach.* Upper Saddle River, N.J.: Prentice Hall, 2001.

Chapter Two
1. Interesting facts for real football devotees on the Cleveland Browns vs. Denver Broncos rivalry: roll the clock forward one year to January 1988. The same two teams met in the same AFC Conference Championship game. Was the outcome the same?

With 1:12 left in the game, Denver led 38–31, and the ball rested on the exact same spot on the field as it did a year earlier, the Denver 2-yard line. Only this time, the Browns had possession of the ball and were in a position to score, setting up an opportunity to put the game into sudden-death overtime and avenge the prior year's defeat. The Browns were in control of the outcome of this game. Cleveland quarterback Bernie Kozar took the snap and handed off to All-Pro running back Earnest Byner, who was "rocked" just short of the goal line by Denver defensive back, Jeremiah Castille. Byner fumbled the ball, and Denver recovered. Game over. Denver won its second consecutive AFC Conference Championship. Lesson: moving the ball is important, but in the end, you must protect the ball and execute the "basics" if you really want to win big games!

2. Reeves, B., and Smith, R. (eds.). *Pro Football's Greatest Quarterbacks.* St. Louis, Mo.: Sporting News, 2005.

3. Longenecker, C. O., and Simonetti, J. A. *Getting Results: Five Absolutes for High Performance.* San Francisco: Jossey-Bass, 2001.

4. Longenecker, C. O., and Scazzero, J. A. "Improving Service Quality: A Tale of Two Operations." *Managing Service Quality,* 2000, *10*(4), 227–232.

5. Longenecker, C. O., Neubert, M. J., and Fink, L. S. "Causes and Consequences of Managerial Failure in Rapidly Changing Organizations."*Business Horizons,* 2007, *50*(2), 145–155.

6. Reicher, A. E., Wanous, J. P., and Austin, J. T. "Understanding and Managing Cynicism About Organizational Change." *Academy of Management Executive,* 1997, *11*(1), 48–59.

Chapter Three

1. Smith, D. *Taking Charge of Change: 10 Principles for Managing People and Performance.* Reading, Mass.: Addison-Wesley, 1996.

2. Kinni, T. B., and Kinni, D. *No Substitute for Victory: Lessons in Strategy and Leadership from General Douglas MacArthur.* Upper Saddle River, N.J.: Prentice Hall, 2005.

Chapter Four

1. Drucker, P. *Managing for Results.* New York: HarperCollins, 1964.

2. Goleman, D. "Leadership That Gets Results." *Harvard Business Review,* Mar.–Apr. 2000, pp. 78–90.

Chapter Five

1. Kotter, J. "Leading Change: Why Transformation Efforts Fail." *Harvard Business Review*, 1995, *93*(2), 59–67; Murray, E., and Richardson, P. "Fast Forward: A New Framework for Rapid Organizational Change." *Ivey Business Journal*, Mar.–Apr. 2003, pp. 1–5.
2. Woodward, S., and Hendry, C. "Leading and Coping with Change." *Journal of Change Management*, 2004, *4*(2), 155–183.

Chapter Six

1. Ault, R., Walton, R., and Childers, M. *What Works: A Decade of Change at Champion International.* San Francisco: Jossey-Bass, 1998.
2. Longenecker, C. O., and Scazzero, J. A. "Improving Service Quality: A Tale of Two Operations." *Managing Service Quality*, 2000, *10*(4), 227–232.
3. Longenecker, C. O., and Neubert, M. J. "The Management Development Needs of Front-Line Managers: Voices from the Field." *Career Development International*, 2003, *8*(4), 210–218.

Chapter Seven

1. Ivancevich, J., and Lidwell, W. *Guidelines for Excellence in Management.* Cincinnati, Ohio: South-Western Educational, 2004.
2. Kleiner, A., and Roth, G. *Oil Change: Perspectives on Corporate Transformation.* New York: Oxford University Press, 2000.

Chapter Eight

1. Ashenden, R., Silagy, C., and Weller, D. "A Systematic Review of Promoting Lifestyle Change in General Practice." *Family Practice*, 1997, *14*(2), 160–176; Maxwell, J. C. *Thinking for a Change: 11 Ways Highly Successful People Approach Life and Work.* New York: Warner Business Books, 2003.
2. Deutschman, A. "Change or Die." *Fast Company*, May 2005, pp. 54–62.
3. Ornish, D. *Dr. Dean Ornish's Program for Reversing Heart Disease.* New York: Ballantine Books, 1996.
4. Longenecker, C. O., and Fink, L. S. "How Top Managers Develop: A Field Study." *Organizational Development and Learning: An International Journal*, 2006, *20*(5), 18–20.

5. Fitz-Enz, J. *The 8 Practices of Exceptional Companies.* New York: AMACOM, 1997.

Chapter Nine

1. Senge, P. *The Fifth Discipline.* New York: Doubleday, 1990.
2. Drew, S., and Smith, P. "The Learning Organization: Change Proofing and Strategy." *Learning Organization,* 1995, *2*(1), 4–14.
3. Abrashoff, D. M. *It's Your Ship: Management Lessons from the Best Damn Ship in the Navy.* New York: Warner Books, 2002.
4. Longenecker, C. O., and Stansfield, T. C. "Why Plant Managers Fail: Causes and Consequences." *Industrial Management,* Jan.–Feb. 2000, pp. 24–32.
5. McLagan, P. "Success with Change." *TD,* Dec. 2002, pp. 44–53.
6. Wick, C. W., and Stanton Leon, L. *The Learning Edge.* New York: McGraw-Hill, 1993.
7. Longenecker, C. O., and Simonetti, J. A. *Getting Results: Five Absolutes for High Performance.* San Francisco: Jossey-Bass, 2001.
8. Baumbusch, R. "Internal Best Practices: Turning Knowledge into Results." *Strategy and Leadership,* 1997, *25*(4), 44–45.
9. Beeman, D., and Sharkey, T. "The Use and Abuse of Corporate Politics." *Business Horizons,* Mar.–Apr. 1987, pp. 54–63.

ACKNOWLEDGMENTS

Like all projects, this effort would not be possible without the support and input of a great many great people. First, we want to thank all the **players,** which must start with all the business leaders who served as participants in this project. Without your playing time experience, the game never begins. Second, we want to thank our great **coaches** at Jossey-Bass for helping us get the ball in the end zone with the publication of this book, and especially our head coach and editor, Neal Maillet, and his awesome team of professionals. Third, we want a special thanks to our top-performing **"money players"** who were influential in the creation of this book: Dr. Larry "You Should Do It" Fink, Melissa "Get it Done" Rieman, and Denise "It Can Be Done" Turk.

We also want to acknowledge the key **trainers** and **strength coaches** who have played significant roles in our lives and who have helped properly prepare us for the game that we are competing in. These great people include Coach Tom Amstutz, Dr. Sonny Ariss, Mrs. Brewer, Al Bush, Ken Chaloupek, Jay Coykendall, Dr. Dale Dwyer, Dr. Denny Gioia, Tom Handel, Tom (the Man) Hoover, Ron Lora, Mark McCabe, Dr. Nagi Naganathan, Bob Napierala, Dr. Mitch Newbert, Coach Gary Pinkel, Dave Risley, Ken Shaner, Dr. Jack Simonetti, Dr. Hank Sims, Tony Siravo, Jeff Smith, Dr. Chuck Snow, Dan Streb, Bill Swonger, Bob Weaver, and Jim Zare.

We are very thankful for having had the opportunity and pleasure of playing with a number of great business **quarterbacks,** including Mark Allen, Gary Bentley, Dr. Al Bianco, Dr. Sheri Caldwell, John Caponigro, Lee Childers, Dan Corbin, Andy Cosgrove, Lee Cremer, Tony Damon, Larry Davenport, Chris Endress, Rod Filcek, Dr. Tom Gutteridge, Bob Hays, Carrie Herr, Doug Homer, Tim Iorio, Dr. Lloyd Jacobs, Bill Kieffer, Dave LaHote, Tom Lause, Scott Libbe, Bill Logie, John Mallin, Mike McCartney, John Meier, Hal Miller,

Janie Miller, Joe Napoli, John Nechiporchik, Dr. Randy Oostra, Ron Ranallo, Anne Rex, Mike Riccio, Steve Rindskopf, John Szuch, Brian Varano, Skip Vermilya, John Walton, and Don Warner. Thank you for being play makers for your franchises.

A special thanks to the **key players** on the field during our most recent two-minute drills: Beth Foor, Dan Holman, Todd Jurski, Phil Leinbach, John LePla, Dr. Paul Longenecker, Rick Longenecker, Pat Madigan, Ronda Massey, Bridget Metzger, Michelle Reimer, Jack Schaffer, Jamie Smith, and Theresa Smith.

We also want to recognize the support of our **fans,** who include our coworkers, students, program participants, mentees, and family members who make life truly enjoyable and give us tremendous faith in the future. And a special thanks to the University of Toledo's College of Business Administration for being a great **franchise** and providing support for our ongoing research and mission to "develop lifelong leaders for the world of business."

Proverbs 27:17 says, "As iron sharpens iron, so one person can sharpen another." We want to thank all the people in our lives who have helped sharpen us and who know that we desire to do the same in all that we do! It is our prayer and hope that this book might be used to make a real difference in the lives of readers and the organizations that they are responsible for leading. Remember that leading change is never a spectator sport!

June 2007   Clinton O. Longenecker
Toledo, Ohio   Greg R. Papp
                                                         Timothy C. Stansfield

ABOUT THE AUTHORS

Clinton O. Longenecker is an award-winning business educator and is the Stranahan Professor of Leadership and Organizational Excellence in the College of Business Administration at the University of Toledo. His teaching and research interests are in leadership, management effectiveness, organization development, and all facets of rapid performance improvement. During his academic career he has been the recipient of fifteen awards for outstanding teaching and research and of several industry awards, including the Ernst & Young Entrepreneur of the Year Award. He was selected Best Professor of Northwest Ohio by the *Toledo City Paper* in 2005, 2006, and 2007.

Clint has published over 120 articles and papers in leading academic and professional journals, including the *Sloan Management Review, Academy of Management Executive, Business Horizons, Industrial Management, Journal of Compensation and Benefits,* and *Organizational Dynamics.* He is also featured in several educational videos based on his research, including the award-winning CRM training film "Effective Performance Appraisal" and the Society of Manufacturing Engineer's "Continuous Improvement in Manufacturing," and he is a frequent media commentator on front-page business issues. His most recent book, *Getting Results: Five Absolutes for High Performance* (Jossey-Bass, 2001), describes the best practices of over two thousand high-performance managers and has been translated into seven languages.

Clint is a nationally recognized authority on rapid performance improvement and leadership and is an active management consultant, educator, and executive coach whose clients include a wide variety of Fortune 500 firms and entrepreneurial enterprises, including SSOE, ProMedica Health Systems, Eaton Corporation, Roadway Express, Dana Corporation, Howard Hughes Medical Institute, and MFC. He has also served as a visiting lecturer at the University of the West Indies–Barbados and has lectured and worked extensively in Haiti, Poland, Hungary, Zimbabwe, and Russia. Clint is an exceptional and popular speaker and has recently been described by *Career Publications* as "one of the top motivational speakers in the U.S. who can blend cutting edge research, common sense, humor and conviction into a call for better performance that we can all relate to and really do something with."

Clint holds a B.B.A. in marketing and an M.B.A. in management, both from the University of Toledo, and a Ph.D. in management from the Pennsylvania State University. He was a college football player at the University of Toledo and was the recipient of a four-year athletic scholarship. Clint continues to work with the football team and to mentor players at the University of Toledo. He can be reached at 419-530-2368 or clinton.longenecker@utoledo.edu, or visit his website at www.businessfaculty.utoledo.edu/clongen.

Greg R. Papp is the founder and president of Cube Culture Corporation, an enterprise dedicated to assisting organizations in developing better methods for creating high performance in administrative and office environments. With over thirty years of professional and executive experience in finance and engineering at Fortune 500 organizations, including General Motors, Ford, and Allied-Signal, Greg brings a wealth of knowledge and new ideas to his clients. Over the course of his career, Greg has led change initiatives across a wide spectrum of business functions within plant, division, sector, and corporate areas of responsibility. He has been an instructor, leader, and team member on hundreds of improvement initiatives using various leading-edge tools, including Lean initiatives, Six Sigma techniques, Ford Quality Circles, Ford QOS, and GE Workout. In addition, he is an adjunct faculty member at the University of Toledo's Executive Center for Global Competitiveness.

Prior to founding Cube Culture, Greg was the corporate controller of Aeroquip-Vickers Corporation, a $2 billion firm providing engineered materials and services to the automotive, industrial, and aerospace industries. Greg is also the founder of the Process Improvement Networking Group (PING), which brings executives of major corporations together to leverage ideas for improving business processes. PING is dedicated to creating a platform for executives to share process improvement practices in administrative, financial, and human resource management functions.

Greg is a sought-after speaker, trainer, seminar leader, and executive coach who helps leaders look for ways not only to improve performance but to do it quicker than their competitors. Greg's clients include Cooper Tire, La-Z-Boy, Owens Corning, Pilkington, and Owens Illinois. He has also served as a judge for several quality and business excellence awards, including the Ohio Excellence Award.

Greg received an M.B.A. from the University of Arizona and a B.S. in industrial engineering from General Motors Institute (Kettering University). He has also participated in advanced management education programs at Harvard Business School, the University of Michigan, and the Kellogg School of Business Management. Greg can be reached at 419-867-0852 or gregp@ cubeculture.com, or visit his website at www.cubeculture.com.

Timothy C. Stansfield is the founder and president of IET, Inc., and has over twenty-five years of manufacturing and management consulting experience in more than twelve hundred different manufacturing plants worldwide. IET is a leading world-class manufacturing and engineering consulting enterprise whose international clients include NASA, General Motors, Leggett & Platt, Kraft Foods, Philip Morris, Lear Corporation, and Gillette. IET specializes in designing and executing manufacturing solutions to help clients compete in a global manufacturing environment and provides strategic manufacturing design and management support for operations throughout North America, as well as in South America, Europe, and Asia. The company has received a wide variety of industry awards for engineering and human resource excellence. In addition to Tim's administrative responsibilities in leading IET, he is actively involved as an executive coach, educator, and thought leader across the manufacturing landscape.

Tim has been the recipient of numerous industry and academic recognitions, including Ernst & Young's Entrepreneur of the Year Award, and has received the Distinguished Alumnus Award at the University of Toledo in both the College of Engineering and the College of Business. He holds professional engineering licenses in the states of Ohio, Michigan, North Carolina, Iowa, Illinois, and New York.

Tim has published numerous articles in leading professional journals, such as *Business Horizons, Industrial Management, IE Solutions,* and *International Journal of Productivity and Performance Management.* His research centers on manufacturing productivity, effective plant management, goal setting and feedback, and production launch success. He is an adjunct faculty member in the College of Business Administration, the College of Engineering, and the Executive Center for Global Competitiveness at the University of Toledo.

Tim holds a Ph.D. in manufacturing management, an M.B.A. in management, an M.A. in history, and a B.S. in industrial engineering, all from the University of Toledo, where Clint Longenecker was his teacher and mentor. Tim can be reached at 419-385-1233 or at stansfield@ieteng.com, or visit his website at www.ieteng.com.

See You at the Game!

To learn more about our collaborative work on real and rapid organizational improvement or to become part of our Two-Minute Drill team, please visit our TMD website, www.twominutedrill.org, for a complete listing of rapid performance improvement services. We encourage you to share a personal rapid improvement story with us to become eligible for our Two-Minute Drill Hall of Fame, and to consider joining our Quarterback Club. See our website for a listing of eligibility guidelines.

No spectators allowed!

INDEX

CPSIA information can be obtained at www.ICGtesting.com
Printed in the USA
LVOW04s0738210115

423651LV00003B/16/P